The R

Pocket WORLD ATLAS

The RANDOM HOUSE *Pocket* WORLD ATLAS

RANDOM HOUSE
NEW YORK

The Random House Pocket World Atlas

All inquiries should be addressed to
Random House Reference,
Random House, Inc.,
New York, NY.

Published in the United States by Random House, Inc., and simultaneously in Canada by Random House of Canada Limited.

This edition was originally published in the United Kingdom by Helicon Publishing Ltd.

Printed and bound in Italy by Giunti Industrie Grafiche

Library of Congress Cataloging-in-Publication Data Is Available

First Edition
0987654321
May 2002

ISBN: 0-375-71984-9

Contents

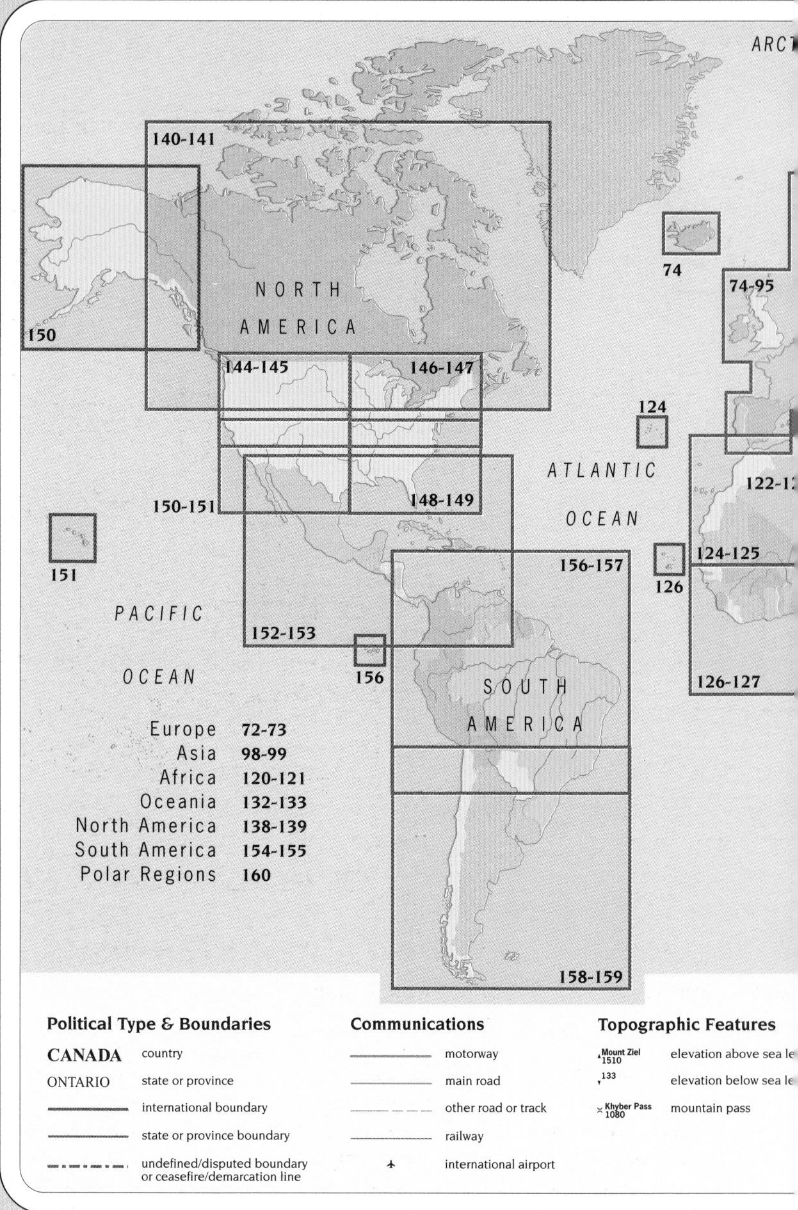
ARC
140-141
150
NORTH
AMERICA
74
74-95
144-145
146-147
124
ATLANTIC
OCEAN
150-151
148-149
122-1
151
156-157
124-125
126
PACIFIC
152-153
156
OCEAN
SOUTH
AMERICA
126-127
Europe 72-73
Asia 98-99
Africa 120-121
Oceania 132-133
North America 138-139
South America 154-155
Polar Regions 160
158-159
Political Type & Boundaries
CANADA country
ONTARIO state or province
international boundary
state or province boundary
undefined/disputed boundary or ceasefire/demarcation line
Communications
motorway
main road
other road or track
railway
international airport
Topographic Features
Mount Ziel 1510 elevation above sea le
133 elevation below sea le
Khyber Pass 1080 mountain pass

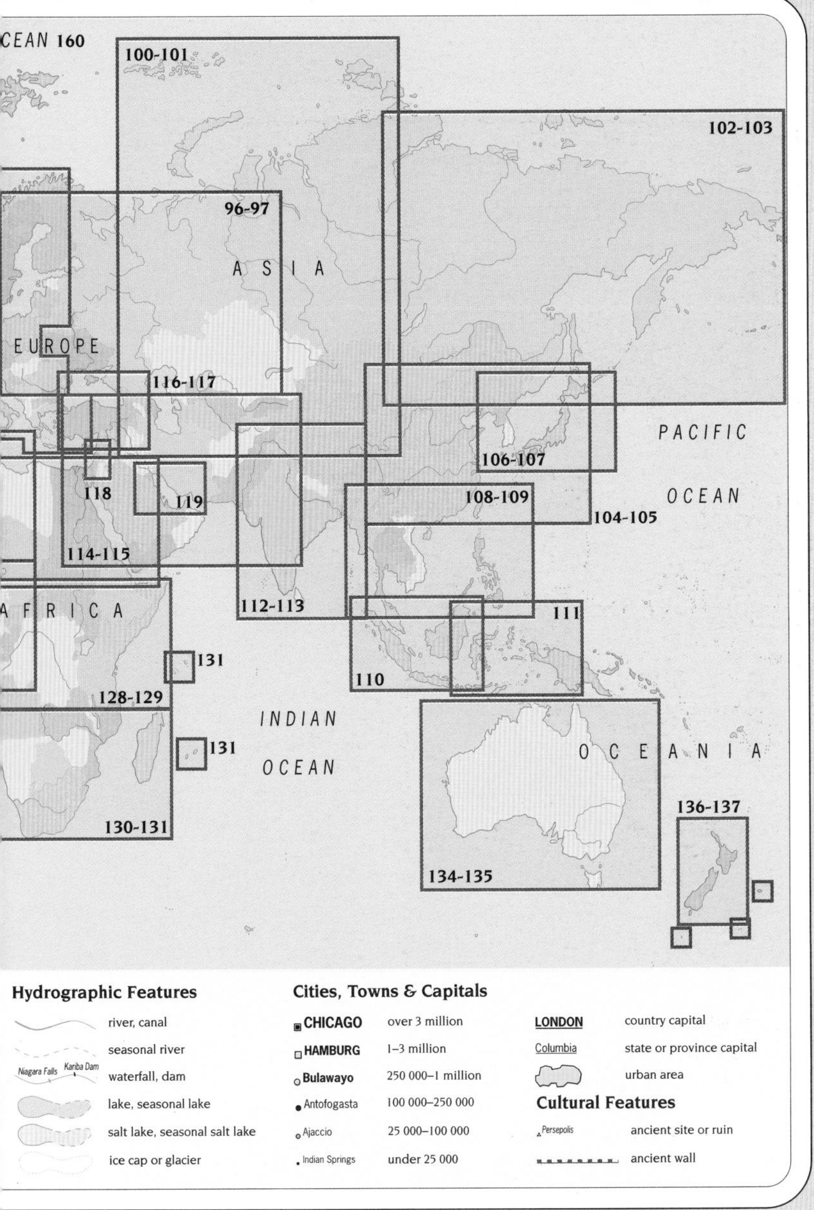

CEAN 160
100-101
102-103
96-97
ASIA
EUROPE
116-117
PACIFIC
OCEAN
106-107
118
119
108-109
104-105
114-115
AFRICA
112-113
111
131
110
128-129
INDIAN
OCEAN
131
OCEANIA
136-137
130-131
134-135
Hydrographic Features
river, canal
seasonal river
Niagara Falls
Kariba Dam
waterfall, dam
lake, seasonal lake
salt lake, seasonal salt lake
ice cap or glacier
Cities, Towns & Capitals
CHICAGO
over 3 million
HAMBURG
1–3 million
Bulawayo
250 000–1 million
Antofogasta
100 000–250 000
Ajaccio
25 000–100 000
Indian Springs
under 25 000
LONDON
country capital
Columbia
state or province capital
urban area
Cultural Features
Persepolis
ancient site or ruin
ancient wall

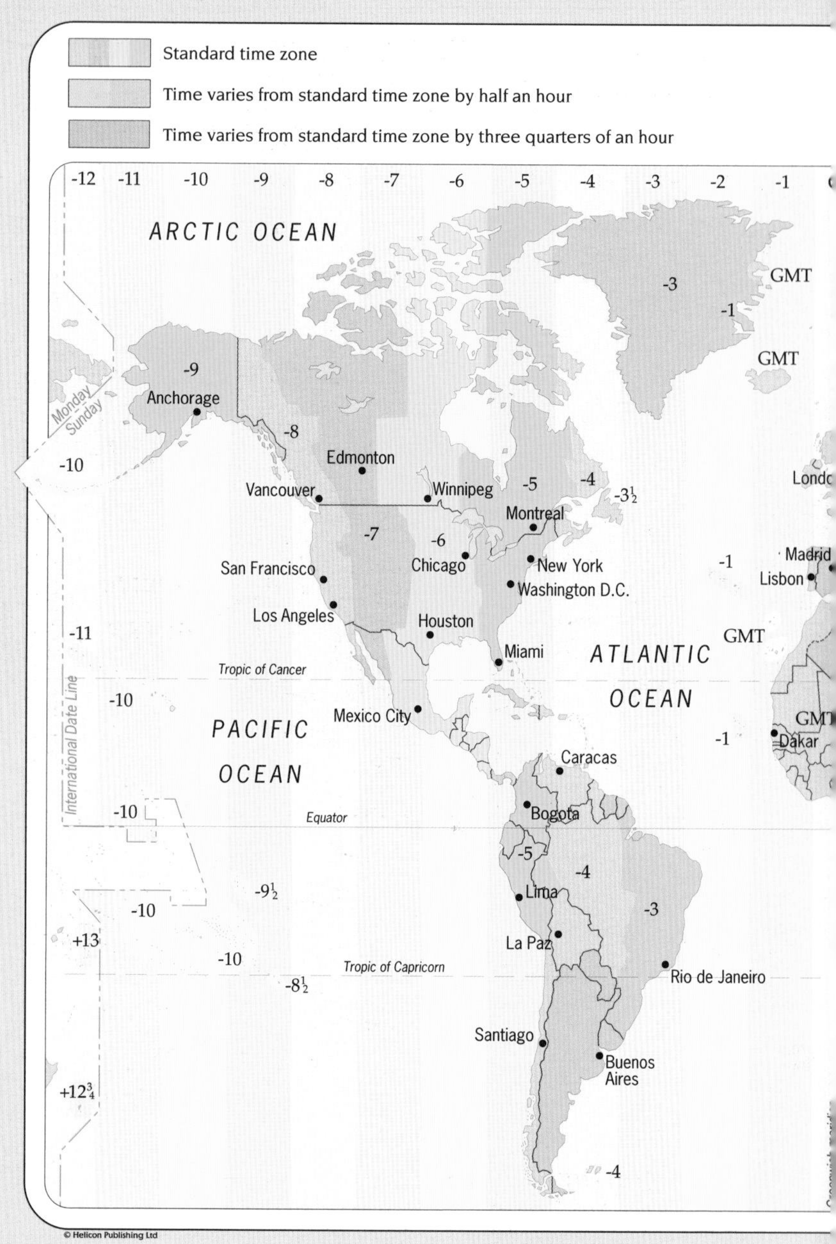

Standard time zone
Time varies from standard time zone by half an hour
Time varies from standard time zone by three quarters of an hour
-12
-11
-10
-9
-8
-7
-6
-5
-4
-3
-2
-1
ARCTIC OCEAN
GMT
-3
-1
GMT
-9
Anchorage
Monday
Sunday
-8
-10
Edmonton
Vancouver
Winnipeg
-5
-4
$-3\frac{1}{2}$
Montreal
-7
-6
San Francisco
Chicago
New York
Washington D.C.
-1
Madrid
Lisbon
Los Angeles
Houston
-11
Miami
ATLANTIC
OCEAN
GMT
Tropic of Cancer
International Date Line
-10
Mexico City
PACIFIC
OCEAN
Dakar
-1
Caracas
-10
Bogota
Equator
-5
-4
$-9\frac{1}{2}$
Lima
-10
-3
+13
La Paz
-10
Tropic of Capricorn
Rio de Janeiro
$-8\frac{1}{2}$
Santiago
Buenos Aires
$+12\frac{3}{4}$
-4

Time zones

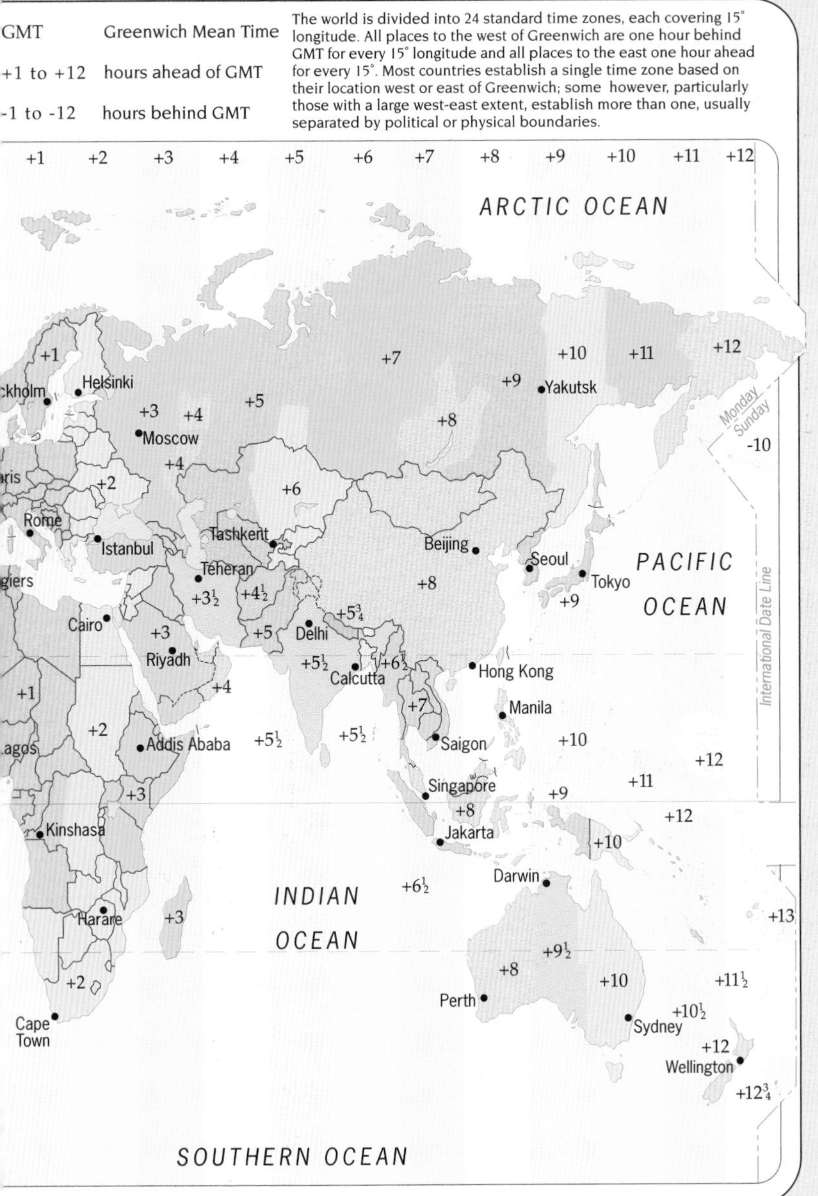
GMT Greenwich Mean Time
+1 to +12 hours ahead of GMT
-1 to -12 hours behind GMT
The world is divided into 24 standard time zones, each covering 15° longitude. All places to the west of Greenwich are one hour behind GMT for every 15° longitude and all places to the east one hour ahead for every 15°. Most countries establish a single time zone based on their location west or east of Greenwich; some however, particularly those with a large west-east extent, establish more than one, usually separated by political or physical boundaries.
+1 +2 +3 +4 +5 +6 +7 +8 +9 +10 +11 +12
ARCTIC OCEAN
PACIFIC OCEAN
INDIAN OCEAN
SOUTHERN OCEAN
International Date Line
Monday
Sunday
-10
+13
+11½
+10½
+12¾
Helsinki
Moscow
Rome
Istanbul
Tashkent
Teheran
Cairo
Riyadh
Addis Ababa
Kinshasa
Harare
Cape Town
Delhi
Calcutta
Beijing
Seoul
Tokyo
Yakutsk
Hong Kong
Manila
Saigon
Singapore
Jakarta
Darwin
Perth
Sydney
Wellington
+3½
+4½
+5¾
+5½
+6½
+9½

Nations of the World

Afghanistan

Map page 114

National name Dowlat-e Eslāmi-ye Afghānestān/ Islamic State of Afghanistan

Area 652,225 sq km/ 251,825 sq mi

Capital Kābul

Major towns/cities Kandahār, Herāt, Mazār-e Sharīf, Jalālābād, Konduz, Qal'eh-ye Now

Physical features mountainous in centre and northeast (Hindu Kush mountain range; Khyber and Salang passes, Wakhan salient, and Panjshir Valley), plains in north and southwest, Amu Darya (Oxus) River, Helmand River, Lake Saberi

Currency afgháni

GNP per capita (PPP) (US$) 800 (1999 est)

Resources natural gas, coal, iron ore, barytes, lapis lazuli, salt, talc, copper, chrome, gold, silver, asbestos, small petroleum reserves

Population 22,720,000 (2000 est)

Population density (per sq km) 34 (1999 est)

Language Pashto, Dari (both official), Uzbek, Turkmen, Balochi, Pashai

Religion Muslim (84% Sunni, 15% Shiite), other 1%

Time difference GMT+4.5

Albania

Map page 94

National name Republika e Shqipërisë/Republic of Albania

Area 28,748 sq km/ 11,099 sq mi

Capital Tirana

Major towns/cities Durrës, Shkodër, Elbasan, Vlorë, Korçë

Major ports Durrës

Physical features mainly mountainous, with rivers flowing east-west, and a narrow coastal plain

Currency lek

GNP per capita (PPP) (US$) 2,892 (1999)

Resources chromite (one of world's largest producers), copper, coal, nickel, petroleum and natural gas

Population 3,113,000 (2000 est)

Population density (per sq km) 108 (1999 est)

Language Albanian (official), Greek

Religion Muslim, Albanian Orthodox, Roman Catholic

Time difference GMT +1

Algeria

Map page 124

National name Al-Jumhuriyyat al-Jaza'iriyya ad-Dimuqratiyya ash-Sha'biyya/ Democratic People's Republic of Algeria

Area 2,381,741 sq km/ 919,590 sq mi

Capital Algiers (Arabic al-Jaza'ir)

Major towns/cities Oran, Annaba, Blida, Sétif, Constantine

Major ports Oran (Ouahran), Annaba (Bône)

Physical features coastal plains backed by mountains in north, Sahara desert in south; Atlas mountains, Barbary Coast, Chott Melrhir depression, Hoggar mountains

Currency Algerian dinar

GNP per capita (PPP) (US$) 4,753 (1999)

Resources natural gas and petroleum, iron ore, phosphates, lead, zinc, mercury, silver, salt, antimony, copper

Population 31,471,000 (2000 est)

Population density (per sq km) 13 (1999 est)

Language Arabic (official), Berber, French

Religion Sunni Muslim (state religion) 99%, Christian and Jewish 1%

Time difference GMT +/-0

Andorra

Map page 86

National name Principat d'Andorra/Principality of Andorra
Area 468 sq km/ 181 sq mi
Capital Andorra la Vella
Major towns/cities Les Escaldes
Physical features mountainous, with narrow valleys; the eastern Pyrenees, Valira River
Currency French franc and Spanish peseta
GNP per capita (PPP) (US$) 18,000 (1996 est)
Resources iron, lead, aluminium, hydroelectric power
Population 78,000 (2000 est)
Population density (per sq km) 146 (1999 est)
Language Catalan (official), Spanish, French
Religion Roman Catholic (92%)
Time difference GMT +1

Angola

Map page 120

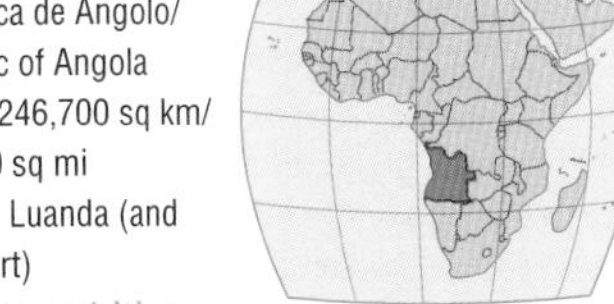

National name República de Angolo/ Republic of Angola
Area 1,246,700 sq km/ 481,350 sq mi
Capital Luanda (and chief port)
Major towns/cities Lobito, Benguela, Huambo, Lubango, Malanje, Namibe, Kuito
Major ports Huambo, Lubango, Malanje
Physical features narrow coastal plain rises to vast interior plateau with rainforest in northwest; desert in south; Cuanza, Cuito, Cubango, and Cunene rivers
Currency kwanza
GNP per capita (PPP) (US$) 632 (1999)
Resources petroleum, diamonds, granite, iron ore, marble, salt, phosphates, manganese, copper
Population 12,878,000 (2000 est)
Population density (per sq km) 10 (1999 est)
Language Portuguese (official), Bantu, other native dialects
Religion Roman Catholic 38%, Protestant 15%, animist 47%
Time difference GMT +1

Antigua and Barbuda

Map page 152

Area 440 sq km/ 169 sq mi (Antigua 280 sq km/108 sq mi, Barbuda 161 sq km/ 62 sq mi, plus Redonda 1 sq km/ 0.4 sq mi)
Capital St. John's (on Antigua) (and chief port)
Major towns/cities Codrington (on Barbuda)
Physical features low-lying tropical islands of limestone and coral with some higher volcanic outcrops; no rivers and low rainfall result in frequent droughts and deforestation. Antigua is the largest of the Leeward Islands; Redonda is an uninhabited island of volcanic rock rising to 305 m/1,000 ft
Currency East Caribbean dollar
GNP per capita (PPP) (US$) 8,959 (1999 est)
Population 68,000 (2000 est)
Population density (per sq km) 246 (1999 est)
Language English (official), local dialects
Religion Christian (mostly Anglican)
Time difference GMT -4

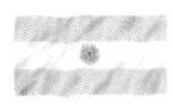

Argentina

Map page 158

National name República Argentina/ Argentine Republic
Area 2,780,400 sq km/ 1,073,518 sq mi
Capital Buenos Aires
Major towns/cities Rosario, Córdoba, San Miguel de Tucumán, Mendoza, Santa Fé, La Plata
Major ports La Plata and Bahía Blanca

Physical features mountains in west, forest and savannah in north, pampas (treeless plains) in east-central area, Patagonian plateau in south; rivers Colorado, Salado, Paraná, Uruguay, Río de La Plata estuary; Andes mountains, with Aconcagua the highest peak in western hemisphere; Iguaçu Falls
Territories disputed claim to the Falkland Islands (Islas Malvinas), and part of Antarctica
Currency peso (= 10,000 australs, which it replaced in 1992)
GNP per capita (PPP) (US$) 11,324 (1999)
Resources coal, crude oil, natural gas, iron ore, lead ore, zinc ore, tin, gold, silver, uranium ore, marble, borates, granite
Population 37,032,000 (2000 est)
Population density (per sq km) 13 (1999 est)
Language Spanish (official) (95%), Italian (3%), English, German, French
Religion predominantly Roman Catholic (state-supported), 2% protestant, 2% Jewish
Time difference GMT -3

Armenia

Map page 116

National name Hayastani Hanrapetoutioun/ Republic of Armenia
Area 29,800 sq km/ 11,505 sq mi
Capital Yerevan
Major towns/cities Gyumri (formerly Leninakan), Vanadzor (formerly Kirovakan), Hrazdan, Aboyvan
Physical features mainly mountainous (including Mount Ararat), wooded
Currency dram (replaced Russian rouble in 1993)
GNP per capita (PPP) (US$) 2,210 (1999)
Resources copper, zinc, molybdenum, iron, silver, marble, granite
Population 3,520,000 (2000 est)
Population density (per sq km) 118 (1999 est)
Language Armenian (official)
Religion Armenian Orthodox
Time difference GMT +4

Australia

Map page 134

National name Commonwealth of Australia
Area 7,682,850 sq km/ 2,966,136 sq mi
Capital Canberra
Major towns/cities Adelaide, Alice Springs, Brisbane, Darwin, Melbourne, Perth, Sydney, Hobart, Newcastle, Wollongong
Physical features Ayers Rock; Arnhem Land; Gulf of Carpentaria; Cape York Peninsula; Great Australian Bight; Great Sandy Desert; Gibson Desert; Great Victoria Desert; Simpson Desert; the Great Barrier Reef; Great Dividing Range and Australian Alps in the east (Mount Kosciusko, 2,229 m/7,136 ft, Australia's highest peak). The fertile southeast region is watered by the Darling, Lachlan, Murrumbridgee, and Murray rivers. Lake Eyre basin and Nullarbor Plain in the south
Territories Norfolk Island, Christmas Island, Cocos (Keeling) Islands, Ashmore and Cartier Islands, Coral Sea Islands, Heard Island and McDonald Islands, Australian Antarctic Territory
Currency Australian dollar
GNP per capita (PPP) (US$) 22,448 (1999)
Resources coal, iron ore (world's third-largest producer), bauxite, copper, zinc (world's second-largest producer), nickel (world's fifth-largest producer), uranium, gold, diamonds
Population 18,886,000 (2000 est)
Population density (per sq km) 2 (1999 est)
Language English (official), Aboriginal languages
Religion Anglican 26%, Roman Catholic 26%, other Christian 24%
Time difference GMT +8/10

Austria

Map page 88

National name Republik Österreich/Republic of Austria
Area 83,859 sq km/32,367 sq mi
Capital Vienna

Major towns/cities Graz, Linz, Salzburg, Innsbruck, Klagenfurt
Physical features landlocked mountainous state, with Alps in west and south (Austrian Alps, including Grossglockner and Brenner and Semmering passes, Lechtaler and Allgauer Alps north of River Inn, Carnic Alps on Italian border) and low relief in east where most of the population is concentrated; River Danube
Currency schilling
GNP per capita (PPP) (US$) 23,808 (1999)
Resources lignite, iron, kaolin, gypsum, talcum, magnesite, lead, zinc, forests
Population 8,211,000 (2000 est)
Population density (per sq km) 98 (1999 est)
Language German (official)
Religion Roman Catholic 78%, Protestant 5%
Time difference GMT +1

Azerbaijan

Map page 116

National name Azärbaycan Respublikasi/ Republic of Azerbaijan
Area 86,600 sq km/ 33,436 sq mi
Capital Baku
Major towns/cities Gäncä, Sumqayit, Naxçivan, Xankändi, Mingäçevir
Physical features Caspian Sea with rich oil reserves; the country ranges from semidesert to the Caucasus Mountains
Currency manat (replaced Russian rouble in 1993)
GNP per capita (PPP) (US$) 2,322 (1999)
Resources petroleum, natural gas, iron ore, aluminium, copper, barytes, cobalt, precious metals, limestone, salt
Population 7,734,000 (2000 est)
Population density (per sq km) 89 (1999 est)
Language Azeri (official), Russian
Religion Shiite Muslim 68%, Sunni Muslim 27%, Russian Orthodox 3%, Armenian Orthodox 2%
Time difference GMT +4

The Bahamas

Map page 152

National name Commonwealth of the Bahamas
Area 13,880 sq km/ 5,383 sq mi
Capital Nassau (on New Providence island)
Major towns/cities Freeport (on Grand Bahama)
Physical features comprises 700 tropical coral islands and about 1,000 cays; the Exumas are a narrow spine of 365 islands; only 30 of the desert islands are inhabited; Blue Holes of Andros, the world's longest and deepest submarine caves
Currency Bahamian dollar
GNP per capita (PPP) (US$) 13,955 (1999 est)
Resources aragonite (extracted from seabed), chalk, salt
Population 307,000 (2000 est)
Population density (per sq km) 22 (1999 est)
Language English (official), Creole
Religion Christian 94% (Baptist 32%, Roman Catholic 19%, Anglican 20%, other Protestant 23%)
Time difference GMT -5

Bahrain

Map page 119

National name Dawlat al-Bahrayn/State of Bahrain
Area 688 sq km/ 266 sq mi
Capital Al Manāmah (on Bahrain island)
Major towns/cities Sitra, Al Muharraq, Jidd Ḩafş, Madinat 'Īsá
Physical features archipelago of 35 islands in Arabian Gulf, composed largely of sand-covered limestone; generally poor and infertile soil; flat and hot; causeway linking Bahrain to mainland

Saudi Arabia
Currency Bahraini dinar
GNP per capita (PPP) (US$) 11,527 (1999 est)
Resources petroleum and natural gas
Population 617,000 (2000 est)
Population density (per sq km) 882 (1999 est)
Language Arabic (official), Farsi, English, Urdu
Religion 85% Muslim (Shiite 60%, Sunni 40%), Christian; Islam is the state religion
Time difference GMT +3

Bangladesh

Map page 112

National name Gana Prajatantri Bangladesh/People's Republic of Bangladesh
Area 144,000 sq km/55,598 sq mi
Capital Dhaka
Major towns/cities Rajshahi, Khulna, Chittagong, Sylhet, Rangpur, Narayanganj
Major ports Chittagong, Khulna
Physical features flat delta of rivers Ganges (Padma) and Brahmaputra (Jamuna), the largest estuarine delta in the world; annual rainfall of 2,540 mm/100 in; some 75% of the land is less than 3 m/10 ft above sea level; hilly in extreme southeast and northeast
Currency taka
GNP per capita (PPP) (US$) 1,475 (1999)
Resources natural gas, coal, limestone, china clay, glass sand
Population 129,155,000 (2000 est)
Population density (per sq km) 881 (1999 est)
Language Bengali (official), English
Religion Muslim 88%, Hindu 11%; Islam is the state religion
Time difference GMT +6

Barbados

Map page 152

Area 430 sq km/166 sq mi
Capital Bridgetown
Major towns/cities Speightstown, Holetown, Oistins
Physical features most easterly island of the West Indies; surrounded by coral reefs; subject to hurricanes June-November; highest point Mount Hillaby 340 m/1,115 ft
Currency Barbados dollar
GNP per capita (PPP) (US$) 12,260 (1998)
Resources petroleum and natural gas
Population 270,000 (2000 est)
Population density (per sq km) 625 (1999 est)
Language English (official), Bajan (a Barbadian English dialect)
Religion 40% Anglican, 8% Pentecostal, 6% Methodist, 4% Roman Catholic
Time difference GMT -4

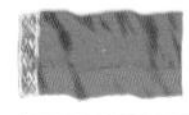

Belarus

Map page 96

National name Respublika Belarus/Republic of Belarus
Area 207,600 sq km/80,154 sq mi
Capital Minsk (Belorussian Mensk)
Major towns/cities Homyel', Vitsyebsk, Mahilyow, Babruysk, Hrodna, Brest
Physical features more than 25% forested; rivers Dvina, Dnieper and its tributaries, including the Pripet and Beresina; the Pripet Marshes in the east; mild and damp climate
Currency Belarus rouble, or zaichik
GNP per capita (PPP) (US$) 6,518 (1999)
Resources petroleum, natural gas, peat, salt, coal, lignite
Population 10,236,000 (2000 est)
Population density (per sq km) 50 (1999 est)
Language Belorussian (official), Russian, Polish

Religion 80% Eastern Orthodox; Baptist, Roman Catholic Muslim, and Jewish minorities
Time difference GMT +2

Belgium

Map page 80

National name Royaume de Belgique (French), Koninkrijk België (Flemish)/Kingdom of Belgium
Area 30,510 sq km/ 11,779 sq mi
Capital Brussels
Major towns/cities Antwerp, Ghent, Liège, Charleroi, Brugge, Mons, Namur, Louvain
Major ports Antwerp, Oostende, Zeebrugge
Physical features fertile coastal plain in northwest, central rolling hills rise eastwards, hills and forest in southeast; Ardennes Forest; rivers Schelde and Meuse
Currency Belgian franc
GNP per capita (PPP) (US$) 24,200 (1999)
Resources coal, coke, natural gas, iron
Population 10,161,000 (2000 est)
Population density (per sq km) 333 (1999 est)
Language Flemish (a Dutch dialect, known as Vlaams; official) (spoken by 56%, mainly in Flanders, in the north), French (especially the dialect Walloon; official) (spoken by 32%, mainly in Wallonia, in the south), German (0.6%; mainly near the eastern border)
Religion Roman Catholic 75%, various Protestant denominations
Time difference GMT +1

Belize

Map page 152

Area 22,963 sq km/ 8,866 sq mi
Capital Belmopan
Major towns/cities Belize, Dangriga, Orange Walk, Corozal, San Ignacio
Major ports Belize, Dangriga, Punta Gorda
Physical features tropical swampy coastal plain, Maya Mountains in south; over 90% forested
Currency Belize dollar
GNP per capita (PPP) (US$) 4,492 (1999)
Population 241,000 (2000 est)
Population density (per sq km) 10 (1999 est)
Language English (official), Spanish (widely spoken), Creole dialects
Religion Roman Catholic 62%, Protestant 30%
Time difference GMT -6

Benin

Map page 126

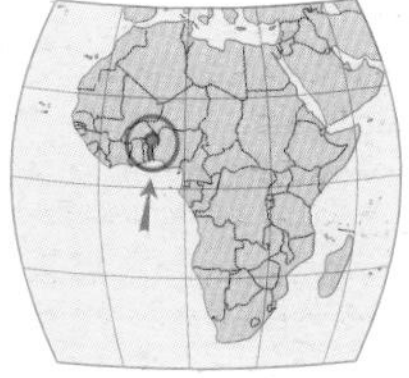

National name République du Bénin/ Republic of Benin
Area 112,622 sq km/ 43,483 sq mi
Capital Porto-Novo (official), Cotonou (de facto)
Major towns/cities Abomey, Natitingou, Parakou, Kandi, Ouidah, Djougou, Bohicon, Cotonou
Major ports Cotonou
Physical features flat to undulating terrain; hot and humid in south; semiarid in north; coastal lagoons with fishing villages on stilts; Niger River in northeast
Currency franc CFA
GNP per capita (PPP) (US$) 886 (1999)
Resources petroleum, limestone, marble
Population 6,097,000 (2000 est)
Population density (per sq km) 53 (1999 est)
Language French (official), Fon (47%), Yoruba (9%) (both in the south), six major tribal languages in the north
Religion animist 70%, Muslim 15%, Christian 15%
Time difference GMT +1

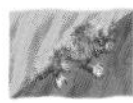

Bhutan

Map page 112

National name Druk-yul/Kingdom of Bhutan
Area 47,500 sq km/18,147 sq mi

Capital Thimphu
Major towns/cities Paro, Punakha, Mongar, Phuntsholing, Tashigang
Physical features occupies southern slopes of the Himalayas; Gangkar Punsum (7,529 m/24,700 ft) is one of the world's highest unclimbed peaks; cut by valleys formed by tributaries of the Brahmaputra; thick forests in south
Currency ngultrum, although the Indian rupee is also accepted
GNP per capita (PPP) (US$) 1,496 (1999 est)
Resources limestone, gypsum, coal, slate, dolomite, lead, talc, copper
Population 2,124,000 (2000 est)
Population density (per sq km) 44 (1999 est)
Language Dzongkha (a Tibetan dialect; official), Tibetan, Sharchop, Bumthap, Nepali, English
Religion 70% Mahayana Buddhist (state religion), 25% Hindu
Time difference GMT +6

Bolivia

Map page 156

National name República de Bolivia/ Republic of Bolivia
Area 1,098,581 sq km/ 424,162 sq mi
Capital La Paz (seat of government), Sucre (legal capital and seat of the judiciary)
Major towns/cities Santa Cruz, Cochabamba, Oruro, El Alto, Potosí, Tarija
Physical features high plateau (Altiplano) between mountain ridges (cordilleras); forest and lowlands (llano) in east; Andes; lakes Titicaca (the world's highest navigable lake, 3,800 m/12,500 ft) and Poopó
Currency boliviano
GNP per capita (PPP) (US$) 2,193 (1999)
Resources petroleum, natural gas, tin (world's fifth-largest producer), zinc, silver, gold, lead, antimony, tungsten, copper
Population 8,329,000 (2000 est)
Population density (per sq km) 7 (1999 est)
Language Spanish (official) (4%), Aymara, Quechua
Religion Roman Catholic 90% (state-recognized)
Time difference GMT -4

Bosnia-Herzegovina

Map page 92

National name Bosna i Hercegovina/ Bosnia-Herzegovina
Area 51,129 sq km/ 19,740 sq mi
Capital Sarajevo
Major towns/cities Banja Luka, Mostar, Prijedor, Tuzla, Zenica, Bihac, Gorazde
Physical features barren, mountainous country, part of the Dinaric Alps; limestone gorges; 20 km/12 mi of coastline with no harbour
Currency dinar
GNP per capita (PPP) (US$) 450 (1996 est)
Resources copper, lead, zinc, iron ore, coal, bauxite, manganese
Population 3,972,000 (2000 est)
Population density (per sq km) 75 (1999 est)
Language Serbian, Croat, Bosnian
Religion 40% Muslim, 31% Serbian Orthodox, 15% Roman Catholic
Time difference GMT +1

Botswana

Map page 130

National name Republic of Botswana
Area 582,000 sq km/ 224,710 sq mi
Capital Gaborone
Major towns/cities Mahalapye, Serowe, Francistown, Selebi-Phikwe, Molepolole, Maun
Physical features Kalahari Desert in southwest (70-

80% of national territory is desert), plains (Makgadikgadi salt pans) in east, fertile lands and Okavango Delta in north
Currency franc CFA
GNP per capita (PPP) (US$) 6,032 (1999)
Resources diamonds (world's third-largest producer), copper-nickel ore, coal, soda ash, gold, cobalt, salt, plutonium, asbestos, chromite, iron, silver, manganese, talc, uranium
Population 1,622,000 (2000 est)
Population density (per sq km) 3 (1999 est)
Language English (official), Setswana (national)
Religion Christian 50%, animist 50%
Time difference GMT +2

Brazil

Map page 154

National name República Federativa do Brasil/Federative Republic of Brazil
Area 8,511,965 sq km/ 3,286,469 sq mi
Capital Brasília
Major towns/cities São Paulo, Belo Horizonte, Nova Iguaçu, Rio de Janeiro, Belém, Recife, Porto Alegre, Salvador, Curitiba, Manaus, Fortaleza
Major ports Rio de Janeiro, Belém, Recife, Porto Alegre, Salvador
Physical features the densely forested Amazon basin covers the northern half of the country with a network of rivers; south is fertile; enormous energy resources, both hydroelectric (Itaipú Reservoir on the Paraná, and Tucuruí on the Tocantins) and nuclear (uranium ores); mostly tropical climate
Currency real
GNP per capita (PPP) (US$) 6,317 (1999)
Resources iron ore (world's second-largest producer), tin (world's fourth-largest producer), aluminium (world's fourth-largest producer), gold, phosphates, platinum, bauxite, uranium, manganese, coal, copper, petroleum, natural gas, hydroelectric power, forests
Population 170,115,000 (2000 est)
Population density (per sq km) 20 (1999 est)
Language Portuguese (official), Spanish, English, French, 120 Indian languages
Religion Roman Catholic 70%; Indian faiths
Time difference GMT -2/5

Brunei

Map page 110

National name Negara Brunei Darussalam/State of Brunei
Area 5,765 sq km/ 2,225 sq mi
Capital Bandar Seri Begawan (and chief port)
Major towns/cities Seria, Kuala Belait
Physical features flat coastal plain with hilly lowland in west and mountains in east (Mount Pagon 1,850 m/ 6,070 ft); 75% of the area is forested; the Limbang valley splits Brunei in two, and its cession to Sarawak in 1890 is disputed by Brunei; tropical climate; Temburong, Tutong, and Belait rivers
Currency Bruneian dollar, although the Singapore dollar is also accepted
GNP per capita (PPP) (US$) 24,824 (1999 est)
Resources petroleum, natural gas
Population 328,000 (2000 est)
Population density (per sq km) 56 (1999 est)
Language Malay (official), Chinese (Hokkien), English
Religion Muslim 66%, Buddhist 14%, Christian 10%
Time difference GMT +8

Bulgaria

Map page 92

National name Republika Bulgaria/Republic of Bulgaria
Area 110,912 sq km/ 42,823 sq mi
Capital Sofia
Major towns/cities Plovdiv, Varna, Ruse,

Burgas, Stara Zagora, Pleven
Major ports Burgas, Varna
Physical features lowland plains in north and southeast separated by mountains (Balkan and Rhodope) that cover three-quarters of the country; River Danube in north
Currency lev
GNP per capita (PPP) (US$) 4,914 (1999)
Resources coal, iron ore, manganese, lead, zinc, petroleum
Population 8,225,000 (2000 est)
Population density (per sq km) 75 (1999 est)
Language Bulgarian (official), Turkish
Religion Eastern Orthodox Christian, Muslim, Jewish, Roman Catholic, Protestant
Time difference GMT +2

Burkina Faso

Map page 126

Area 274,122 sq km/ 105,838 sq mi
Capital Ouagadougou
Major towns/cities Bobo-Dioulasso, Koudougou, Banfora, Ouahigouya, Tenkodogo
Physical features landlocked plateau with hills in west and southeast; headwaters of the River Volta; semiarid in north, forest and farmland in south; linked by rail to Abidjan in Côte d'Ivoire, Burkina Faso's only outlet to the sea
Currency franc CFA
GNP per capita (PPP) (US$) 898 (1999 est)
Resources manganese, zinc, limestone, phosphates, diamonds, gold, antimony, marble, silver, lead
Population 11,937,000 (2000 est)
Population density (per sq km) 42 (1999 est)
Language French (official), 50 Sudanic languages (90%)
Religion animist 40%, Sunni Muslim 50%, Christian (mainly Roman Catholic) 10%
Time difference GMT+/-0

Burundi

Map page 128

National name Republika y'Uburundi/ République du Burundi/ Republic of Burundi
Area 27,834 sq km/ 10,746 sq mi
Capital Bujumbura
Major towns/cities Gitega, Bururi, Ngozi, Muyinga, Ruyigi, Kayanaza
Physical features landlocked grassy highland straddling watershed of Nile and Congo; Lake Tanganyika, Great Rift Valley
Currency Burundi franc
GNP per capita (PPP) (US$) 553 (1999 est)
Resources nickel, gold, tungsten, phosphates, vanadium, uranium, peat, petroleum deposits have been detected
Population 6,695,000 (2000 est)
Population density (per sq km) 236 (1999 est)
Language Kirundi, French (both official), Kiswahili
Religion Roman Catholic 62%, Pentecostalist 5%, Anglican 1%, Muslim 1%, animist
Time difference GMT +2

Cambodia

Map page 108

National name Preah Réaché'anachâkr Kâmpuchéa/Kingdom of Cambodia
Area 181,035 sq km/ 69,897 sq mi
Capital Phnum Penh
Major towns/cities Bătdâmbâng, Kâmpōng Cham, Siĕmréab, Prey Vêng
Major ports Kâmpōng Cham
Physical features mostly flat, forested plains with mountains in southwest and north; Mekong River runs north-south; Lake Tonle Sap
Currency Cambodian riel
GNP per capita (PPP) (US$) 1,286 (1999 est)
Resources phosphates, iron ore, gemstones, bauxite,

silicon, manganese
Population 11,168,000 (2000 est)
Population density (per sq km) 66 (1999 est)
Language Khmer (official), French
Religion Theravada Buddhist 95%, Muslim, Roman Catholic
Time difference GMT +7

Cameroon

Map page 126

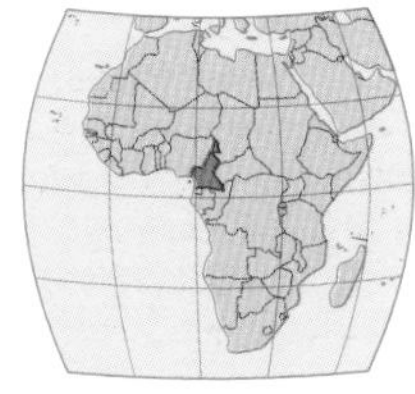

National name République du Cameroun/Republic of Cameroon
Area 475,440 sq km/ 183,567 sq mi
Capital Yaoundé
Major towns/cities Garoua, Douala, Nkongsamba, Maroua, Bamenda, Bafoussam, Ngaoundéré
Major ports Douala
Physical features desert in far north in the Lake Chad basin, mountains in west, dry savannah plateau in the intermediate area, and dense tropical rainforest in south; Mount Cameroon 4,070 m/13,358 ft, an active volcano on the coast, west of the Adamawa Mountains
Currency franc CFA
GNP per capita (PPP) (US$) 1,444 (1999)
Resources petroleum, natural gas, tin ore, limestone, bauxite, iron ore, uranium, gold
Population 15,085,000 (2000 est)
Population density (per sq km) 31 (1999 est)
Language French, English (both official; often spoken in pidgin), Sudanic languages (in the north), Bantu languages (elsewhere); there has been some discontent with the emphasis on French - there are 163 indigenous peoples with their own African languages
Religion animist 50%, Christian 33%, Muslim 16%
Time difference GMT +1

Canada

Map page 140

Area 9,970,610 sq km/ 3,849,652 sq mi
Capital Ottawa
Major towns/cities Toronto, Montréal, Vancouver, Edmonton, Calgary, Winnipeg, Québec, Hamilton, Saskatoon, Halifax, London, Kitchener, Mississauga, Laval, Surrey
Physical features mountains in west, with low-lying plains in interior and rolling hills in east; St. Lawrence Seaway, Mackenzie River; Great Lakes; Arctic Archipelago; Rocky Mountains; Great Plains or Prairies; Canadian Shield; Niagara Falls; climate varies from temperate in south to arctic in north; 45% of country forested
Currency Canadian dollar
GNP per capita (PPP) (US$) 23,725 (1999)
Resources petroleum, natural gas, coal, copper (world's third-largest producer), nickel (world's second-largest producer), lead (world's fifth-largest producer), zinc (world's largest producer), iron, gold, uranium, timber
Population 31,147,000 (2000 est)
Population density (per sq km) 3 (1999 est)
Language English (60%), French (24%) (both official), American Indian languages, Inuktitut (Inuit)
Religion Roman Catholic 45%, various Protestant denominations
Time difference GMT -3.5/9

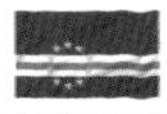

Cape Verde

Map page 126

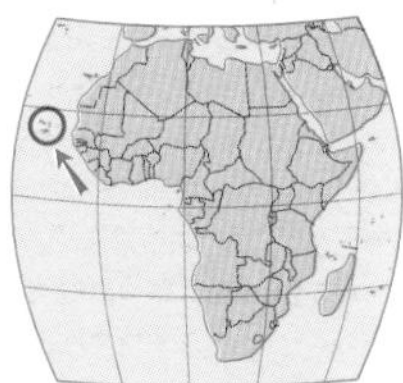

National name República de Cabo Verde/Republic of Cape Verde
Area 4,033 sq km/ 1,557 sq mi
Capital Praia
Major towns/cities Mindelo, Santa Maria
Major ports Mindelo

Physical features archipelago of ten volcanic islands 565 km/350 mi west of Senegal; the windward (Barlavento) group includes Santo Antão, São Vicente, Santa Luzia, São Nicolau, Sal, and Boa Vista; the leeward (Sotovento) group comprises Maio, São Tiago, Fogo, and Brava; all but Santa Luzia are inhabited
Currency Cape Verde escudo
GNP per capita (PPP) (US$) 3,497 (1999 est)
Resources salt, pozzolana (volcanic rock), limestone, basalt, kaolin
Population 428,000 (2000 est)
Population density (per sq km) 104 (1999 est)
Language Portuguese (official), Creole
Religion Roman Catholic 93%, Protestant (Nazarene Church)
Time difference GMT -1

Central African Republic

Map page 128

National name République Centrafricaine/Central African Republic
Area 622,436 sq km/ 240,322 sq mi
Capital Bangui
Major towns/cities Berbérati, Bouar, Bambari, Bossangoa, Carnot, Kaga Bandoro
Physical features landlocked flat plateau, with rivers flowing north and south, and hills in northeast and southwest; dry in north, rainforest in southwest; mostly wooded; Kotto and Mbali river falls; the Oubangui River rises 6 m/20 ft at Bangui during the wet season (June-November)
Currency franc CFA
GNP per capita (PPP) (US$) 1,131 (1999 est)
Resources gem diamonds and industrial diamonds, gold, uranium, iron ore, manganese, copper
Population 3,615,000 (2000 est)
Population density (per sq km) 6 (1999 est)
Language French (official), Sangho (national), Arabic, Hunsa, Swahili
Religion Protestant 25%, Roman Catholic 25%, animist 24%, Muslim 15%
Time difference GMT +1

Chad

Map page 122

National name République du Tchad/ Republic of Chad
Area 1,284,000 sq km/ 495,752 sq mi
Capital Ndjamena (formerly Fort Lamy)
Major towns/cities Sarh, Moundou, Abéché, Bongor, Doba, Kélo, Koumra
Physical features landlocked state with mountains (Tibetsi) and part of Sahara Desert in north; moist savannah in south; rivers in south flow northwest to Lake Chad
Currency franc CFA
GNP per capita (PPP) (US$) 816 (1999 est)
Resources petroleum, tungsten, tin ore, bauxite, iron ore, gold, uranium, limestone, kaolin, titanium
Population 7,651,000 (2000 est)
Population density (per sq km) 6 (1999 est)
Language French, Arabic (both official), over 100 African languages
Religion Muslim 50%, Christian 25%, animist 25%
Time difference GMT +1

Chile

Map page 158

National name República de Chile/ Republic of Chile
Area 756,950 sq km/ 292,258 sq mi
Capital Santiago
Major towns/cities Concepción, Viña del Mar, Valparaíso, Talcahuano, Puente Alto, Temuco, Antofagasta
Major ports Valparaíso, Antofagasta, Arica, Iquique,

Punta Arenas
Physical features Andes mountains along eastern border, Atacama Desert in north, fertile central valley, grazing land and forest in south
Territories Easter Island, Juan Fernández Islands, part of Tierra del Fuego, claim to part of Antarctica
Currency Chilean peso
GNP per capita (PPP) (US$) 8,370 (1999)
Resources copper (world's largest producer), gold, silver, iron ore, molybdenum, cobalt, iodine, saltpetre, coal, natural gas, petroleum, hydroelectric power
Population 15,211,000 (2000 est)
Population density (per sq km) 20 (1999 est)
Language Spanish (official)
Religion Roman Catholic 80%, Protestant 13%, atheist and nonreligious 6%
Time difference GMT -4

China

Map page 98

National name Zhonghua Renmin Gongheguo (Zhongguo)/People's Republic of China
Area 9,572,900 sq km/ 3,696,000 sq mi
Capital Beijing (or Peking)
Major towns/cities Shanghai, Hong Kong, Chongqing, Tianjin, Guangzhou (English Canton), Shenyang (formerly Mukden), Wuhan, Nanjing, Harbin, Chengdu, Xi'an
Major ports Tianjin, Shanghai, Hong Kong, Qingdao, Guangzhou
Physical features two-thirds of China is mountains or desert (north and west); the low-lying east is irrigated by rivers Huang He (Yellow River), Chang Jiang (Yangtze-Kiang), Xi Jiang (Si Kiang)
Territories Paracel Islands
Currency yuan
GNP per capita (PPP) (US$) 3,291 (1999)
Resources coal, graphite, tungsten, molybdenum, antimony, tin (world's largest producer), lead (world's fifth-largest producer), mercury, bauxite, phosphate rock, iron ore (world's largest producer), diamonds, gold, manganese, zinc (world's third-largest producer), petroleum, natural gas, fish
Population 1,277,558,000 (2000 est)
Population density (per sq km) 133 (1999 est)
Language Chinese (dialects include Mandarin (official), Yue (Cantonese), Wu (Shanghaiese), Minbai, Minnah, Xiang, Gan, and Hakka)
Religion Taoist, Confucianist, and Buddhist; Muslim 2-3%; Christian about 1% (divided between the 'patriotic' church established in 1958 and the 'loyal' church subject to Rome); Protestant 3 million
Time difference GMT +8

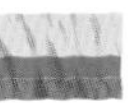

Colombia

Map page 156

National name República de Colombia/ Republic of Colombia
Area 1,141,748 sq km/ 440,828 sq mi
Capital Bogotá
Major towns/cities Medellín, Cali, Barranquilla, Cartagena, Bucaramanga, Cúcuta, Ibagué
Major ports Barranquilla, Cartagena, Buenaventura
Physical features the Andes mountains run north-south; flat coastland in west and plains (llanos) in east; Magdalena River runs north to Caribbean Sea; includes islands of Providencia, San Andrés, and Mapelo; almost half the country is forested
Currency Colombian peso
GNP per capita (PPP) (US$) 5,709 (1999 est)
Resources petroleum, natural gas, coal, nickel, emeralds (accounts for about half of world production), gold, manganese, copper, lead, mercury, platinum, limestone, phosphates
Population 42,321,000 (2000 est)
Population density (per sq km) 36 (1999 est)
Language Spanish (official) (95%)
Religion Roman Catholic
Time difference GMT -5

Comoros

Map page 130

National name Jumhuriyyat al-Qumur al-Itthadiyah al-Islamiyah (Arabic), République fédérale islamique des Comores (French)/Federal Islamic Republic of the Comoros
Area 1,862 sq km/718 sq mi
Capital Moroni
Major towns/cities Mutsamudu, Domoni, Fomboni, Mitsamiouli
Physical features comprises the volcanic islands of Njazídja, Nzwani, and Mwali (formerly Grande Comore, Anjouan, Moheli); at northern end of Mozambique Channel in Indian Ocean between Madagascar and coast of Africa
Currency Comorian franc
GNP per capita (PPP) (US$) 1,360 (1999 est)
Population 694,000 (2000 est)
Population density (per sq km) 363 (1999 est)
Language Arabic, French (both official), Comorian (a Swahili and Arabic dialect), Makua
Religion Muslim; Islam is the state religion
Time difference GMT +3

Congo, Democratic Republic of

Map page 128

National name République Démocratique du Congo/Democratic Republic of Congo
Area 2,344,900 sq km/905,366 sq mi
Capital Kinshasa
Major towns/cities Lubumbashi, Kananga, Mbuji-Mayi, Kisangani, Kolwezi, Likasi, Boma
Major ports Matadi, Kalemie
Physical features Congo River basin has tropical rainforest (second-largest remaining in world) and savannah; mountains in east and west; lakes Tanganyika, Albert, Edward; Ruwenzori Range
Currency congolese franc
GNP per capita (PPP) (US$) 731 (1999 est)
Resources petroleum, copper, cobalt (65% of world's reserves), manganese, zinc, tin, uranium, silver, gold, diamonds (one of the world's largest producers of industrial diamonds)
Population 51,654,000 (2000 est)
Population density (per sq km) 21 (1999 est)
Language French (official), Swahili, Lingala, Kikongo, Tshiluba (all national languages), over 200 other languages
Religion Roman Catholic 41%, Protestant 32%, Kimbanguist 13%, animist 10%, Muslim 1-5%
Time difference GMT +1/2

Congo

Map page 126

National name République du Congo/Republic of Congo
Area 342,000 sq km/132,046 sq mi
Capital Brazzaville
Major towns/cities Pointe-Noire, Nkayi, Loubomo, Bouenza, Mossendjo, Ouésso, Owando
Major ports Pointe-Noire
Physical features narrow coastal plain rises to central plateau, then falls into northern basin; Congo River on the border with the Democratic Republic of Congo; half the country is rainforest
Currency franc CFA
GNP per capita (PPP) (US$) 897 (1999)
Resources petroleum, natural gas, lead, zinc, gold, copper, phosphate, iron ore, potash, bauxite
Population 2,943,000 (2000 est)
Population density (per sq km) 8 (1999 est)
Language French (official), Kongo, Monokutuba and Lingala (both patois), and other dialects
Religion Christian 50%, animist 48%, Muslim 2%
Time difference GMT +1

Costa Rica

Map page 152

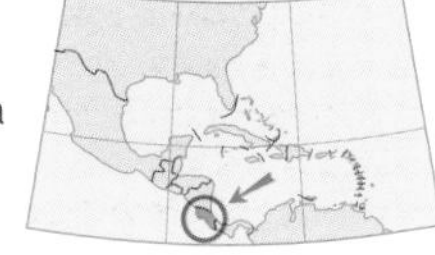

National name República de Costa Rica/Republic of Costa Rica
Area 51,100 sq km/ 19,729 sq mi
Capital San José
Major towns/cities Alajuela, Cartago, Limón, Puntarenas, San Isidro, Desamparados
Major ports Limón, Puntarenas
Physical features high central plateau and tropical coasts; Costa Rica was once entirely forested, containing an estimated 5% of the Earth's flora and fauna
Currency colón
GNP per capita (PPP) (US$) 5,770 (1999 est)
Resources gold, salt, hydro power
Population 4,023,000 (2000 est)
Population density (per sq km) 77 (1999 est)
Language Spanish (official)
Religion Roman Catholic 95% (state religion)
Time difference GMT -6

Côte d'Ivoire

Map page 126

National name République de la Côte d'Ivoire/Republic of the Ivory Coast
Area 322,463 sq km/ 124,502 sq mi
Capital Yamoussoukro
Major towns/cities Abidjan, Bouaké, Daloa, Man, Korhogo, Gagnoa
Major ports Abidjan, San Pedro
Physical features tropical rainforest (diminishing as exploited) in south; savannah and low mountains in north; coastal plain; Vridi canal, Kossou dam, Monts du Toura
Currency franc CFA
GNP per capita (PPP) (US$) 1,546 (1999)
Resources petroleum, natural gas, diamonds, gold, nickel, reserves of manganese, iron ore, bauxite
Population 14,786,000 (2000 est)
Population density (per sq km) 45 (1999 est)
Language French (official), over 60 ethnic languages
Religion animist 17%, Muslim 39% (mainly in north), Christian 26% (mainly Roman Catholic in south)
Time difference GMT +/-0

Croatia

Map page 92

National name Republika Hrvatska/Republic of Croatia
Area 56,538 sq km/ 21,829 sq mi
Capital Zagreb
Major towns/cities Osijek, Split, Dubrovnik, Rijeka, Zadar, Pula
Major ports chief port: Rijeka (Fiume); other ports: Zadar, Šibenik, Split, Dubrovnik
Physical features Adriatic coastline with large islands; very mountainous, with part of the Karst region and the Julian and Styrian Alps; some marshland
Currency kuna
GNP per capita (PPP) (US$) 6,915 (1999)
Resources petroleum, natural gas, coal, lignite, bauxite, iron ore, salt
Population 4,473,000 (2000 est)
Population density (per sq km) 79 (1999 est)
Language Croat (official), Serbian
Religion Roman Catholic (Croats) 76.5%; Orthodox Christian (Serbs) 11%, Protestant 1.4%, Muslim 1.2%
Time difference GMT +1

Cuba

Map page 152

National name República de Cuba/Republic of Cuba
Area 110,860 sq km/42,803 sq mi
Capital Havana
Major towns/cities Santiago de Cuba, Camagüey,

Holguín, Guantánamo, Santa Clara, Bayamo, Cienfuegos

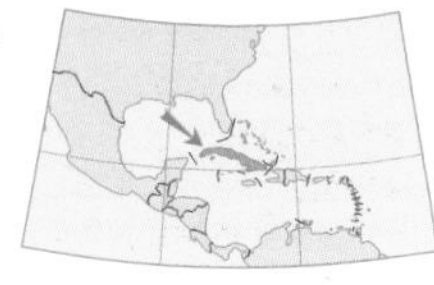

Physical features comprises Cuba and smaller islands including Isle of Youth; low hills; Sierra Maestra mountains in southeast; Cuba has 3,380 km/2,100 mi of coastline, with deep bays, sandy beaches, coral islands and reefs
Currency Cuban peso
GNP per capita (PPP) (US$) N/A
Resources iron ore, copper, chromite, gold, manganese, nickel, cobalt, silver, salt
Population 11,201,000 (2000 est)
Population density (per sq km) 101 (1999 est)
Language Spanish (official)
Religion Roman Catholic; also Episcopalians and Methodists
Time difference GMT -5

Cyprus

Map page 94

National name Kipriakí Dimokratía/Greek Republic of Cyprus (south); Kibris Cumhuriyeti/Turkish Republic of Northern Cyprus (north)

Area 9,251 sq km/3,571 sq mi (3,335 sq km/ 1,287 sq mi is Turkish-occupied)
Capital Nicosia (divided between Greek and Turkish Cypriots)
Major towns/cities Limassol, Larnaka, Pafos, Lefkosià, Famagusta
Major ports Limassol, Larnaka, and Pafos (Greek); Keryneia and Famagusta (Turkish)
Physical features central plain between two east-west mountain ranges
Currency Cyprus pound and Turkish lira
GNP per capita (PPP) (US$) 18,395 (1999 est)
Resources copper precipitates, beutonite, umber and other ochres
Population 786,000 (2000 est)
Population density (per sq km) 84 (1999 est)
Language Greek, Turkish (both official), English
Religion Greek Orthodox 78%, Sunni Muslim 18%, Maronite, Armenian Apostolic
Time difference GMT +2

Czech Republic

Map page 76

National name Ceská Republika/Czech Republic
Area 78,864 sq km/ 30,449 sq mi
Capital Prague
Major towns/cities Brno, Ostrava, Olomouc, Liberec, Plzen, Hradec Králové, České Budějovice
Physical features mountainous; rivers: Morava, Labe (Elbe), Vltava (Moldau)
Currency koruna (based on the Czechoslovak koruna)
GNP per capita (PPP) (US$) 12,289 (1999)
Resources coal, lignite
Population 10,244,000 (2000 est)
Population density (per sq km) 130 (1999 est)
Language Czech (official), Slovak
Religion Roman Catholic 39%, atheist 30%, Protestant 5%, Orthodox 3%
Time difference GMT +1

Denmark

Map page 74

National name Kongeriget Danmark/Kingdom of Denmark
Area 43,075 sq km/ 16,631 sq mi
Capital Copenhagen
Major towns/cities Århus, Odense, Ålborg, Esbjerg, Randers, Kolding, Horsens

Major ports Århus, Odense, Ålborg, Esbjerg
Physical features comprises the Jutland peninsula and about 500 islands (100 inhabited) including Bornholm in the Baltic Sea; the land is flat and

cultivated; sand dunes and lagoons on the west coast and long inlets on the east; the main island is Sjælland (Zealand), where most of Copenhagen is located (the rest is on the island of Amager)
Territories the dependencies of Faroe Islands and Greenland
Currency Danish krone
GNP per capita (PPP) (US$) 24,280 (1999)
Resources crude petroleum, natural gas, salt, limestone
Population 5,293,000 (2000 est)
Population density (per sq km) 123 (1999 est)
Language Danish (official), German
Religion Evangelical Lutheran 87% (national church), other Protestant and Roman Catholic 3%
Time difference GMT +1

Djibouti

Map page 122

National name Jumhouriyya Djibouti/ Republic of Djibouti
Area 23,200 sq km/ 8,957 sq mi
Capital Djibouti (and chief port)
Major towns/cities Tadjoura, Obock, Dikhil, Ali-Sabieh
Physical features mountains divide an inland plateau from a coastal plain; hot and arid
Currency Djibouti franc
GNP per capita (PPP) (US$) 1,200 (1999 est)
Population 638,000 (2000 est)
Population density (per sq km) 27 (1999 est)
Language French (official), Issa (Somali), Afar, Arabic
Religion Sunni Muslim
Time difference GMT +3

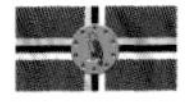

Dominica

Map page 152

National name Commonwealth of Dominica
Area 751 sq km/290 sq mi
Capital Roseau
Major towns/cities Portsmouth, Marigot, Mahaut, Atkinson, Grand Bay
Major ports Roseau, Portsmouth, Berekua, Marigot
Physical features second-largest of the Windward Islands, mountainous central ridge with tropical rainforest
Currency East Caribbean dollar, although the pound sterling and French franc are also accepted
GNP per capita (PPP) (US$) 4,825 (1999)
Resources pumice, limestone, clay
Population 71,000 (2000 est)
Population density (per sq km) 100 (1999 est)
Language English (official), a Dominican patois (which reflects earlier periods of French rule)
Religion Roman Catholic 80%
Time difference GMT -4

Dominican Republic

Map page 152

National name República Dominicana/ Dominican Republic
Area 48,442 sq km/ 18,703 sq mi
Capital Santo Domingo
Major towns/cities Santiago, La Romana, San Pedro de Macoris, La Vega, San Juan, San Cristóbal
Physical features comprises eastern two-thirds of island of Hispaniola; central mountain range with fertile valleys; Pico Duarte 3,174 m/10,417 ft, highest point in Caribbean islands
Currency Dominican Republic peso
GNP per capita (PPP) (US$) 4,653 (1999 est)
Resources ferro-nickel, gold, silver
Population 8,495,000 (2000 est)
Population density (per sq km) 173 (1999 est)
Language Spanish (official)
Religion Roman Catholic
Time difference GMT -4

Ecuador

Map page 156

National name República del Ecuador/ Republic of Ecuador
Area 270,670 sq km/ 104,505 sq mi
Capital Quito
Major towns/cities Guayaquil, Cuenca, Machala, Portoviejo, Manta, Ambato, Santo Domingo
Major ports Guayaquil
Physical features coastal plain rises sharply to Andes Mountains, which are divided into a series of cultivated valleys; flat, low-lying rainforest in the east; Galapagos Islands; Cotopaxi, the world's highest active volcano. Ecuador is crossed by the Equator, from which it derives its name
Currency sucre
GNP per capita (PPP) (US$) 2,605 (1999)
Resources petroleum, natural gas, gold, silver, copper, zinc, antimony, iron, uranium, lead, coal
Population 12,646,000 (2000 est)
Population density (per sq km) 46 (1999 est)
Language Spanish (official), Quechua, Jivaro, other indigenous languages
Religion Roman Catholic
Time difference GMT -5

Egypt

Map page 122

National name Jumhuriyyat Misr al-'Arabiyya/Arab Republic of Egypt
Area 1,001,450 sq km/ 386,659 sq mi
Capital Cairo
Major towns/cities El Giza, Shubrâ el Kheima, Alexandria, Port Said, El-Mahalla el-Koubra, El Mansûra, Suez
Major ports Alexandria, Port Said, Suez, Dumyât, Shubra Al Khayma
Physical features mostly desert; hills in east; fertile land along Nile valley and delta; cultivated and settled area is about 35,500 sq km/13,700 sq mi; Aswan High Dam and Lake Nasser; Sinai
Currency Egyptian pound
GNP per capita (PPP) (US$) 3,303 (1999)
Resources petroleum, natural gas, phosphates, manganese, uranium, coal, iron ore, gold
Population 68,470,000 (2000 est)
Population density (per sq km) 67 (1999 est)
Language Arabic (official), Coptic (derived from ancient Egyptian), English, French
Religion Sunni Muslim 90%, Coptic Christian and other Christian 6%
Time difference GMT +2

El Salvador

Map page 152

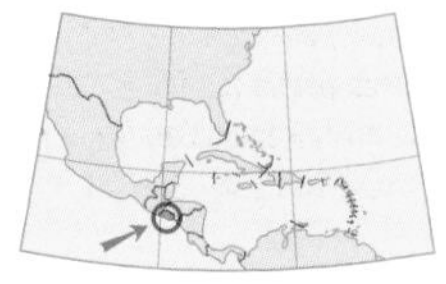

National name República de El Salvador/Republic of El Salvador
Area 21,393 sq km/ 8,259 sq mi
Capital San Salvador
Major towns/cities Santa Ana, San Miguel, Nueva San Salvador, Apopa, Delgado
Physical features narrow coastal plain, rising to mountains in north with central plateau
Currency US dollar (replaced Salvadorean colón in 2001)
GNP per capita (PPP) (US$) 4,048 (1999 est)
Resources salt, limestone, gypsum
Population 6,276,000 (2000 est)
Population density (per sq km) 288 (1999 est)
Language Spanish (official), Nahuatl
Religion about 75% Roman Catholic, Protestant
Time difference GMT -6

Equatorial Guinea

Map page 126

National name República de Guinea Ecuatorial/Republic of Equatorial Guinea

Area 28,051 sq km/ 10,830 sq mi
Capital Malabo
Major towns/cities Bata, Mongomo, Ela Nguema, Mbini, Campo Yaunde, Los Angeles
Physical features comprises mainland Río Muni, plus the small islands of Corisco, Elobey Grande and Elobey Chico, and Bioko (formerly Fernando Po) together with Annobón (formerly Pagalu); nearly half the land is forested; volcanic mountains on Bioko
Currency franc CFA
GNP per capita (PPP) (US$) 3,545 (1999 est)
Resources petroleum, natural gas, gold, uranium, iron ore, tantalum, manganese
Population 453,000 (2000 est)
Population density (per sq km) 16 (1999 est)
Language Spanish (official), pidgin English, a Portuguese patois (on Annobón, whose people were formerly slaves of the Portuguese), Fang and other African patois (on Río Muni)
Religion Roman Catholic, Protestant, animist
Time difference GMT +1

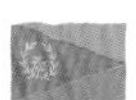

Eritrea

Map page 122

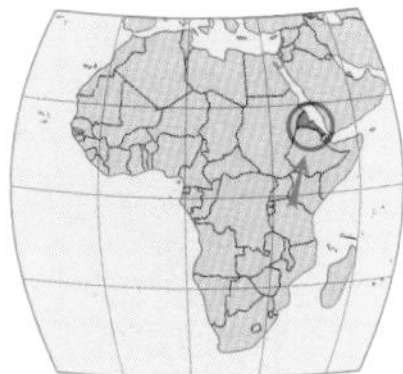

National name Hagere Eretra al-Dawla al-Iritra/ State of Eritrea
Area 125,000 sq km/ 48,262 sq mi
Capital Asmara
Major towns/cities Assab, Keren, Massawa, Adi Ugri, Ed
Major ports Assab, Massawa
Physical features coastline along the Red Sea 1,000 km/620 mi; narrow coastal plain that rises to an inland plateau; Dahlak Islands
Currency Ethiopian nakfa
GNP per capita (PPP) (US$) 1,012 (1999 est)
Resources gold, silver, copper, zinc, sulphur, nickel, chrome, potash, basalt, limestone, marble, sand, silicates
Population 3,850,000 (2000 est)
Population density (per sq km) 30 (1999 est)
Language Tigre, Tigrinya, Arabic, English, Afar, Amharic, Kunama, Italian
Religion mainly Sunni Muslim and Coptic Christian, some Roman Catholic, Protestant, and animist
Time difference GMT +3

Estonia

Map page 74

National name Eesti Vabariik/Republic of Estonia
Area 45,000 sq km/ 17,374 sq mi
Capital Tallinn
Major towns/cities Tartu, Narva, Kohtla-Järve, Pärnu
Physical features lakes and marshes in a partly forested plain; 774 km/481 mi of coastline; mild climate; Lake Peipus and Narva River forming boundary with Russian Federation; Baltic islands, the largest of which is Saaremaa
Currency kroon
GNP per capita (PPP) (US$) 7,826 (1999)
Resources oilshale, peat, phosphorite ore, superphosphates
Population 1,396,000 (2000 est)
Population density (per sq km) 31 (1999 est)
Language Estonian (official), Russian
Religion Eastern Orthodox, Evangelical Lutheran, Russian Orthodox, Muslim, Judaism
Time difference GMT +2

Ethiopia

Map page 120

National name Ya'Ityopya Federalawi Dimokrasiyawi Repeblik/Federal Democratic Republic of Ethiopia
Area 1,096,900 sq km/423,513 sq mi
Capital Addis Ababa
Major towns/cities Dirē Dawa, Harar, Nazrēt, Desē, Gonder, Mek'ele, Bahir Dar
Physical features a high plateau with central

mountain range divided by Rift Valley; plains in east; source of Blue Nile River; Danakil and Ogaden deserts
Currency Ethiopian birr
GNP per capita (PPP) (US$) 599 (1999)
Resources gold, salt, platinum, copper, potash. Reserves of petroleum have not been exploited
Population 62,565,000 (2000 est)
Population density (per sq km) 56 (1999 est)
Language Amharic (official), Arabic, Tigrinya, Orominga, about 100 other local languages
Religion Muslim 45%, Ethiopian Orthodox Church (which has had its own patriarch since 1976) 35%, animist 12%, other Christian 8%
Time difference GMT +3

Fiji

Map page 132

National name Matanitu Ko Viti/ Republic of the Fiji Islands
Area 18,333 sq km/ 7,078 sq mi
Capital Suva
Major towns/cities Lautoka, Nadi, Ba, Labasa, Nausori
Major ports Lautoka, Levuka
Physical features comprises about 844 Melanesian and Polynesian islands and islets (about 100 inhabited), the largest being Viti Levu (10,429 sq km/4,028 sq mi) and Vanua Levu (5,556 sq km/2,146 sq mi); mountainous, volcanic, with tropical rainforest and grasslands; almost all islands surrounded by coral reefs; high volcanic peaks
Currency Fiji dollar
GNP per capita (PPP) (US$) 4,536 (1999)
Resources gold, silver, copper
Population 817,000 (2000 est)
Population density (per sq km) 44 (1999 est)
Language English (official), Fijian, Hindi
Religion Methodist 37%, Hindu 38%, Muslim 8%, Roman Catholic 8%, Sikh
Time difference GMT +12

Finland

Map page 74

National name Suomen Tasavalta (Finnish)/ Republiken Finland (Swedish)/Republic of Finland
Area 338,145 sq km/ 130,557 sq mi
Capital Helsinki (Swedish Helsingfors)
Major towns/cities Tampere, Turku, Espoo, Vantaa, Oulu
Major ports Turku, Oulu
Physical features most of the country is forest, with low hills and about 60,000 lakes; one-third is within the Arctic Circle; archipelago in south includes Åland Islands; Helsinki is the most northerly national capital on the European continent. At the 70th parallel there is constant daylight for 73 days in summer and 51 days of uninterrupted night in winter.
Currency markka
GNP per capita (PPP) (US$) 21,209 (1999)
Resources copper ore, lead ore, gold, zinc ore, silver, peat, hydro power, forests
Population 5,176,000 (2000 est)
Population density (per sq km) 15 (1999 est)
Language Finnish (93%), Swedish (6%) (both official), Saami (Lapp), Russian
Religion Evangelical Lutheran 87%, Greek Orthodox 1%
Time difference GMT +2

France

Map page 84

National name République Française/French Republic
Area (including Corsica) 543,965 sq km/ 210,024 sq mi
Capital Paris
Major towns/cities Lyon, Lille, Bordeaux, Toulouse,

Nantes, Marseille, Nice, Strasbourg, Montpellier, Rennes, Le Havre
Major ports Marseille, Nice, Le Havre
Physical features rivers Seine, Loire, Garonne, Rhône; mountain ranges Alps, Massif Central, Pyrenees, Jura, Vosges, Cévennes; Auvergne mountain region; Mont Blanc (4,810 m/15,781 ft); Ardennes forest; Riviera; caves of Dordogne with relics of early humans; the island of Corsica
Territories Guadeloupe, French Guiana, Martinique, Réunion, St. Pierre and Miquelon, Southern and Antarctic Territories, New Caledonia, French Polynesia, Wallis and Futuna, Mayotte, Bassas da India, Clipperton Island, Europa Island, Glorioso Islands, Juan de Nova Island, Tromelin Island
Currency franc
GNP per capita (PPP) (US$) 21,897 (1999)
Resources coal, petroleum, natural gas, iron ore, copper, zinc, bauxite
Population 59,080,000 (2000 est)
Population density (per sq km) 108 (1999 est)
Language French (official; regional languages include Basque, Breton, Catalan, Corsican, and Provençal)
Religion Roman Catholic, about 90%; also Muslim, Protestant, and Jewish minorities
Time difference GMT +1

Gabon

Map page 126

National name République Gabonaise/Gabonese Republic
Area 267,667 sq km/103,346 sq mi
Capital Libreville
Major towns/cities Port-Gentil, Franceville (or Masuku), Lambaréné, Oyem, Mouila
Major ports Port-Gentil and Owendo
Physical features virtually the whole country is tropical rainforest; narrow coastal plain rising to hilly interior with savannah in east and south; Ogooué River flows north-west
Currency franc CFA
GNP per capita (PPP) (US$) 5,325 (1999)
Resources petroleum, natural gas, manganese (one of world's foremost producers and exporters), iron ore, uranium, gold, niobium, talc, phosphates
Population 1,226,000 (2000 est)
Population density (per sq km) 4 (1999 est)
Language French (official), Fang (in the north), Bantu languages, and other local dialects
Religion Christian 60% (mostly Roman Catholic), animist about 4%, Muslim 1%
Time difference GMT +1

The Gambia

Map page 126

National name Republic of the Gambia
Area 10,402 sq km/4,016 sq mi
Capital Banjul
Major towns/cities Brikama, Bakau, Farafenni, Gunjur, Basse
Physical features consists of narrow strip of land along the River Gambia; river flanked by low hills
Currency dalasi
GNP per capita (PPP) (US$) 1,492 (1999)
Resources ilmenite, zircon, rutile, petroleum (well discovered, but not exploited)
Population 1,305,000 (2000 est)
Population density (per sq km) 122 (1999 est)
Language English (official), Mandinka, Fula, Wolof, other indigenous dialects
Religion Muslim 85%, with animist and Christian minorities
Time difference GMT +/-0

Georgia

Map page 116

National name Sak'art'velo/Georgia
Area 69,700 sq km/26,911 sq mi
Capital T'bilisi
Major towns/cities K'ut'aisi, Rust'avi, Bat'umi,

Zugdidi, Gori

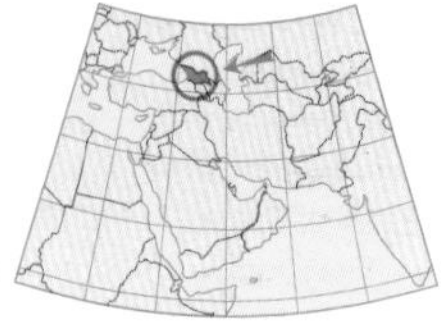

Physical features largely mountainous with a variety of landscape from the subtropical Black Sea shores to the ice and snow of the crest line of the Caucasus; chief rivers are Kura and Rioni

Currency lari

GNP per capita (PPP) (US$) 3,606 (1999)

Resources coal, manganese, barytes, clay, petroleum and natural gas deposits, iron and other ores, gold, agate, marble, alabaster, arsenic, tungsten, mercury

Population 4,968,000 (2000 est)

Population density (per sq km) 72 (1999 est)

Language Georgian (official), Russian, Abkazian, Armenian, Azeri

Religion Georgian Orthodox, also Muslim

Time difference GMT +3

Germany

Map page 78

National name Bundesrepublik Deutschland/Federal Republic of Germany

Area 357,041 sq km/ 137,853 sq mi

Capital Berlin

Major towns/cities Koln, Hamburg, Munich, Essen, Frankfurt am Main, Dortmund, Stuttgart, Düsseldorf, Leipzig, Dresden, Hannover

Major ports Hamburg, Kiel, Bremerhaven, Rostock

Physical features flat in north, mountainous in south with Alps; rivers Rhine, Weser, Elbe flow north, Danube flows southeast, Oder and Neisse flow north along Polish frontier; many lakes, including Müritz; Black Forest, Harz Mountains, Erzgebirge (Ore Mountains), Bavarian Alps, Fichtelgebirge, Thüringer Forest

Currency Deutschmark

GNP per capita (PPP) (US$) 22,404 (1999)

Resources lignite, hard coal, potash salts, crude oil, natural gas, iron ore, copper, timber, nickel, uranium

Population 82,220,000 (2000 est)

Population density (per sq km) 230 (1999 est)

Language German (official)

Religion Protestant (mainly Lutheran) 38%, Roman Catholic 34%

Time difference GMT +1

Ghana

Map page 126

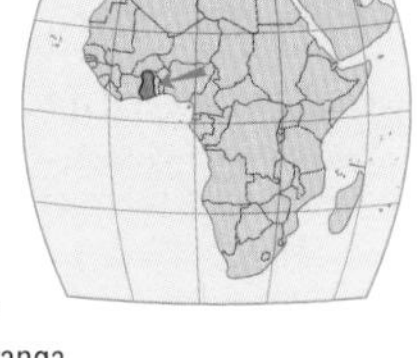

National name Republic of Ghana

Area 238,540 sq km/ 92,100 sq mi

Capital Accra

Major towns/cities Kumasi, Tamale, Tema, Sekondi, Takoradi, Cape Coast, Koforidua, Bolgatanga, Obuasi

Major ports Sekondi, Tema

Physical features mostly tropical lowland plains; bisected by River Volta

Currency cedi

GNP per capita (PPP) (US$) 1,793 (1999 est)

Resources diamonds, gold, manganese, bauxite

Population 20,212,000 (2000 est)

Population density (per sq km) 83 (1999 est)

Language English (official), Ga, other African languages

Religion Christian 40%, animist 32%, Muslim 16%

Time difference GMT +/-0

Greece

Map page 94

National name Elliniki Dimokratia/Hellenic Republic

Area 131,957 sq km/ 50,948 sq mi

Capital Athens

Major towns/cities Thessaloniki, Peiraias, Patra, Iraklion, Larisa, Peristerio, Kallithéa

Major ports Peiraias, Thessaloniki, Patra, Iraklion

Physical features mountainous (Mount Olympus); a large number of islands, notably Crete, Corfu, and Rhodes, and Cyclades and Ionian Islands
Currency drachma
GNP per capita (PPP) (US$) 14,595 (1999)
Resources bauxite, nickel, iron pyrites, magnetite, asbestos, marble, salt, chromite, lignite
Population 10,645,000 (2000 est)
Population density (per sq km) 81 (1999 est)
Language Greek (official)
Religion Greek Orthodox, over 96%; about 1% Muslim
Time difference GMT +2

Grenada

Map page 152

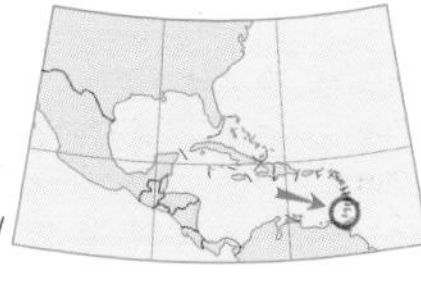

Area (including the southern Grenadine Islands, notably Carriacou and Petit Martinique) 344 sq km/ 133 sq mi
Capital St. George's
Major towns/cities Grenville, Sauteurs, Victoria, Gouyave
Physical features southernmost of the Windward Islands; mountainous; Grand-Anse beach; Annandale Falls; the Great Pool volcanic crater
Currency East Caribbean dollar
GNP per capita (PPP) (US$) 5,847 (1999)
Population 94,000 (2000 est)
Population density (per sq km) 286 (1999 est)
Language English (official), some French-African patois
Religion Roman Catholic 53%, Anglican about 14%, Seventh Day Adventist, Pentecostal, Methodist
Time difference GMT -4

Guatemala

Map page 152

National name República de Guatemala/Republic of Guatemala
Area 108,889 sq km/42,042 sq mi
Capital Guatemala
Major towns/cities Quezaltenango, Escuintla, Puerto Barrios (naval base), Chinautla
Physical features mountainous; narrow coastal plains; limestone tropical plateau in north; frequent earthquakes
Currency quetzal
GNP per capita (PPP) (US$) 3,517 (1999 est)
Resources petroleum, antimony, gold, silver, nickel, lead, iron, tungsten
Population 11,385,000 (2000 est)
Population density (per sq km) 102 (1999 est)
Language Spanish (official), 22 Mayan languages (45%)
Religion Roman Catholic 70%, Protestant 10%, traditional Mayan
Time difference GMT -6

Guinea

Map page 126

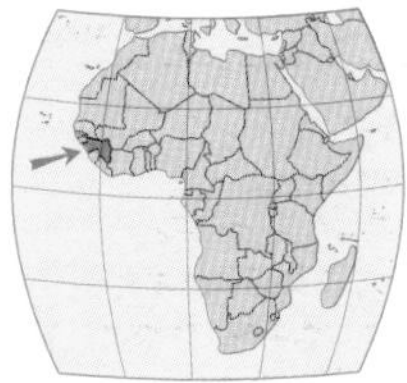

National name République de Guinée/ Republic of Guinea
Area 245,857 sq km/ 94,925 sq mi
Capital Conakry
Major towns/cities Labé, Nzérékoré, Kankan, Kindia, Mamou, Siguiri
Physical features flat coastal plain with mountainous interior; sources of rivers Niger, Gambia, and Senegal; forest in southeast; Fouta Djallon, area of sandstone plateaux, cut by deep valleys
Currency Guinean franc
GNP per capita (PPP) (US$) 1,761 (1999)
Resources bauxite (world's top exporter of bauxite and second-largest producer of bauxite ore), alumina, diamonds, gold, granite, iron ore, uranium, nickel, cobalt, platinum
Population 7,430,000 (2000 est)
Population density (per sq km) 30 (1999 est)
Language French (official), Susu, Pular (Fulfude), Malinke, and other African languages
Religion Muslim 85%, Christian 6%, animist
Time difference GMT +/-0

Guinea-Bissau

Map page 126

National name República da Guiné-Bissau/Republic of Guinea-Bissau
Area 36,125 sq km/ 13,947 sq mi
Capital Bissau (and chief port)
Major towns/cities Bafatá, Bissorã, Bolama, Gabú, Bubaque, Cacheu, Catió, Farim
Physical features flat coastal plain rising to savannah in east
Currency Guinean peso
GNP per capita (PPP) (US$) 595 (1999)
Resources bauxite, phosphate, petroleum (largely unexploited)
Population 1,213,000 (2000 est)
Population density (per sq km) 33 (1999 est)
Language Portuguese (official), Crioulo (a Cape Verdean dialect of Portuguese), African languages
Religion animist 58%, Muslim 40%, Christian 5% (mainly Roman Catholic)
Time difference GMT +/-0

Guyana

Map page 156

National name Cooperative Republic of Guyana
Area 214,969 sq km/ 82,999 sq mi
Capital Georgetown (and chief port)
Major towns/cities Linden, New Amsterdam, Bartica, Corriverton
Major ports New Amsterdam
Physical features coastal plain rises into rolling highlands with savannah in south; mostly tropical rainforest; Mount Roraima; Kaietur National Park, including Kaietur Falls on the Potaro (tributary of Essequibo) 250 m/821 ft
Currency Guyanese dollar
GNP per capita (PPP) (US$) 3,242 (1999 est)
Resources gold, diamonds, bauxite, copper, tungsten, iron, nickel, quartz, molybdenum
Population 861,000 (2000 est)
Population density (per sq km) 4 (1999 est)
Language English (official), Hindi, American Indian languages
Religion Christian 57%, Hindu 34%, Sunni Muslim 9%
Time difference GMT -3

Haiti

Map page 152

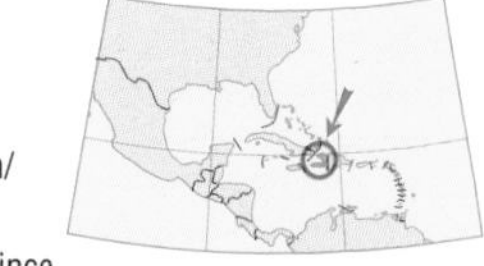

National name République d'Haïti/ Republic of Haiti
Area 27,750 sq km/ 10,714 sq mi
Capital Port-au-Prince
Major towns/cities Cap-Haïtien, Gonaïves, Les Cayes, St. Marc, Carrefour, Delmas
Physical features mainly mountainous and tropical; occupies western third of Hispaniola Island in Caribbean Sea
Currency gourde
GNP per capita (PPP) (US$) 1,407 (1999 est)
Resources marble, limestone, calcareous clay, unexploited copper and gold deposits
Population 8,222,000 (2000 est)
Population density (per sq km) 291 (1999 est)
Language French (20%), Creole (both official)
Religion Christian 95% (of which 70% are Roman Catholic), voodoo 4%
Time difference GMT -5

Honduras

Map page 152

National name República de Honduras/ Republic of Honduras
Area 112,100 sq km/ 43,281 sq mi
Capital Tegucigalpa
Major towns/cities San Pedro Sula, La Ceiba, El Progreso, Choluteca, Juticalpa, Danlí

Major ports La Ceiba
Physical features narrow tropical coastal plain with mountainous interior, Bay Islands, Caribbean reefs
Currency lempira
GNP per capita (PPP) (US$) 2,254 (1999 est)
Resources lead, zinc, silver, gold, tin, iron, copper, antimony
Population 6,485,000 (2000 est)
Population density (per sq km) 56 (1999 est)
Language Spanish (official), English, American Indian languages
Religion Roman Catholic 97%
Time difference GMT -6

Hungary

Map page 76

National name Magyar Köztársaság/Republic of Hungary
Area 93,032 sq km/ 35,919 sq mi
Capital Budapest
Major towns/cities Miskolc, Debrecen, Szeged, Pécs, Győr, Nyíregyháza, Székesfehérvár, Kecskemét
Physical features Great Hungarian Plain covers eastern half of country; Bakony Forest, Lake Balaton, and Transdanubian Highlands in the west; rivers Danube, Tisza, and Raba; more than 500 thermal springs
Currency forint
GNP per capita (PPP) (US$) 10,479 (1999)
Resources lignite, brown coal, natural gas, petroleum, bauxite, hard coal
Population 10,036,000 (2000 est)
Population density (per sq km) 108 (1999 est)
Language Hungarian (official)
Religion Roman Catholic 65%, Calvinist 20%, other Christian denominations, Jewish, atheist
Time difference GMT +1

Iceland

Map page 74

National name Lýðveldið Ísland/Republic of Iceland
Area 103,000 sq km/39,768 sq mi
Capital Reykjavík
Major towns/cities Akureyri, Kópavogur, Hafnarfjördur, Keflavík, Vestmannaeyjar
Physical features warmed by the Gulf Stream; glaciers and lava fields cover 75% of the country; active volcanoes (Hekla was once thought the gateway to Hell), geysers, hot springs, and new islands created offshore (Surtsey in 1963); subterranean hot water heats 85% of Iceland's homes; Sidujokull glacier moving at 100 metres a day
Currency krona
GNP per capita (PPP) (US$) 26,283 (1999)
Resources aluminium, diatomite, hydroelectric and thermal power, fish
Population 281,000 (2000 est)
Population density (per sq km) 3 (1999 est)
Language Icelandic (official)
Religion Evangelical Lutheran about 90%, other Protestant and Roman Catholic about 4%
Time difference GMT +/-0

India

Map page 112

National name Bharat (Hindi)/India; Bharatiya Janarajya (unofficial)/ Republic of India
Area 3,166,829 sq km/ 1,222,713 sq mi
Capital New Delhi

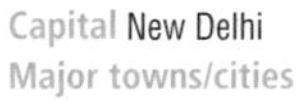

Major towns/cities Mumbai (formerly Bombay), Kolkata (formerly Calcutta), Chennai (formerly Madras), Bangalore, Hyderabad, Ahmadabad, Kanpur, Pune, Nagpur, Bhopal, Jaipur, Lucknow, Surat
Major ports Kolkata, Mumbai, Chennai
Physical features Himalayas on northern border; plains around rivers Ganges, Indus, Brahmaputra; Deccan peninsula south of the Narmada River forms plateau between Western and Eastern Ghats mountain ranges; desert in west; Andaman and Nicobar Islands, Lakshadweep (Laccadive Islands)

Currency rupee
GNP per capita (PPP) (US$) 2,149 (1999 est)
Resources coal, iron ore, copper ore, bauxite, chromite, gold, manganese ore, zinc, lead, limestone, crude oil, natural gas, diamonds
Population 1,013,662,000 (2000 est)
Population density (per sq km) 315 (1999 est)
Language Hindi, English, Assamese, Bengali, Gujarati, Kannada, Kashmiri, Konkani, Malayalam, Manipuri, Marathi, Nepali, Oriya, Punjabi, Sanskrit, Sindhi, Tamil, Telugu, Urdu (all official), more than 1,650 dialects
Religion Hindu 80%, Sunni Muslim 10%, Christian 2.5%, Sikh 2%, Buddhist, Jewish
Time difference GMT +5.5

Indonesia

Map page 110

National name Republik Indonesia/Republic of Indonesia
Area 1,904,569 sq km/ 735,354 sq mi
Capital Jakarta
Major towns/cities Surabaya, Bandung, Medan, Semarang, Palembang, Tangerang, Tanjungkarang-Telukbetung, Ujung Pandang, Malang
Major ports Surabaya, Semarang (Java), Ujung Pandang (Sulawesi)
Physical features comprises 13,677 tropical islands (over 6,000 of them are inhabited): the Greater Sundas (including Java, Madura, Sumatra, Sulawesi, and Kalimantan (part of Borneo)), the Lesser Sunda Islands/Nusa Tenggara (including Bali, Lombok, Sumbawa, Flores, Sumba, Alor, Lomblen, Timor, Roti, and Savu), Maluku/Moluccas (over 1,000 islands including Ambon, Ternate, Tidore, Tanimbar, and Halmahera), and Irian Jaya (part of New Guinea); over half the country is tropical rainforest; it has the largest expanse of peatlands in the tropics
Currency rupiah
GNP per capita (PPP) (US$) 2,439 (1999)
Resources petroleum (principal producer of petroleum in the Far East), natural gas, bauxite, nickel (world's third-largest producer), copper, tin (world's second-largest producer), gold, coal, forests
Population 212,107,000 (2000 est)
Population density (per sq km) 110 (1999 est)
Language Bahasa Indonesia (closely related to Malay; official), Javanese, Dutch, over 550 regional languages and dialects
Religion Muslim 87%, Protestant 6%, Roman Catholic 3%, Hindu 2% and Buddhist 1% (the continued spread of Christianity, together with an Islamic revival, have led to greater religious tensions)
Time difference GMT +7/9

Iran

Map page 114

National name Jomhûrî-ye Eslâmi-ye Îrân/Islamic Republic of Iran
Area 1,648,000 sq km/ 636,292 sq mi
Capital Teheran
Major towns/cities Eşfahān, Mashhad, Tabrīz, Shīrāz, Ahvāz, Kermānshāh, Qom, Karaj
Major ports Abādān
Physical features plateau surrounded by mountains, including Elburz and Zagros; Lake Rezayeh; Dasht-e-Kavir desert; occupies islands of Abu Musa, Greater Tunb and Lesser Tunb in the Gulf
Currency rial
GNP per capita (PPP) (US$) 5,163 (1999)
Resources petroleum, natural gas, coal, magnetite, gypsum, iron ore, copper, chromite, salt, bauxite, decorative stone
Population 67,702,000 (2000 est)
Population density (per sq km) 41 (1999 est)
Language Farsi (official), Kurdish, Turkish, Arabic, English, French
Religion Shiite Muslim (official) 91%, Sunni Muslim 8%; Zoroastrian, Christian, Jewish, and Baha'i comprise about 1%
Time difference GMT +3.5

Iraq

Map page 114

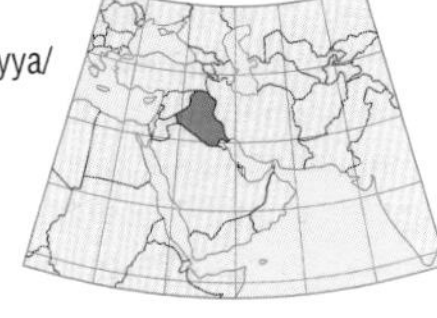

National name al-Jumhuriyya al'Iraqiyya/ Republic of Iraq
Area 434,924 sq km/ 167,924 sq mi
Capital Baghdād
Major towns/cities Al Mawşil, Al Başrah, Kirkūk, Al Ḩillah, An Najaf, An Nāşirīyah, Arbīl
Major ports Al Başrah
Physical features mountains in north, desert in west; wide valley of rivers Tigris and Euphrates running northwest-southeast; canal linking Baghdād and The Gulf opened in 1992
Currency Iraqi dinar
GNP per capita (PPP) (US$) N/A
Resources petroleum, natural gas, sulphur, phosphates
Population 23,115,000 (2000 est)
Population density (per sq km) 52 (1999 est)
Language Arabic (80%) (official), Kurdish (15%), Assyrian, Armenian
Religion Shiite Muslim 60%, Sunni Muslim 37%, Christian 3%
Time difference GMT +3

Ireland, Republic of

Map page 82

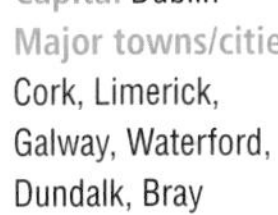

National name Poblacht Na hÉireann/Republic of Ireland
Area 70,282 sq km/ 27,135 sq mi
Capital Dublin
Major towns/cities Cork, Limerick, Galway, Waterford, Dundalk, Bray
Major ports Cork, Dun Laoghaire, Limerick, Waterford, Galway
Physical features central plateau surrounded by hills; rivers Shannon, Liffey, Boyne; Bog of Allen; Macgillicuddy's Reeks, Wicklow Mountains; Lough Corrib, lakes of Killarney; Galway Bay and Aran Islands
Currency Irish pound, or punt Eireannach
GNP per capita (PPP) (US$) 19,180 (1999)
Resources lead, zinc, peat, limestone, gypsum, petroleum, natural gas, copper, silver
Population 3,730,000 (2000 est)
Population density (per sq km) 53 (1999 est)
Language Irish Gaelic, English (both official)
Religion Roman Catholic 92%, Church of Ireland, other Protestant denominations 3%
Time difference GMT +/-0

Israel

Map page 118

National name Medinat Israel/State of Israel
Area 20,800 sq km/ 8,030 sq mi (as at 1949 armistice)
Capital Jerusalem (not recognized by the United Nations)
Major towns/cities Tel Aviv-Yafo, Haifa, Bat-Yam, Ḩolon, Ramat Gan, Petah Tiqwa, Rishon le Ẕiyyon, Be'ér Sheva'
Major ports Tel Aviv-Yafo, Haifa, 'Akko (formerly Acre), Elat
Physical features coastal plain of Sharon between Haifa and Tel Aviv noted since ancient times for its fertility; central mountains of Galilee, Samaria, and Judea; Dead Sea, Lake Tiberias, and River Jordan Rift Valley along the east are below sea level; Negev Desert in the south; Israel occupies Golan Heights, West Bank, East Jerusalem, and Gaza Strip (the last was awarded limited autonomy, with West Bank town of Jericho, in 1993)
Currency shekel
GNP per capita (PPP) (US$) 16,867 (1999)
Resources potash, bromides, magnesium, sulphur, copper ore, gold, salt, petroleum, natural gas
Population 6,217,000 (2000 est)
Population density (per sq km) 293 (1999 est)
Language Hebrew, Arabic (both official), English, Yiddish, other European and west Asian languages
Religion Israel is a secular state, but the predominant faith is Judaism 80%; also Sunni Muslim (about

15%), Christian, and Druze
Time difference GMT +2

Italy

Map page 90

National name Repubblica Italiana/Italian Republic
Area 301,300 sq km/ 116,331 sq mi
Capital Rome
Major towns/cities Milan, Naples, Turin, Palermo, Genoa, Bologna, Florence
Major ports Naples, Genoa, Palermo, Bari, Catania, Trieste
Physical features mountainous (Maritime Alps, Dolomites, Apennines) with narrow coastal lowlands; continental Europe's only active volcanoes: Vesuvius, Etna, Stromboli; rivers Po, Adige, Arno, Tiber, Rubicon; islands of Sicily, Sardinia, Elba, Capri, Ischia, Lipari, Pantelleria; lakes Como, Maggiore, Garda
Currency lira
GNP per capita (PPP) (US$) 20,751 (1999)
Resources lignite, lead, zinc, mercury, potash, sulphur, fluorspar, bauxite, marble, petroleum, natural gas, fish
Population 57,298,000 (2000 est)
Population density (per sq km) 190 (1999 est)
Language Italian (official), German and Ladin (in the north), French (in the Valle d'Aosta region), Greek and Albanian (in the south)
Religion Roman Catholic 98% (state religion)
Time difference GMT +1

Jamaica

Map page 152

Area 10,957 sq km/ 4,230 sq mi
Capital Kingston
Major towns/cities Montego Bay, Spanish Town, Portmore, May Pen
Physical features mountainous tropical island; Blue Mountains (so called because of the haze over them)
Currency Jamaican dollar
GNP per capita (PPP) (US$) 3,276 (1999)
Resources bauxite (one of world's major producers), marble, gypsum, silica, clay
Population 2,583,000 (2000 est)
Population density (per sq km) 234 (1999 est)
Language English (official), Jamaican Creole
Religion Protestant 70%, Rastafarian
Time difference GMT -5

Japan

Map page 106

National name Nihon-koku/State of Japan
Area 377,535 sq km/ 145,766 sq mi
Capital Tōkyō
Major towns/cities Yokohama, Ōsaka, Nagoya, Fukuoka, Kita-Kyūshū, Kyōto, Sapporo, Kobe, Kawasaki, Hiroshima
Major ports Ōsaka, Nagoya, Yokohama, Kobe
Physical features mountainous, volcanic (Mount Fuji, volcanic Mount Aso, Japan Alps); comprises over 1,000 islands, the largest of which are Hokkaido, Honshu, Kyushu, and Shikoku
Currency yen
GNP per capita (PPP) (US$) 24,041 (1999)
Resources coal, iron, zinc, copper, natural gas, fish
Population 126,714,000 (2000 est)
Population density (per sq km) 335 (1999 est)
Language Japanese (official), Ainu
Religion Shinto, Buddhist (often combined), Christian (less than 1%)
Time difference GMT +9

Jordan

Map page 114

National name Al-Mamlaka al-Urduniyya al-Hashemiyyah/Hashemite Kingdom of Jordan
Area 89,206 sq km/34,442 sq mi (excluding the West

Bank 5,879 sq km/ 2,269 sq mi)

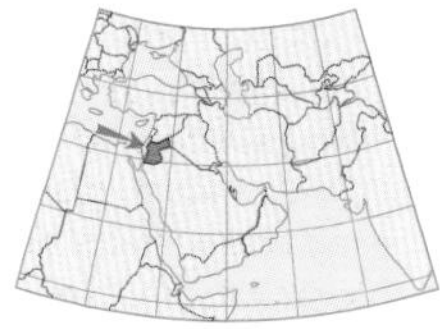

Capital Ammān
Major towns/cities Zarqā', Irbid, Ma'ān
Major ports Aqaba
Physical features desert plateau in east; Rift Valley separates east and west banks of River Jordan
Currency Jordanian dinar
GNP per capita (PPP) (US$) 3,542 (1999)
Resources phosphates, potash, shale
Population 6,669,000 (2000 est)
Population density (per sq km) 73 (1999 est)
Language Arabic (official), English
Religion over 90% Sunni Muslim (official religion), small communities of Christians and Shiite Muslims
Time difference GMT +2

Kazakhstan

Map page 100

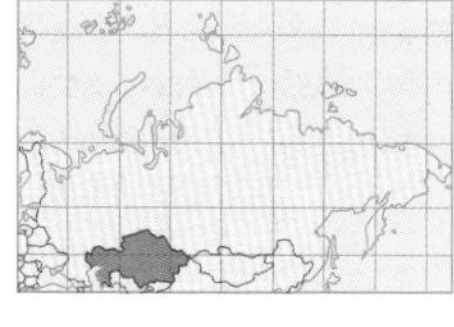

National name Kazak Respublikasy/ Republic of Kazakhstan
Area 2,717,300 sq km/ 1,049,150 sq mi
Capital Astana (formerly Akmola)
Major towns/cities Qaraghandy, Pavlodar, Semey, Petropavl, Shymkent
Physical features Caspian and Aral seas, Lake Balkhash; Steppe region; natural gas and oil deposits in the Caspian Sea
Currency tenge
GNP per capita (PPP) (US$) 4,408 (1999)
Resources petroleum, natural gas, coal, bauxite, chromium, copper, iron ore, lead, titanium, magnesium, tungsten, molybdenum, gold, silver, manganese
Population 16,223,000 (2000 est)
Population density (per sq km) 6 (1999 est)
Language Kazakh (related to Turkish; official), Russian
Religion Sunni Muslim 50-60%, Russian Orthodox 30-35%
Time difference GMT +6

Kenya

Map page 128

National name Jamhuri ya Kenya/Republic of Kenya

Area 582,600 sq km/ 224,941 sq mi
Capital Nairobi
Major towns/cities Mombasa, Kisumu, Nakuru, Eldoret, Nyeri
Major ports Mombasa
Physical features mountains and highlands in west and centre; coastal plain in south; arid interior and tropical coast; semi-desert in north; Great Rift Valley, Mount Kenya, Lake Nakuru (salt lake with world's largest colony of flamingos), Lake Turkana (Rudolf)
Currency Kenyan shilling
GNP per capita (PPP) (US$) 975 (1999)
Resources soda ash, fluorspar, salt, limestone, rubies, gold, vermiculite, diatonite, garnets
Population 30,080,000 (2000 est)
Population density (per sq km) 51 (1999 est)
Language English, Kiswahili (both official), many local dialects
Religion Roman Catholic 28%, Protestant 8%, Muslim 6%, traditional tribal religions
Time difference GMT +3

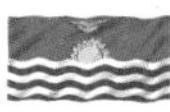

Kiribati

Map page 132

National name Ribaberikan Kiribati/ Republic of Kiribati
Area 717 sq km/ 277 sq mi
Capital Bairiki (on Tarawa atoll)
Major towns/cities principal islands are the Gilbert Islands, the Phoenix Islands, the Line Islands, Banaba
Major ports Bairiki, Betio (on Tarawa)
Physical features comprises 33 Pacific coral islands: the Kiribati (Gilbert), Rawaki (Phoenix), Banaba (Ocean Island), and three of the Line Islands

including Kiritimati (Christmas Island); island groups crossed by Equator and International Date Line
Currency Australian dollar
GNP per capita (PPP) (US$) 3,186 (1999)
Resources phosphate, salt
Population 83,000 (2000 est)
Population density (per sq km) 107 (1999 est)
Language English (official), Gilbertese
Religion Roman Catholic, Protestant (Congregationalist)
Time difference GMT -10/-11

Kuwait

Map page 119

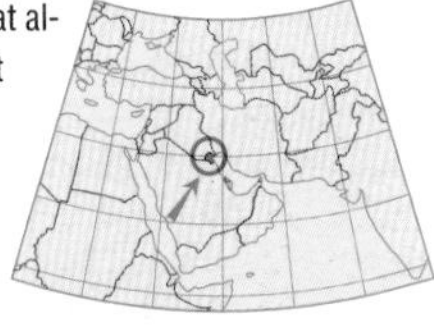

National name Dowlat al-Kuwayt/State of Kuwait
Area 17,819 sq km/ 6,879 sq mi
Capital Kuwait (and chief port)
Major towns/cities as-Salimiya, Ḩawallī, Al Farwānīyah, Abraq Kheetan, Al Jahrah, Al Aḩmadī, Al Fuḩayḩil
Physical features hot desert; islands of Faylakah, Bubiyan, and Warbah at northeast corner of Arabian Peninsula
Currency Kuwaiti dinar
GNP per capita (PPP) (US$) 24,270 (1997)
Resources petroleum, natural gas, mineral water
Population 1,972,000 (2000 est)
Population density (per sq km) 106 (1999 est)
Language Arabic (78%) (official), English, Kurdish (10%), Farsi (4%)
Religion Sunni Muslim 45%, Shiite Muslim 40%; Christian, Hindu, and Parsi about 5%
Time difference GMT +3

Kyrgyzstan

Map page 100

National name Kyrgyz Respublikasy/Kyrgyz Republic
Area 198,500 sq km/76,640 sq mi
Capital Bishkek (formerly Frunze)
Major towns/cities Osh, Karakol, Kyzyl-Kiya, Tokmak, Djalal-Abad
Physical features mountainous, an extension of the Tien Shan range
Currency som
GNP per capita (PPP) (US$) 2,223 (1999)
Resources petroleum, natural gas, coal, gold, tin, mercury, antimony, zinc, tungsten, uranium
Population 4,699,000 (2000 est)
Population density (per sq km) 24 (1999 est)
Language Kyrgyz (a Turkic language; official), Russian
Religion Sunni Muslim 70%, Russian Orthodox 20%
Time difference GMT +5

Laos

Map page 108

National name Sathalanalat Praxathipatai Paxaxôn Lao/Democratic People's Republic of Laos
Area 236,790 sq km/ 91,424 sq mi
Capital Vientiane
Major towns/cities Louangphrabang (the former royal capital), Pakxé, Savannakhet
Physical features landlocked state with high mountains in east; Mekong River in west; rainforest covers nearly 60% of land
Currency new kip
GNP per capita (PPP) (US$) 1,726 (1999)
Resources coal, tin, gypsum, baryte, lead, zinc, nickel, potash, iron ore; small quantities of gold, silver, precious stones
Population 5,433,000 (2000 est)
Population density (per sq km) 22 (1999 est)
Language Lao (official), French, English, ethnic languages
Religion Theravada Buddhist 85%, animist beliefs among mountain dwellers
Time difference GMT +7

Latvia

Map page 74

National name Latvijas Republika/Republic of Latvia
Area 63,700 sq km/ 24,594 sq mi
Capital Rīga
Major towns/cities Daugavpils, Liepāja, Jūrmala, Jelgava, Ventspils
Major ports Ventspils, Liepāja
Physical features wooded lowland (highest point 312 m/1,024 ft), marshes, lakes; 472 km/293 mi of coastline; mild climate
Currency lat
GNP per capita (PPP) (US$) 5,938 (1999)
Resources peat, gypsum, dolomite, limestone, amber, gravel, sand
Population 2,357,000 (2000 est)
Population density (per sq km) 38 (1999 est)
Language Latvian (official)
Religion Lutheran, Roman Catholic, Russian Orthodox
Time difference GMT +2

Lebanon

Map page 118

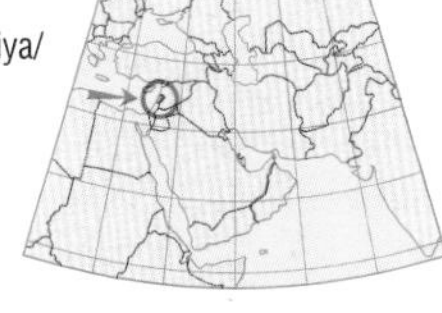

National name Jumhouria al-Lubnaniya/ Republic of Lebanon
Area 10,452 sq km/ 4,035 sq mi
Capital Beirut (and chief port)
Major towns/cities Tripoli, Zahlé, Baabda, Ba'albek, Jezzine
Major ports Tripoli, Soûr, Saïda, Joûnié
Physical features narrow coastal plain; fertile Bekka valley running north-south between Lebanon and Anti-Lebanon mountain ranges
Currency Lebanese pound
GNP per capita (PPP) (US$) 4,129 (1999)
Resources there are no commercially viable mineral deposits; small reserves of lignite and iron ore
Population 3,282,000 (2000 est)
Population density (per sq km) 310 (1999 est)
Language Arabic (official), French, Armenian, English
Religion Muslim 70% (Shiite 35%, Sunni 23%, Druze 7%, other 5%); Christian 30% (mainly Maronite 19%), Druze 3%; other Christian denominations including Greek Orthodox, Armenian, and Roman Catholic
Time difference GMT +2

Lesotho

Map page 130

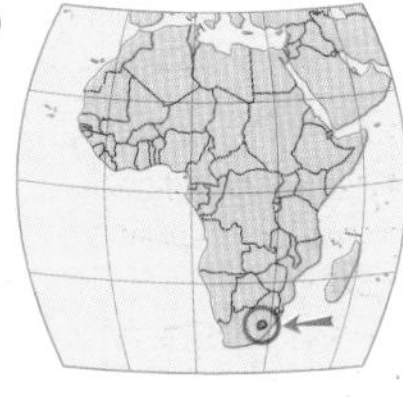

National name Mmuso oa Lesotho/Kingdom of Lesotho
Area 30,355 sq km/ 11,720 sq mi
Capital Maseru
Major towns/cities Qacha's Nek, Teyateyaneng, Mafeteng, Hlotse, Roma, Quthing
Physical features mountainous with plateaux, forming part of South Africa's chief watershed
Currency loti
GNP per capita (PPP) (US$) 2,058 (1999)
Resources diamonds, uranium, lead, iron ore; believed to have petroleum deposits
Population 2,153,000 (2000 est)
Population density (per sq km) 69 (1999 est)
Language English (official), Sesotho, Zulu, Xhosa
Religion Protestant 42%, Roman Catholic 38%, indigenous beliefs
Time difference GMT +

Liberia

Map page 126

National name Republic of Liberia
Area 111,370 sq km/ 42,999 sq mi
Capital Monrovia (and chief port)
Major towns/cities Bensonville, Gbarnga,

Voinjama, Buchanan
Major ports Buchanan, Greenville
Physical features forested highlands; swampy tropical coast where six rivers enter the sea
Currency Liberian dollar
GNP per capita (PPP) (US$) N/A
Resources iron ore, diamonds, gold, barytes, kyanite
Population 3,154,000 (2000 est)
Population density (per sq km) 26 (1999 est)
Language English (official), over 20 Niger-Congo languages
Religion animist 70%, Sunni Muslim 20%, Christian 10%
Time difference GMT +/-0

Libya

Map page 122

National name Al-Jamahiriyya al-'Arabiyya al-Libiyya ash-Sha'biyya al-Ishtirakiyya al-'Uzma/Great Libyan Arab Socialist People's State of the Masses
Area 1,759,540 sq km/679,358 sq mi
Capital Tripoli
Major towns/cities Banghāzī, Mişrātah, Az Zāwīyah, Tubruq, Ajdābiyā, Darnah
Major ports Banghāzī, Mişrāta, Az Zāwīyah, Tubruq, Ajdābiyā, Darnah
Physical features flat to undulating plains with plateaux and depressions stretch southwards from the Mediterranean coast to an extremely dry desert interior
Currency Libyan dinar
GNP per capita (PPP) (US$) N/A
Resources petroleum, natural gas, iron ore, potassium, magnesium, sulphur, gypsum
Population 5,605,000 (2000 est)
Population density (per sq km) 3 (1999 est)
Language Arabic (official), Italian, English
Religion Sunni Muslim 97%
Time difference GMT +1

Liechtenstein

Map page 88

National name Fürstentum Liechtenstein/Principality of Liechtenstein
Area 160 sq km/62 sq mi
Capital Vaduz
Major towns/cities Balzers, Schaan, Eschen
Physical features landlocked Alpine; includes part of Rhine Valley in west
Currency Swiss franc
GNP per capita (PPP) (US$) 24,000 (1998 est)
Resources hydro power
Population 33,000 (2000 est)
Population density (per sq km) 199 (1999 est)
Language German (official), an Alemannic dialect
Religion Roman Catholic 80%, Protestant 7%
Time difference GMT +1

Lithuania

Map page 74

National name Lietuvos Respublika/Republic of Lithuania
Area 65,200 sq km/25,173 sq mi
Capital Vilnius
Major towns/cities Kaunas, Klaipėda, Šiauliai, Panevėžys
Physical features central lowlands with gentle hills in west and higher terrain in southeast; 25% forested; some 3,000 small lakes, marshes, and complex sandy coastline; River Nenumas
Currency litas
GNP per capita (PPP) (US$) 6,093 (1999)
Resources small deposits of petroleum, natural gas, peat, limestone, gravel, clay, sand
Population 3,670,000 (2000 est)
Population density (per sq km) 56 (1999 est)
Language Lithuanian (official)
Religion predominantly Roman Catholic; Evangelical Lutheran, also Russian Orthodox, Evangelical

Reformist, and Baptist
Time difference GMT +2

Luxembourg

Map page 80

National name Grand-Duché de Luxembourg/Grand Duchy of Luxembourg
Area 2,586 sq km/ 998 sq mi
Capital Luxembourg
Major towns/cities Esch, Differdange, Dudelange, Pétange
Physical features on the River Moselle; part of the Ardennes (Oesling) forest in north
Currency Luxembourg franc
GNP per capita (PPP) (US$) 38,247 (1999)
Resources iron ore
Population 431,000 (2000 est)
Population density (per sq km) 165 (1999 est)
Language Letzeburgisch (a German-Moselle-Frankish dialect; official), English
Religion Roman Catholic about 95%, Protestant and Jewish 4%
Time difference GMT +1

Macedonia

Map page 94

National name Republika Makedonija/Republic of Macedonia (official internal name); Poranesna Jugoslovenska Republika Makedonija/ Former Yugoslav Republic of Macedonia (official international name)
Area 25,700 sq km/9,922 sq mi
Capital Skopje
Major towns/cities Bitola, Prilep, Kumanovo, Tetovo
Physical features mountainous; rivers: Struma, Vardar; lakes: Ohrid, Prespa, Scutari; partly Mediterranean climate with hot summers
Currency Macedonian denar
GNP per capita (PPP) (US$) 4,339 (1999)
Resources coal, iron, zinc, chromium, manganese, lead, copper, nickel, silver, gold
Population 2,024,000 (2000 est)
Population density (per sq km) 78 (1999 est)
Language Macedonian (related to Bulgarian; official), Albanian
Religion Christian, mainly Orthodox 67%; Muslim 30%
Time difference GMT +1

Madagascar

Map page 130

National name Repoblikan'i Madagasikara/ République de Madagascar/Republic Madagascar
Area 587,041 sq km/ 226,656 sq mi
Capital Antananarivo
Major towns/cities Antsirabe, Mahajanga, Fianarantsoa, Toamasina, Ambatondrazaka
Major ports Toamasina, Antsirañana, Mahajanga
Physical features temperate central highlands; humid valleys and tropical coastal plains; arid in south
Currency Malagasy franc
GNP per capita (PPP) (US$) 766 (1999)
Resources graphite, chromite, mica, titanium ore, small quantities of precious stones, bauxite and coal deposits, petroleum reserves
Population 15,942,000 (2000 est)
Population density (per sq km) 26 (1999 est)
Language Malagasy, French (both official), local dialects
Religion over 50% traditional beliefs, Roman Catholic, Protestant about 40%, Muslim 7%
Time difference GMT +3

Malawi

Map page 130

National name Republic of Malawi
Area 118,484 sq km/45,735 sq mi

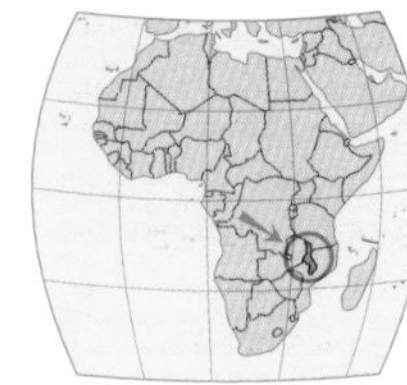

Capital Lilongwe
Major towns/cities Blantyre, Mzuzu, Zomba
Physical features landlocked narrow plateau with rolling plains; mountainous west of Lake Nyasa
Currency Malawi kwacha
GNP per capita (PPP) (US$) 581 (1999)
Resources marble, coal, gemstones, bauxite and graphite deposits, reserves of phosphates, uranium, glass sands, asbestos, vermiculite
Population 10,925,000 (2000 est)
Population density (per sq km) 90 (1999 est)
Language English, Chichewa (both official), other Bantu languages
Religion Protestant 50%, Roman Catholic 20%, Muslim 2%, animist
Time difference GMT +2

Malaysia

Map page 110

National name Persekutuan Tanah Malaysia/Federation of Malaysia
Area 329,759 sq km/ 127,319 sq mi
Capital Kuala Lumpur
Major towns/cities Johor Bahru, Ipoh, George Town (on Penang island), Kuala Terengganu, Kuala Bahru, Petaling Jaya, Kelang, Kuching (on Sarawak), Kota Kinabalu (on Sabah)
Major ports Kelang
Physical features comprises peninsular Malaysia (the nine Malay states - Johore, Kedah, Kelantan, Negri Sembilan, Pahang, Perak, Perlis, Selangor, Terengganu - plus Malacca and Penang); states of Sabah and Sarawak on the island of Borneo; and the federal territory of Kuala Lumpur; 75% tropical rainforest; central mountain range; Mount Kinabalu, the highest peak in southeast Asia, is in Sabah; swamps in east; Niah caves (Sarawak)
Currency ringgit
GNP per capita (PPP) (US$) 7,963 (1999)
Resources tin, bauxite, copper, iron ore, petroleum, natural gas, forests
Population 22,244,000 (2000 est)
Population density (per sq km) 66 (1999 est)
Language Bahasa Malaysia (Malay; official), English, Chinese, Tamil, Iban, many local dialects
Religion Muslim (official) about 53%, Buddhist 19%, Hindu, Christian, local beliefs
Time difference GMT +8

Maldives

Map page 112

National name Divehi Raajjeyge Jumhuriyya/ Republic of the Maldives
Area 298 sq km/ 115 sq mi
Capital Malé
Physical features comprises 1,196 coral islands, grouped into 12 clusters of atolls, largely flat, none bigger than 13 sq km/5 sq mi, average elevation 1.8 m/6 ft; 203 are inhabited
Currency rufiya
GNP per capita (PPP) (US$) 3,545 (1999)
Resources coral (mining was banned as a measure against the encroachment of the sea)
Population 286,000 (2000 est)
Population density (per sq km) 933 (1999 est)
Language Divehi (a Sinḥalese dialect; official), English, Arabic
Religion Sunni Muslim
Time difference GMT +5

Mali

Map page 124

National name République du Mali/Republic of Mali
Area 1,240,142 sq km/478,818 sq mi
Capital Bamako
Major towns/cities Mopti, Kayes, Ségou, Tombouctou, Sikasso
Physical features landlocked state with River Niger

and savannah in south; part of the Sahara in north; hills in northeast; Senegal River and its branches irrigate the southwest
Currency franc CFA
GNP per capita (PPP) (US$) 693 (1999)
Resources iron ore, uranium, diamonds, bauxite, manganese, copper, lithium, gold
Population 11,234,000 (2000 est)
Population density (per sq km) 9 (1999 est)
Language French (official), Bambara, other African languages
Religion Sunni Muslim 80%, animist, Christian
Time difference GMT +/-0

Malta

Map page 90

National name Repubblika ta'Malta/Republic of Malta
Area 320 sq km/ 124 sq mi
Capital Valletta (and chief port)
Major towns/cities Rabat, Birkirkara, Qormi, Sliema
Major ports Marsaxlokk, Valletta
Physical features includes islands of Gozo 67 sq km/ 26 sq mi and Comino 3 sq km/1 sq mi
Currency Maltese lira
GNP per capita (PPP) (US$) 15,066 (1999 est)
Resources stone, sand; offshore petroleum reserves were under exploration 1988-95
Population 389,000 (2000 est)
Population density (per sq km) 1,206 (1999 est)
Language Maltese, English (both official)
Religion Roman Catholic 98%
Time difference GMT +1

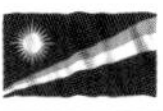

Marshall Islands

Map page 132

National name Majol/Republic of the Marshall Islands
Area 181 sq km/ 70 sq mi
Capital Dalap-Uliga-Darrit (on Majuro atoll)
Major towns/cities Ebeye (the only other town)
Physical features comprises the Ratak and Ralik island chains in the West Pacific, which together form an archipelago of 31 coral atolls, 5 islands, and 1,152 islets
Currency US dollar
GNP per capita (PPP) (US$) 1,860 (1999 est)
Resources phosphates
Population 64,000 (2000 est)
Population density (per sq km) 343 (1999 est)
Language Marshallese, English (both official)
Religion Christian (mainly Protestant) and Baha'i
Time difference GMT +12

Mauritania

Map page 124

National name Al-Jumhuriyya al-Islamiyya al-Mawritaniyya/ République Islamique Arabe et Africaine de Mauritanie/Islamic Republic of Mauritania
Area 1,030,700 sq km/397,953 sq mi
Capital Nouakchott (and chief port)
Major towns/cities Nouâdhibou, Kaédi, Zouérat, Kiffa, Rosso, Atâr
Major ports Nouâdhibou
Physical features valley of River Senegal in south; remainder arid and flat
Currency ouguiya
GNP per capita (PPP) (US$) 1,522 (1999 est)
Resources copper, gold, iron ore, gypsum, phosphates, sulphur, peat

Population 2,670,000 (2000 est)
Population density (per sq km) 3 (1999 est)
Language Hasaniya Arabic (official), Pulaar, Soninke, Wolof (all national languages), French (particularly in the south)
Religion Sunni Muslim (state religion)
Time difference GMT +/-0

Mauritius

Map page 130

National name Republic of Mauritius
Area 1,865 sq km/720 sq mi
Capital Port Louis (and chief port)
Major towns/cities Beau Bassin, Rose Hill, Curepipe, Quatre Bornes, Vacoas-Phoenix
Physical features mountainous, volcanic island surrounded by coral reefs; the island of Rodrigues is part of Mauritius; there are several small island dependencies
Currency Mauritian rupee
GNP per capita (PPP) (US$) 8,652 (1999)
Population 1,158,000 (2000 est)
Population density (per sq km) 616 (1999 est)
Language English (official), French, Creole (36%), Bhojpuri (32%), other Indian languages
Religion Hindu over 50%, Christian (mainly Roman Catholic) about 30%, Muslim 17%
Time difference GMT +4

Mexico

Map page 152

National name Estados Unidos Mexicanos/United States of Mexico
Area 1,958,201 sq km/ 756,061 sq mi
Capital Mexico City
Major towns/cities Guadalajara, Monterrey, Puebla, Ciudad Juárez, Tijuana
Major ports 49 ocean ports
Physical features partly arid central highlands; Sierra Madre mountain ranges east and west; tropical coastal plains; volcanoes, including Popocatepetl; Rio Grande
Currency Mexican peso
GNP per capita (PPP) (US$) 7,719 (1999)
Resources petroleum, natural gas, zinc, salt, silver, copper, coal, mercury, manganese, phosphates, uranium, strontium sulphide
Population 98,881,000 (2000 est)
Population density (per sq km) 50 (1999 est)
Language Spanish (official), Nahuatl, Maya, Zapoteco, Mixteco, Otomi
Religion Roman Catholic about 90%
Time difference GMT -6/8

Micronesia, Federated States of

Map page 132

National name Federated States of Micronesia (FSM)
Area 700 sq km/ 270 sq mi
Capital Palikir (in Pohnpei island state)
Major towns/cities Kolonia (in Pohnpei), Weno (in Truk), Lelu (in Kosrae)
Physical features an archipelago of 607 equatorial, volcanic islands in the West Pacific
Currency US dollar
GNP per capita (PPP) (US$) 3,860 (1999 est)
Population 119,000 (2000 est)
Population density (per sq km) 165 (1999 est)
Language English (official), eight officially recognized local languages (including Trukese, Pohnpeian, Yapese, and Kosrean), a number of other dialects
Religion Christianity (mainly Roman Catholic in Yap state, Protestant elsewhere)
Time difference GMT +10 (Chuuk and Yap); +11 (Kosrae and Pohnpei)

Moldova

Map page 92

National name Republica Moldova/Republic of Moldova
Area 33,700 sq km/ 13,011 sq mi
Capital Chişinău (Russian Kishinev)
Major towns/cities Tiraspol, Bălţi, Tighina
Physical features hilly land lying largely between the rivers Prut and Dniester; northern Moldova comprises the level plain of the Bălţi Steppe and uplands; the climate is warm and moderately continental
Currency leu
GNP per capita (PPP) (US$) 2,358 (1999)
Resources lignite, phosphorites, gypsum, building materials; petroleum and natural gas deposits discovered in the early 1990s were not yet exploited in 1996
Population 4,380,000 (2000 est)
Population density (per sq km) 130 (1999 est)
Language Moldovan (official), Russian, Gaganz (a Turkish dialect)
Religion Eastern Orthodox 98.5%; remainder Jewish
Time difference GMT +2

Monaco

Map page 84

National name Principauté de Monaco/Principality of Monaco
Area 1.95 sq km/ 0.75 sq mi
Physical features steep and rugged; surrounded landwards by French territory; being expanded by filling in the sea
Currency French franc
GNP per capita (PPP) (US$) 27,000 (1999 est)
Population 34,000 (2000 est)
Population density (per sq km) 16,074 (1999 est)
Language French (official), Monégasgne (a mixture

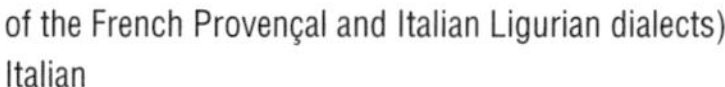

of the French Provençal and Italian Ligurian dialects), Italian
Religion Roman Catholic about 90%
Time difference GMT +1

Mongolia

Map page 102

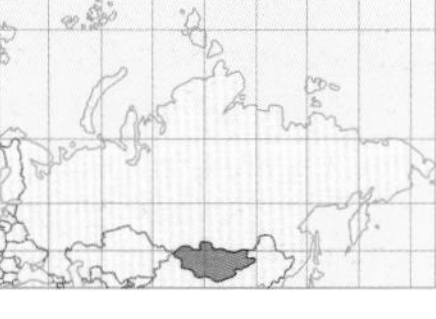

National name Mongol Uls/State of Mongolia
Area 1,565,000 sq km/ 604,246 sq mi
Capital Ulaanbaatar
Major towns/cities Darhan, Choybalsan, Erdenet
Physical features high plateau with desert and steppe (grasslands); Altai Mountains in southwest; salt lakes; part of Gobi desert in southeast; contains both the world's southernmost permafrost and northernmost desert
Currency tugrik
GNP per capita (PPP) (US$) 1,496 (1999)
Resources copper, nickel, zinc, molybdenum, phosphorites, tungsten, tin, fluorospar, gold, lead; reserves of petroleum discovered in 1994
Population 2,662,000 (2000 est)
Population density (per sq km) 2 (1999 est)
Language Khalkha Mongolian (official), Kazakh (in the province of Bagan-Ölgiy), Chinese, Russian, Turkic languages
Religion there is no state religion, but traditional lamaism (Mahayana Buddhism) is gaining new strength; the Sunni Muslim Kazakhs of Western Mongolia have also begun the renewal of their religious life, and Christian missionary activity has increased
Time difference GMT +8

Morocco

Map page 124

National name Al-Mamlaka al-Maghribyya/Kingdom of Morocco
Area 458,730 sq km/ 177,115 sq mi (excluding Western Sahara)
Capital Rabat

Major towns/cities Casablanca, Marrakech, Fès, Oujda, Kénitra, Tétouan, Meknès

Major ports Casablanca, Tanger, Agadir

Physical features mountain ranges, including the Atlas Mountains northeast-southwest; fertile coastal plains in west

Currency dirham

GNP per capita (PPP) (US$) 3,190 (1999)

Resources phosphate rock and phosphoric acid, coal, iron ore, barytes, lead, copper, manganese, zinc, petroleum, natural gas, fish

Population 28,351,000 (2000 est)

Population density (per sq km) 61 (1999 est)

Language Arabic (75%) (official), Berber dialects (25%), French, Spanish

Religion Sunni Muslim; Christian and Jewish minorities

Time difference GMT +/-0

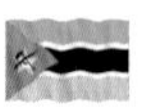

Mozambique

Map page 130

National name República de Moçambique/Republic of Mozambique

Area 799,380 sq km/ 308,640 sq mi

Capital Maputo (and chief port)

Major towns/cities Beira, Nampula, Nacala, Chimoio

Major ports Beira, Nacala, Quelimane

Physical features mostly flat tropical lowland; mountains in west; rivers Zambezi and Limpopo

Currency metical

GNP per capita (PPP) (US$) 797 (1999 est)

Resources coal, salt, bauxite, graphite; reserves of iron ore, gold, precious and semi-precious stones, marble, natural gas (all largely unexploited in 1996)

Population 19,680,000 (2000 est)

Population density (per sq km) 24 (1999 est)

Language Portuguese (official), 16 African languages

Religion animist 48%, Muslim 20%, Roman Catholic 16%, Protestant 16%

Time difference GMT +2

Myanmar (Burma)

Map page 108

National name Pyedawngsu Myanma Naingngan/Union of Myanmar

Area 676,577 sq km/ 261,226 sq mi

Capital Yangon (formerly Rangoon) (and chief port)

Major towns/cities Mandalay, Moulmein, Bago, Bassein, Taung-gyi, Sittwe,

Physical features over half is rainforest; rivers Irrawaddy and Chindwin in central lowlands ringed by mountains in north, west, and east

Currency kyat

GNP per capita (PPP) (US$) 1,200 (1999 est)

Resources natural gas, petroleum, zinc, tin, copper, tungsten, coal, lead, gems, silver, gold

Population 45,611,000 (2000 est)

Population density (per sq km) 70 (1999 est)

Language Burmese (official), English, tribal dialects

Religion Hinayana Buddhist 89%, Christian 5%, Muslim 4%, animist 1.5%

Time difference GMT +6.5

Namibia

Map page 130

National name Republic of Namibia

Area 824,300 sq km/ 318,262 sq mi

Capital Windhoek

Major towns/cities Swakopmund, Rehoboth, Rundu

Major ports Walvis Bay

Physical features mainly desert (Namib and Kalahari); Orange River; Caprivi Strip links Namibia to Zambezi River; includes the enclave of Walvis Bay

(area 1,120 sq km/432 sq mi)
Currency Namibian dollar
GNP per capita (PPP) (US$) 5,369 (1999 est)
Resources uranium, copper, lead, zinc, silver, tin, gold, salt, semi-precious stones, diamonds (one of the world's leading producers of gem diamonds), hydrocarbons, lithium, manganese, tungsten, cadmium, vanadium
Population 1,726,000 (2000 est)
Population density (per sq km) 2 (1999 est)
Language English (official), Afrikaans, German, Ovambo (51%), Nama (12%), Kavango (10%), other indigenous languages
Religion about 90% Christian (Lutheran, Roman Catholic, Dutch Reformed Church, Anglican)
Time difference GMT +1

Nauru

Map page 132

National name Republic of Nauru
Area 21 sq km/8.1 sq mi
Capital Yaren District (seat of government)
Physical features tropical coral island in southwest Pacific; plateau encircled by coral cliffs and sandy beaches
Currency Australian dollar
GNP per capita (PPP) (US$) 11,800 (1994 est)
Resources phosphates
Population 12,000 (2000 est)
Population density (per sq km) 524 (1999 est)
Language Nauruan, English (both official)
Religion majority Protestant, Roman Catholic
Time difference GMT +12

Nepal

Map page 112

National name Nepál Adhirajya/Kingdom of Nepal
Area 147,181 sq km/56,826 sq mi
Capital Kathmandu
Major towns/cities Biratnagar, Lalitpur, Bhadgaon, Pokhara, Birganj, Dahran Bazar
Physical features descends from the Himalayas in the north through foothills to the River Ganges plain in the south; Mount Everest, Mount Kanchenjunga
Currency Nepalese rupee
GNP per capita (PPP) (US$) 1,219 (1999)
Resources lignite, talcum, magnesite, limestone, copper, cobalt
Population 23,930,000 (2000 est)
Population density (per sq km) 159 (1999 est)
Language Nepali (official), Tibetan, numerous local languages
Religion Hindu 90%; Buddhist 5%, Muslim 3%, Christian
Time difference GMT +5.5

Netherlands

Map page 80

National name Koninkrijk der Nederlanden/Kingdom of the Netherlands
Area 41,863 sq km/16,163 sq mi
Capital Amsterdam (official), The Hague (legislative and judicial)
Major towns/cities Rotterdam, Utrecht, Eindhoven, Groningen, Tilburg, Maastricht, Apeldoorn, Nijmegen, Breda
Major ports Rotterdam
Physical features flat coastal lowland; rivers Rhine, Schelde, Maas; Frisian Islands
Territories Aruba, Netherlands Antilles (Caribbean)
Currency guilder
GNP per capita (PPP) (US$) 23,052 (1999)
Resources petroleum, natural gas
Population 15,786,000 (1999 est)
Population density (per sq km) 376 (1999 est)
Language Dutch (official)
Religion atheist 39%, Roman Catholic 31%, Dutch Reformed Church 14%, Calvinist 8%
Time difference GMT +1

New Zealand

Map page 136

National name Aotearoa/New Zealand
Area 268,680 sq km/ 103,737 sq mi
Capital Wellington
Major towns/cities Auckland, Hamilton, Christchurch, Manukau
Major ports Auckland, Wellington
Physical features comprises North Island, South Island, Stewart Island, Chatham Islands, and minor islands; mainly mountainous; Ruapehu in North Island, 2,797 m/9,180 ft, highest of three active volcanoes; geysers and hot springs of Rotorua district; Lake Taupo (616 sq km/238 sq mi), source of Waikato River; Kaingaroa state forest. In South Island are the Southern Alps and Canterbury Plains
Territories Tokelau (three atolls transferred in 1926 from former Gilbert and Ellice Islands colony); Niue Island (one of the Cook Islands, separately administered from 1903: chief town Alafi); Cook Islands are internally self-governing but share common citizenship with New Zealand; Ross Dependency in Antarctica
Currency New Zealand dollar
GNP per capita (PPP) (US$) 16,566 (1999)
Resources coal, clay, limestone, dolomite, natural gas, hydroelectric power, pumice, iron ore, gold, forests
Population 3,862,000 (2000 est)
Population density (per sq km) 14 (1999 est)
Language English (official), Maori
Religion Christian (Anglican 18%, Roman Catholic 14%, Presbyterian 13%)
Time difference GMT +12

Nicaragua

Map page 152

National name República de Nicaragua/Republic of Nicaragua
Area 127,849 sq km/49,362 sq mi
Capital Managua
Major towns/cities León, Chinandega, Masaya, Granada, Estelí
Major ports Corinto, Puerto Cabezas, El Bluff
Physical features narrow Pacific coastal plain separated from broad Atlantic coastal plain by volcanic mountains and lakes Managua and Nicaragua; one of the world's most active earthquake regions
Currency cordoba
GNP per capita (PPP) (US$) 2,154 (1999)
Resources gold, silver, copper, lead, antimony, zinc, iron, limestone, gypsum, marble, bentonite
Population 5,074,000 (2000 est)
Population density (per sq km) 39 (1999 est)
Language Spanish (official), English, American Indian languages
Religion Roman Catholic 95%
Time difference GMT -6

Niger

Map page 124

National name République du Niger/ Republic of Niger
Area 1,186,408 sq km/ 458,072 sq mi
Capital Niamey
Major towns/cities Zinder, Maradi, Tahoua, Agadez, Birnin Konni, Arlit
Physical features desert plains between hills in north and savannah in south; River Niger in southwest, Lake Chad in southeast
Currency franc CFA
GNP per capita (PPP) (US$) 727 (1999)
Resources uranium (one of world's leading producers), phosphates, gypsum, coal, cassiterite, tin, salt, gold; deposits of other minerals (including petroleum, iron ore, copper, lead, diamonds, and tungsten) have been confirmed
Population 10,730,000 (2000 est)
Population density (per sq km) 9 (1999 est)
Language French (official), Hausa (70%), Djerma, other ethnic languages

Religion Sunni Muslim 95%; also Christian, and traditional animist beliefs
Time difference GMT +1

Nigeria

Map page 126

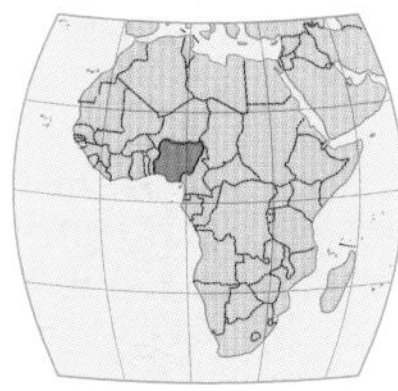

National name Federal Republic of Nigeria
Area 923,773 sq km/ 356,668 sq mi
Capital Abuja
Major towns/cities Ibadan, Lagos, Ogbomosho, Kano, Oshogbo, Ilorin, Abeokuta, Zaria, Port Harcourt
Major ports Lagos, Port Harcourt, Warri, Calabar
Physical features arid savannah in north; tropical rainforest in south, with mangrove swamps along coast; River Niger forms wide delta; mountains in southeast
Currency naira
GNP per capita (PPP) (US$) 744 (1999)
Resources petroleum, natural gas, coal, tin, iron ore, uranium, limestone, marble, forest
Population 111,506,000 (2000 est)
Population density (per sq km) 118 (1999 est)
Language English, French (both official), Hausa, Ibo, Yoruba
Religion Sunni Muslim 50% (in north), Christian 35% (in south), local religions 15%
Time difference GMT +1

North Korea

Map page 106

National name Chosun Minchu-chui Inmin Konghwa-guk/Democratic People's Republic of Korea
Area 120,538 sq km/ 46,539 sq mi
Capital P'yŏngyang
Major towns/cities Hamhŭng, Ch'ŏngjin, Namp'o, Wŏnsan, Sinŭiji
Physical features wide coastal plain in west rising to mountains cut by deep valleys in interior
Currency won
GNP per capita (PPP) (US$) 950 (1999 est)
Resources coal, iron, lead, copper, zinc, tin, silver, gold, magnesite (has 40-50% of world's deposits of magnesite)
Population 24,039,000 (2000 est)
Population density (per sq km) 197 (1999 est)
Language Korean (official)
Religion Buddhist (predominant religion), Chondoist, Christian, traditional beliefs
Time difference GMT +9

Norway

Map page 74

National name Kongeriket Norge/Kingdom of Norway
Area 387,000 sq km/ 149,420 sq mi (including Svalbard and Jan Mayen)
Capital Oslo
Major towns/cities Bergen, Trondheim, Stavanger, Kristiansand, Drammen
Physical features mountainous with fertile valleys and deeply indented coast; forests cover 25%; extends north of Arctic Circle
Territories dependencies in the Arctic (Svalbard and Jan Mayen) and in Antarctica (Bouvet and Peter I Island, and Queen Maud Land)
Currency Norwegian krone
GNP per capita (PPP) (US$) 26,522 (1999)
Resources petroleum, natural gas, iron ore, iron pyrites, copper, lead, zinc, forests
Population 4,465,000 (2000 est)
Population density (per sq km) 14 (1999 est)
Language Norwegian (official), Saami (Lapp), Finnish
Religion Evangelical Lutheran (endowed by state) 88%; other Protestant and Roman Catholic 4%
Time difference GMT +1

Oman

Map page 114

National name Saltanat `Uman/Sultanate of Oman
Area 272,000 sq km/ 105,019 sq mi
Capital Muscat
Major towns/cities Sallālah, Ibrī, Suḩār, Al Buraymī, Nazwá, Sūr, Maţraḩ
Physical features mountains to the north and south of a high arid plateau; fertile coastal strip; Jebel Akhdar highlands; Kuria Muria Islands
Currency Omani rial
GNP per capita (PPP) (US$) 8,690 (1997)
Resources petroleum, natural gas, copper, chromite, gold, salt, marble, gypsum, limestone
Population 2,542,000 (2000 est)
Population density (per sq km) 9 (1999 est)
Language Arabic (official), English, Urdu, other Indian languages
Religion Muslim 75% (predominantly Ibadhi Muslim), about 25% Hindu
Time difference GMT +4

Pakistan

Map page 114

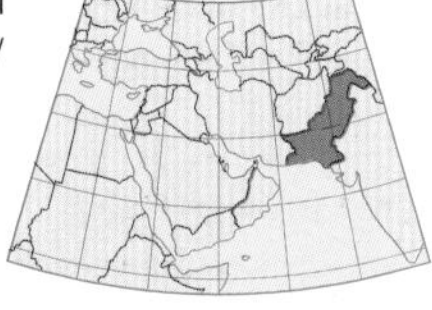

National name Islami Jamhuriyya e Pakistan/ Islamic Republic of Pakistan
Area 803,940 sq km/ 310,321 sq mi
Capital Islamabad
Major towns/cities Lahore, Rawalpindi, Faisalabad, Karachi, Hyderabad, Multan, Peshawar, Gujranwala, Quetta
Major ports Karachi
Physical features fertile Indus plain in east, Baluchistan plateau in west, mountains in north and northwest; the 'five rivers' (Indus, Jhelum, Chenab, Ravi, and Sutlej) feed the world's largest irrigation system; K2 mountain; Khyber Pass
Currency Pakistan rupee
GNP per capita (PPP) (US$) 1,757 (1999)
Resources iron ore, natural gas, limestone, rock salt, gypsum, silica, coal, petroleum, graphite, copper, manganese, chromite
Population 156,483,000 (2000 est)
Population density (per sq km) 189 (1999 est)
Language Urdu (official), English, Punjabi, Sindhi, Pashto, Baluchi, other local dialects
Religion Sunni Muslim 90%, Shiite Muslim 5%; also Hindu, Christian, Parsee, Buddhist
Time difference GMT +5

Palau

Map page 132

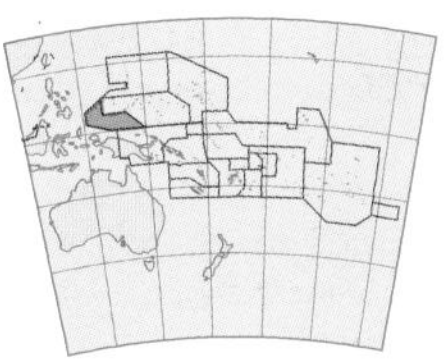

National name Belu'u era Belau/ Republic of Palau
Area 508 sq km/ 196 sq mi
Capital Koror (on Koror island)
Physical features more than 350 (mostly uninhabited) islands, islets, and atolls in the west Pacific; warm, humid climate, susceptible to typhoons
Currency US dollar
GNP per capita (PPP) (US$) N/A
Population 19,000 (2000 est)
Population density (per sq km) 39 (1999 est)
Language Palauan, English (both official in most states)
Religion Christian, principally Roman Catholic; Modekngei (indigenous religion)
Time difference GMT +9

Panama

Map page 152

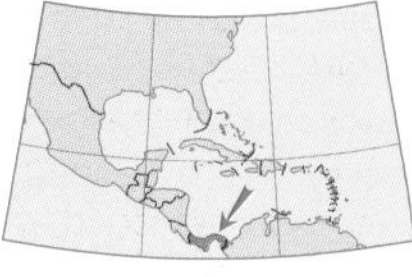

National name República de Panamá/ Republic of Panama
Area 77,100 sq km/ 29,768 sq mi
Capital Panamá
Major towns/cities San Miguelito, Colón, David, La Chorrera, Santiago, Chitré, Changuinola
Major ports Colón, Cristóbal, Balboa

Physical features coastal plains and mountainous interior; tropical rainforest in east and northwest; Archipelago de las Perlas in Gulf of Panama; Panama Canal
Currency balboa
GNP per capita (PPP) (US$) 5,016 (1999)
Resources limestone, clay, salt; deposits of coal, copper, and molybdenum have been discovered
Population 2,856,000 (2000 est)
Population density (per sq km) 36 (1999 est)
Language Spanish (official), English
Religion Roman Catholic 93%
Time difference GMT -5

Papua New Guinea

Map page 132

National name Gau Hedinarai ai Papua-Matamata Guinea/Independent State of Papua New Guinea
Area 462,840 sq km/ 178,702 sq mi
Capital Port Moresby (on East New Guinea)
Major towns/cities Lae, Madang, Arawa, Wewak, Goroka, Rabaul
Major ports Port Moresby, Rabaul
Physical features mountainous; swamps and plains; monsoon climate; tropical islands of New Ireland, New Britain, and Bougainville; Admiralty Islands, D'Entrecasteaux Islands, and Louisiade Archipelago; active volcanoes Vulcan and Tavurvur
Currency kina
GNP per capita (PPP) (US$) 2,263 (1999 est)
Resources copper, gold, silver; deposits of chromite, cobalt, nickel, quartz; substantial reserves of petroleum and natural gas (petroleum production began in 1992)
Population 4,807,000 (2000 est)
Population density (per sq km) 10 (1999 est)
Language English (official), pidgin English, over 700 local languages
Religion Christian 97%, of which 3% Roman Catholic; local pantheistic beliefs
Time difference GMT +10

Paraguay

Map page 158

National name República del Paraguay/ Republic of Paraguay
Area 406,752 sq km/ 157,046 sq mi
Capital Asunción (and chief port)
Major towns/cities Ciudad del Este, Pedro Juan Caballero, San Lorenzo, Fernando de la Mora, Lambare, Luque, Capiatá
Major ports Concepción
Physical features low marshy plain and marshlands; divided by Paraguay River; Paraná River forms southeast boundary
Currency guaraní
GNP per capita (PPP) (US$) 4,193 (1999 est)
Resources gypsum, kaolin, limestone, salt; deposits (not commercially exploited) of bauxite, iron ore, copper, manganese, uranium; deposits of natural gas discovered in 1994; exploration for petroleum deposits ongoing mid-1990s
Population 5,496,000 (2000 est)
Population density (per sq km) 13 (1999 est)
Language Spanish (official), Guaraní (an indigenous Indian language)
Religion Roman Catholic (official religion) 85%; Mennonite, Anglican
Time difference GMT -3/4

Peru

Map page 156

National name República del Perú/ Republic of Peru
Area 1,285,200 sq km/ 496,216 sq mi
Capital Lima
Major towns/cities Arequipa, Iquitos, Chiclayo, Trujillo, Huancayo, Piura, Chimbote
Major ports Callao, Chimbote, Salaverry

Physical features Andes mountains running northwest-southeast cover 27% of Peru, separating Amazon river-basin jungle in northeast from coastal plain in west; desert along coast north-south (Atacama Desert); Lake Titicaca
Currency nuevo sol
GNP per capita (PPP) (US$) 4,387 (1999)
Resources lead, copper, iron, silver, zinc (world's fourth-largest producer), petroleum
Population 25,662,000 (2000 est)
Population density (per sq km) 20 (1999 est)
Language Spanish, Quechua (both official), Aymara, many indigenous dialects
Religion Roman Catholic (state religion) 95%
Time difference GMT -5

Philippines

Map page 108

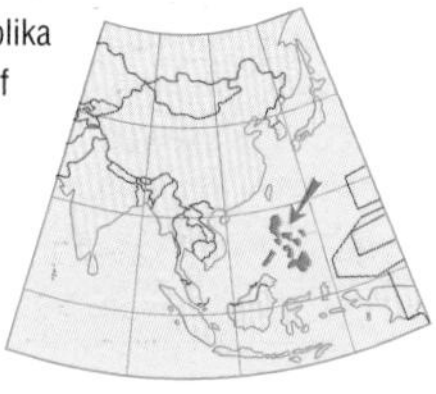

National name Republika Ñg Pilipinas/Republic of the Philippines
Area 300,000 sq km/ 115,830 sq mi
Capital Manila (on Luzon island) (and chief port)
Major towns/cities Quezon City, Davao, Caloocan, Cebu, Bacolod, Cagayan de Oro, Iloilo
Major ports Cebu, Davao (on Mindanao), Iloilo, Zamboanga (on Mindanao)
Physical features comprises over 7,000 islands; volcanic mountain ranges traverse main chain north-south; 50% still forested. The largest islands are Luzon 108,172 sq km/41,754 sq mi and Mindanao 94,227 sq km/36,372 sq mi; others include Samar, Negros, Palawan, Panay, Mindoro, Leyte, Cebu, and the Sulu group; Pinatubo volcano (1,759 m/5,770 ft); Mindanao has active volcano Apo (2,954 m/9,690 ft) and mountainous rainforest
Currency peso
GNP per capita (PPP) (US$) 3,815 (1999)
Resources copper ore, gold, silver, chromium, nickel, coal, crude petroleum, natural gas, forests
Population 75,967,000 (2000 est)
Population density (per sq km) 248 (1999 est)
Language Filipino, English (both official), Spanish, Cebuano, Ilocano, more than 70 other indigenous languages
Religion Christian 94%, mainly Roman Catholic (84%), Protestant; Muslim 4%, local religions
Time difference GMT +8

Poland

Map page 76

National name Rzeczpospolita Polska/ Republic of Poland
Area 312,683 sq km/ 120,726 sq mi
Capital Warsaw
Major towns/cities Łódź, Kraków, Wroclaw, Poznan, Gdansk, Szczecin, Katowice, Bydgoszcz, Lublin
Major ports Gdansk (Danzig), Szczecin (Stettin), Gdynia (Gdingen)
Physical features part of the great plain of Europe; Vistula, Oder, and Neisse rivers; Sudeten, Tatra, and Carpathian mountains on southern frontier
Currency zloty
GNP per capita (PPP) (US$) 7,894 (1999)
Resources coal (world's fifth-largest producer), copper, sulphur, silver, petroleum and natural gas reserves
Population 38,765,000 (2000 est)
Population density (per sq km) 124 (1999 est)
Language Polish (official)
Religion Roman Catholic 95%
Time difference GMT +1

Portugal

Map page 86

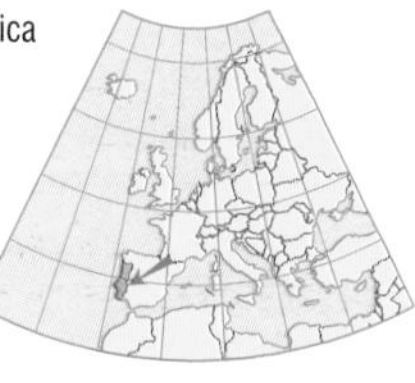

National name República Portuguesa/Republic of Portugal
Area 92,000 sq km/ 35,521 sq mi (including the Azores and Madeira)
Capital Lisbon

Major towns/cities Porto, Coimbra, Amadora, Setúbal, Funchal, Braga, Vila Nova de Gaia
Major ports Porto, Setúbal
Physical features mountainous in the north (Serra da Estrêla mountains); plains in the south; rivers Minho, Douro, Tagus (Tejo), Guadiana
Currency escudo
GNP per capita (PPP) (US$) 15,147 (1999)
Resources limestone, granite, marble, iron, tungsten, copper, pyrites, gold, uranium, coal, forests
Population 9,875,000 (2000 est)
Population density (per sq km) 107 (1999 est)
Language Portuguese (official)
Religion Roman Catholic 97%
Time difference GMT +/-0

Qatar

Map page 119

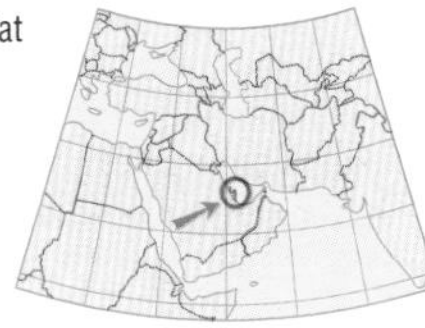

National name Dawlat Qatar/State of Qatar
Area 11,400 sq km/ 4,401 sq mi
Capital Doha (and chief port)
Major towns/cities Dukhān, ad Dawhah, ar-Rayyan, Umm Salal, Musay'īd, aš-Šahniyah
Physical features mostly flat desert with salt flats in south
Currency Qatari riyal
GNP per capita (PPP) (US$) N/A
Resources petroleum, natural gas, water resources
Population 599,000 (2000 est)
Population density (per sq km) 52 (1999 est)
Language Arabic (official), English
Religion Sunni Muslim 95%
Time difference GMT +3

Romania

Map page 92

National name România/Romania
Area 237,500 sq km/91,698 sq mi
Capital Bucharest
Major towns/cities Brasov, Timisoara, Cluj-Napoca, Iaşi, Constanta, Galati, Craiova
Major ports Galati, Constanta, Brăila
Physical features mountains surrounding a plateau, with river plains in south and east. Carpathian Mountains, Transylvanian Alps; River Danube; Black Sea coast; mineral springs
Currency leu
GNP per capita (PPP) (US$) 5,647 (1999)
Resources brown coal, hard coal, iron ore, salt, bauxite, copper, lead, zinc, methane gas, petroleum (reserves expected to be exhausted by mid- to late 1990s)
Population 22,327,000 (2000 est)
Population density (per sq km) 94 (1999 est)
Language Romanian (official), Hungarian, German
Religion Romanian Orthodox 87%; Roman Catholic and Uniate 5%, Reformed/Lutheran 3%, Unitarian 1%
Time difference GMT +2

Russia

Map page 98

National name Rossiiskaya Federatsiya/Russian Federation
Area 17,075,400 sq km/ 6,592,811 sq mi
Capital Moscow
Major towns/cities St. Petersburg, Nizhniy Novgorod, Samara, Yekaterinburg, Novosibirsk, Chelyabinsk, Kazan, Omsk, Perm', Ufa
Physical features fertile Black Earth district; extensive forests; the Ural Mountains with large mineral resources; Lake Baikal, world's deepest lake
Currency rouble
GNP per capita (PPP) (US$) 6,339 (1999)
Resources petroleum, natural gas, coal, peat, copper (world's fourth-largest producer), iron ore, lead, aluminium, phosphate rock, nickel, manganese, gold, diamonds, platinum, zinc, tin
Population 146,934,000 (2000 est)

Population density (per sq km) 9 (1999 est)
Language Russian (official) and many East Slavic, Altaic, Uralic, Caucasian languages
Religion traditionally Russian Orthodox; significant Muslim and Buddhist communities
Time difference GMT +2-12

Rwanda

Map page 128

National name Republika y'u Rwanda/ Republic of Rwanda
Area 26,338 sq km/ 10,169 sq mi
Capital Kigali
Major towns/cities Butare, Ruhengeri, Gisenyi, Kibungo, Cyangugu
Physical features high savannah and hills, with volcanic mountains in northwest; part of lake Kivu; highest peak Mount Karisimbi 4,507 m/ 14,792 ft; Kagera River (whose headwaters are the source of the Nile)
Currency Rwandan franc
GNP per capita (PPP) (US$) 690 (1998)
Resources cassiterite (a tin-bearing ore), wolframite (a tungsten-bearing ore), natural gas, gold, columbo-tantalite, beryl
Population 7,733,000 (2000 est)
Population density (per sq km) 275 (1999 est)
Language Kinyarwanda, French (both official), Kiswahili
Religion about 50% animist; about 40% Christian, mainly Roman Catholic; 9% Muslim
Time difference GMT +2

St. Kitts and Nevis

Map page 152

National name Federation of St. Christopher and St. Nevis
Area 262 sq km/ 101 sq mi (St. Kitts 168 sq km/65 sq mi, Nevis 93 sq km/36 sq mi)
Capital Basseterre (on St. Kitts) (and chief port)
Major towns/cities Charlestown (Nevis), Newcastle, Sandy Point Town, Dieppe Bay Town
Physical features both islands are volcanic; fertile plains on coast; black beaches
Currency East Caribbean dollar
GNP per capita (PPP) (US$) 9,801 (1999)
Population 38,000 (2000 est)
Population density (per sq km) 160 (1999 est)
Language English (official)
Religion Anglican 36%, Methodist 32%, other Protestant 8%, Roman Catholic 10%
Time difference GMT -4

St. Lucia

Map page 152

Area 617 sq km/ 238 sq mi
Capital Castries
Major towns/cities Soufrière, Vieux Fort, Choiseul, Gros Islet
Major ports Vieux-Fort
Physical features mountainous island with fertile valleys; mainly tropical forest; volcanic peaks; Gros and Petit Pitons
Currency East Caribbean dollar
GNP per capita (PPP) (US$) 5,022 (1999)
Resources geothermal energy
Population 154,000 (2000 est)
Population density (per sq km) 252 (1999 est)
Language English (official), French patois
Religion Roman Catholic 85%; Anglican, Protestant
Time difference GMT -4

St. Vincent and the Grenadines

Map page 152

Area 388 sq km/150 sq mi (including islets of the Northern Grenadines 43 sq km/17 sq mi)
Capital Kingstown
Major towns/cities Georgetown, Châteaubelair, Dovers
Physical features volcanic mountains, thickly

forested; La Soufrière volcano
Currency East Caribbean dollar
GNP per capita (PPP) (US$) 4,667 (1999)
Population 114,000 (2000 est)
Population density (per sq km) 355 (1999 est)
Language English (official), French patois
Religion Anglican, Methodist, Roman Catholic
Time difference GMT -4

Samoa

Map page 132

National name 'O la Malo Tu To'atasi o Samoa/Independent State of Samoa
Area 2,830 sq km/ 1,092 sq mi
Capital Apia (on Upolu island) (and chief port)
Major towns/cities Lalomanu, Tuasivi, Falealupo, Falelatai, Taga
Physical features comprises South Pacific islands of Savai'i and Upolu, with two smaller tropical islands and uninhabited islets; mountain ranges on main islands; coral reefs; over half forested
Currency tala, or Samoan dollar
GNP per capita (PPP) (US$) 3,915 (1999)
Population 180,000 (2000 est)
Population density (per sq km) 63 (1999 est)
Language English, Samoan (both official)
Religion Congregationalist; also Roman Catholic, Methodist
Time difference GMT -11

San Marino

Map page 90

National name Serenissima Repubblica di San Marino/Most Serene Republic of San Marino
Area 61 sq km/24 sq mi
Capital San Marino
Major towns/cities Serravalle, Faetano, Fiorentino, Borgo Maggiore, Domagnano
Physical features the slope of Mount Titano
Currency Italian lira
GNP per capita (PPP) (US$) 20,000 (1997 est)
Resources limestone and other building stone
Population 27,000 (2000 est)
Population density (per sq km) 417 (1999 est)
Language Italian (official)
Religion Roman Catholic 95%
Time difference GMT +1

São Tomé and Príncipe

Map page 126

National name República Democrática de São Tomé e Príncipe/ Democratic Republic of São Tomé and Príncipe
Area 1,000 sq km/ 386 sq mi
Capital São Tomé
Major towns/cities Santo António, Sant Ana, Porto Alegre, Neves, Santo Amaro
Physical features comprises two main islands and several smaller ones, all volcanic; thickly forested and fertile
Currency dobra
GNP per capita (PPP) (US$) 1,335 (1999)
Population 147,000 (2000 est)
Population density (per sq km) 161 (1999 est)
Language Portuguese (official), Fang (a Bantu language), Lungwa São Tomé (a Portuguese Creole)
Religion Roman Catholic 80%, animist
Time difference GMT +/-0

Saudi Arabia

Map page 114

National name Al-Mamlaka al-'Arabiyya as-Sa'udiyya/Kingdom of Saudi Arabia

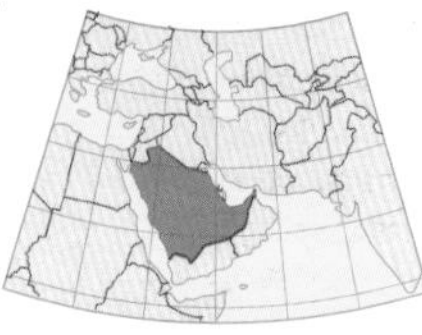

Area 2,200,518 sq km/ 849,620 sq mi
Capital Riyadh
Major towns/cities Jedda, Mecca, Medina, Ad Dammām, Tabūk, Buraydah
Major ports Jedda, Ad Dammām, Jīzān, Yanbu
Physical features desert, sloping to The Gulf from a height of 2,750 m/9,000 ft in the west
Currency riyal
GNP per capita (PPP) (US$) 10,472 (1999 est)
Resources petroleum, natural gas, iron ore, limestone, gypsum, marble, clay, salt, gold, uranium, copper, fish
Population 21,607,000 (2000 est)
Population density (per sq km) 9 (1999 est)
Language Arabic (official), English
Religion Sunni Muslim 85%; there is a Shiite minority
Time difference GMT +3

Senegal

Map page 126

National name République du Sénégal/ Republic of Senegal
Area 196,200 sq km/ 75,752 sq mi
Capital Dakar (and chief port)
Major towns/cities Thiès, Kaolack, Saint-Louis, Ziguinchor, Diourbel, Mbour
Physical features plains rising to hills in southeast; swamp and tropical forest in southwest; River Senegal; The Gambia forms an enclave within Senegal
Currency franc CFA
GNP per capita (PPP) (US$) 1,341 (1999)
Resources calcium phosphates, aluminium phosphates, salt, natural gas; offshore deposits of petroleum to be developed
Population 9,481,000 (2000 est)
Population density (per sq km) 47 (1999 est)
Language French (official), Wolof, other ethnic languages
Religion mainly Sunni Muslim; Christian 4%, animist 1%
Time difference GMT +/-0

Seychelles

Map page 130

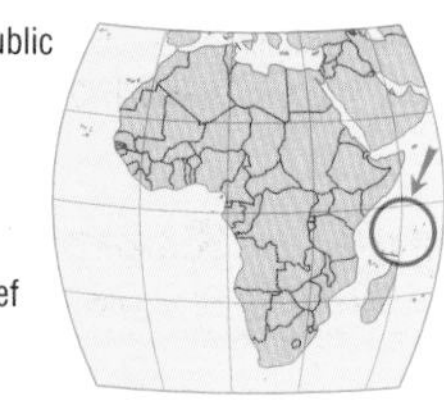

National name Republic of Seychelles
Area 453 sq km/ 174 sq mi
Capital Victoria (on Mahé island) (and chief port)
Major towns/cities Cascade, Anse Boileau, Takamaka
Physical features comprises two distinct island groups: one, the Granitic group, concentrated, the other, the Outer or Coralline group, widely scattered; totals over 100 islands and islets
Currency Seychelles rupee
GNP per capita (PPP) (US$) 10,381 (1999)
Resources guano; natural gas and metal deposits were being explored mid-1990s
Population 77,000 (2000 est)
Population density (per sq km) 174 (1999 est)
Language Creole (an Asian, African, European mixture) (95%), English, French (all official)
Religion Roman Catholic 90%
Time difference GMT +4

Sierra Leone

Map page 126

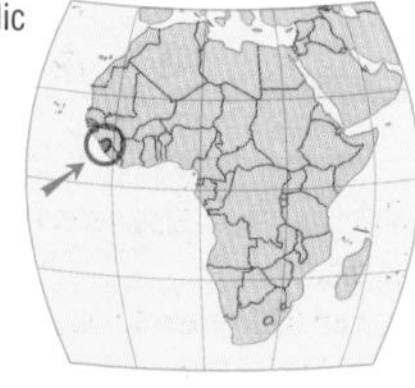

National name Republic of Sierra Leone
Area 71,740 sq km/ 27,698 sq mi
Capital Freetown
Major towns/cities Koidu, Bo, Kenema, Makeni
Major ports Bonthe
Physical features mountains in east; hills and forest; coastal mangrove swamps

Currency leone
GNP per capita (PPP) (US$) 414 (1999)
Resources gold, diamonds, bauxite, rutile (titanium dioxide)
Population 4,854,000 (2000 est)
Population density (per sq km) 66 (1999 est)
Language English (official), Krio (a Creole language), Mende, Limba, Temne
Religion animist 45%, Muslim 44%, Protestant 8%, Roman Catholic 3%
Time difference GMT +/-0

Singapore

Map page 110

National name Repablik Singapura/Republic of Singapore
Area 622 sq km/ 240 sq mi
Capital Singapore
Physical features comprises Singapore Island, low and flat, and 57 small islands; Singapore Island is joined to the mainland by causeway across Strait of Johore
Currency Singapore dollar
GNP per capita (PPP) (US$) 27,024 (1999)
Resources granite
Population 3,567,000 (2000 est)
Population density (per sq km) 5,662 (1999 est)
Language Malay, Mandarin Chinese, Tamil, English (all official), other Indian languages, Chinese dialects
Religion Buddhist, Taoist, Muslim, Hindu, Christian
Time difference GMT +8

Slovak Republic

Map page 76

National name Slovenská Republika/Slovak Republic
Area 49,035 sq km/18,932 sq mi
Capital Bratislava
Major towns/cities Košice, Nitra, Prešov, Banská Bystrica, Zilina, Trnava, Martin
Physical features Western range of Carpathian Mountains, including Tatra and Beskids in north; Danube plain in south; numerous lakes and mineral springs
Currency Slovak koruna (based on Czechoslovak koruna)
GNP per capita (PPP) (US$) 9,811 (1999)
Resources brown coal, lignite, copper, zinc, lead, iron ore, magnesite
Population 5,387,000 (2000 est)
Population density (per sq km) 110 (1999 est)
Language Slovak (official), Hungarian, Czech, other ethnic languages
Religion Roman Catholic (over 50%), Lutheran, Reformist, Orthodox, atheist 10%
Time difference GMT +1

Slovenia

Map page 88

National name Republika Slovenija/Republic of Slovenia
Area 20,251 sq km/ 7,818 sq mi
Capital Ljubljana
Major towns/cities Maribor, Kranj, Celje, Velenje, Koper, Novo Mesto
Major ports Koper
Physical features mountainous; Sava and Drava rivers
Currency tolar
GNP per capita (PPP) (US$) 15,062 (1999)
Resources coal, lead, zinc; small reserves/deposits of natural gas, petroleum, salt, uranium
Population 1,986,000 (2000 est)
Population density (per sq km) 98 (1999 est)
Language Slovene (related to Serbo-Croat; official), Hungarian, Italian
Religion Roman Catholic 70%; Eastern Orthodox, Lutheran, Muslim
Time difference GMT +1

Solomon Islands

Map page 132

Area 27,600 sq km/ 10,656 sq mi
Capital Honiara (on Guadalcanal island) (and chief port)
Major towns/cities Gizo, Auki, Kirakira, Buala
Major ports Yandina
Physical features comprises all but the northernmost islands (which belong to Papua New Guinea) of a Melanesian archipelago stretching nearly 1,500 km/900 mi. The largest is Guadalcanal (area 6,500 sq km/2,510 sq mi); others are Malaita, San Cristobal, New Georgia, Santa Isabel, Choiseul; mainly mountainous and forested
Currency Solomon Island dollar
GNP per capita (PPP) (US$) 1,793 (1999)
Resources bauxite, phosphates, gold, silver, copper, lead, zinc, cobalt, asbestos, nickel
Population 444,000 (2000 est)
Population density (per sq km) 16 (1999 est)
Language English (official), pidgin English, more than 80 Melanesian dialects (85%), Papuan and Polynesian languages
Religion more than 80% Christian; Anglican 34%, Roman Catholic 19%, South Sea Evangelical, other Protestant, animist 5%
Time difference GMT +11

Somalia

Map page 128

National name Jamhuuriyadda Soomaaliya/Republic of Somalia
Area 637,700 sq km/ 246,215 sq mi
Capital Mogadishu (and chief port)
Major towns/cities Hargeysa, Berbera, Kismaayo, Marka
Major ports Berbera, Marka, Kismaayo
Physical features mainly flat, with hills in north
Currency Somali shilling
GNP per capita (PPP) (US$) 600 (1999 est)
Resources chromium, coal, salt, tin, zinc, copper, gypsum, manganese, iron ore, uranium, gold, silver; deposits of petroleum and natural gas have been discovered but remain unexploited
Population 10,097,000 (2000 est)
Population density (per sq km) 15 (1999 est)
Language Somali, Arabic (both official), Italian, English
Religion Sunni Muslim; small Christian community, mainly Roman Catholic
Time difference GMT +3

South Africa

Map page 130

National name Republiek van Suid-Afrika/Republic of South Africa
Area 1,222,081 sq km/ 471,845 sq mi
Capital Cape Town (legislative), Pretoria (administrative), Bloemfontein (judicial)
Major towns/cities Johannesburg, Durban, Port Elizabeth, Vereeniging, Pietermaritzburg, Kimberley, Soweto, Tembisa
Major ports Cape Town, Durban, Port Elizabeth, East London
Physical features southern end of large plateau, fringed by mountains and lowland coastal margin; Drakensberg Mountains, Table Mountain; Limpopo and Orange rivers
Territories Marion Island and Prince Edward Island in the Antarctic
Currency rand
GNP per capita (PPP) (US$) 8,318 (1999)
Resources gold (world's largest producer), coal, platinum, iron ore, diamonds, chromium, manganese, limestone, asbestos, fluorspar, uranium, copper, lead, zinc, petroleum, natural gas
Population 40,377,000 (2000 est)
Population density (per sq km) 33 (1999 est)
Language English, Afrikaans, Xhosa, Zulu, Sesotho

(all official), other African languages
Religion Dutch Reformed Church and other Christian denominations 77%, Hindu 2%, Muslim 1%
Time difference GMT +2

South Korea

Map page 106

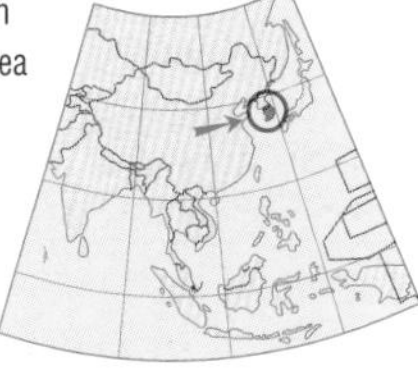

National name Daehan Minguk/Republic of Korea
Area 98,799 sq km/ 38,146 sq mi
Capital Seoul
Major towns/cities Pusan, Taegu, Inch'ŏn, Kwangju, Taejŏn, Songnam
Major ports Pusan, Inch'ŏn
Physical features southern end of a mountainous peninsula separating the Sea of Japan from the Yellow Sea
Currency won
GNP per capita (PPP) (US$) 14,637 (1999)
Resources coal, iron ore, tungsten, gold, molybdenum, graphite, fluorite, natural gas, hydroelectric power, fish
Population 46,844,000 (2000 est)
Population density (per sq km) 473 (1999 est)
Language Korean (official)
Religion Buddhist 48%, Confucian 3%, Christian 47%, mainly Protestant; Chund Kyo (peculiar to Korea, combining elements of Shaman, Buddhist, and Christian doctrines)
Time difference GMT +9

Spain

Map page 86

National name España/Spain
Area 504,750 sq km/ 194,883 sq mi (including the Balearic and Canary islands)
Capital Madrid
Major towns/cities Barcelona, Valencia, Zaragoza, Sevilla, Málaga, Bilbao, Las Palmas (on Gran Canarias island), Murcia, Palma (on Mallorca)
Major ports Barcelona, Valencia, Cartagena, Málaga, Cádiz, Vigo, Santander, Bilbao
Physical features central plateau with mountain ranges, lowlands in south; rivers Ebro, Douro, Tagus, Guadiana, Guadalquivir; Iberian Plateau (Meseta); Pyrenees, Cantabrian Mountains, Andalusian Mountains, Sierra Nevada
Territories Balearic and Canary Islands; in North Africa: Ceuta, Melilla, Alhucemas, Chafarinas Islands, Peñón de Vélez
Currency peseta
GNP per capita (PPP) (US$) 16,730 (1999)
Resources coal, lignite, anthracite, copper, iron, zinc, uranium, potassium salts
Population 39,630,000 (2000 est)
Population density (per sq km) 79 (1999 est)
Language Spanish (Castilian; official), Basque, Catalan, Galician
Religion Roman Catholic 98%
Time difference GMT +1

Sri Lanka

Map page 112

National name Sri Lanka Prajatantrika Samajavadi Janarajaya/Democratic Socialist Republic of Sri Lanka
Area 65,610 sq km/ 25,332 sq mi
Capital Sri Jayewardenapura Kotte
Major towns/cities Colombo, Kandy, Dehiwala-Mount Lavinia, Moratuwa, Jaffna, Galle
Major ports Colombo, Jaffna, Galle, Negombo, Trincomalee
Physical features flat in north and around coast; hills and mountains in south and central interior
Currency Sri Lankan rupee
GNP per capita (PPP) (US$) 3,056 (1999)
Resources gemstones, graphite, iron ore, monazite, rutile, uranium, iemenite sands, limestone, salt, clay
Population 18,827,000 (2000 est)
Population density (per sq km) 284 (1999 est)

Language Sinhala, Tamil (both official), English
Religion Buddhist 69%, Hindu 15%, Muslim 8%, Christian 8%
Time difference GMT +5.5

Sudan

Map page 122

National name Al-Jumhuryyat es-Sudan/Republic of Sudan
Area 2,505,800 sq km/ 967,489 sq mi
Capital Khartoum
Major towns/cities Omdurman, Port Sudan, Juba, Wad Medani, El Obeid, Kassala, Gedaref, Nyala
Major ports Port Sudan
Physical features fertile Nile valley separates Libyan Desert in west from high rocky Nubian Desert in east
Currency Sudanese dinar
GNP per capita (PPP) (US$) 1,298 (1999)
Resources petroleum, marble, mica, chromite, gypsum, gold, graphite, sulphur, iron, manganese, zinc, fluorspar, talc, limestone, dolomite, pumice
Population 29,490,000 (2000 est)
Population density (per sq km) 12 (1999 est)
Language Arabic (51%) (official), 100 local languages
Religion Sunni Muslim 70%; also animist 25%, and Christian 5%
Time difference GMT +2

Suriname

Map page 156

National name Republiek Suriname/ Republic of Suriname
Area 163,820 sq km/ 63,250 sq mi
Capital Paramaribo
Major towns/cities Nieuw Nickerie, Moengo, Brokopondo, Nieuw Amsterdam, Albina, Groningen
Physical features hilly and forested, with flat and narrow coastal plain; Suriname River
Currency Suriname guilder
GNP per capita (PPP) (US$) 3,820 (1998 est)
Resources petroleum, bauxite (one of the world's leading producers), iron ore, copper, manganese, nickel, platinum, gold, kaolin
Population 417,000 (2000 est)
Population density (per sq km) 3 (1999 est)
Language Dutch (official), Spanish, Sranan (Creole), English, Hindi, Javanese, Chinese, various tribal languages
Religion Christian 47%, Hindu 28%, Muslim 20%
Time difference GMT -3.5

Swaziland

Map page 130

National name Umbuso wakaNgwane/Kingdom of Swaziland
Area 17,400 sq km/ 6,718 sq mi
Capital Mbabane, Lobamba
Major towns/cities Manzini, Big Bend, Mhlume, Nhlangano
Physical features central valley; mountains in west (Highveld); plateau in east (Lowveld and Lubombo plateau)
Currency lilangeni
GNP per capita (PPP) (US$) 4,200 (1999)
Resources coal, asbestos, diamonds, gold, tin, kaolin, iron ore, talc, pyrophyllite, silica
Population 1,008,000 (2000 est)
Population density (per sq km) 56 (1999 est)
Language Swazi, English (both official)
Religion about 60% Christian, animist
Time difference GMT +2

Sweden

Map page 74

National name Konungariket Sverige/Kingdom of Sweden

Area 450,000 sq km/ 173,745 sq mi
Capital Stockholm
Major towns/cities Göteborg, Malmö, Uppsala, Norrköping, Västerås, Linköping, Örebro, Helsingborg
Major ports Helsingborg, Malmö, Göteborg, Stockholm
Physical features mountains in west; plains in south; thickly forested; more than 20,000 islands off the Stockholm coast; lakes, including Vänern, Vättern, Mälaren, and Hjälmaren
Currency Swedish krona
GNP per capita (PPP) (US$) 20,824 (1999)
Resources iron ore, uranium, copper, lead, zinc, silver, hydroelectric power, forests
Population 8,910,000 (2000 est)
Population density (per sq km) 20 (1999 est)
Language Swedish (official), Finnish, Saami (Lapp)
Religion Evangelical Lutheran, Church of Sweden (established national church) 90%; Muslim, Jewish
Time difference GMT +1

Switzerland

Map page 88

National name Schweizerische Eidgenossenschaft (German)/Confédération Suisse (French)/ Confederazione Svizzera (Italian)/ Confederaziun Svizra (Romansch)/Swiss Confederation
Area 41,300 sq km/15,945 sq mi
Capital Bern
Major towns/cities Zürich, Geneva, Basel, Lausanne, Luzern, St. Gallen, Winterthur
Major ports river port Basel (on the Rhine)
Physical features most mountainous country in Europe (Alps and Jura mountains); highest peak Dufourspitze 4,634 m/15,203 ft in Apennines
Currency Swiss franc
GNP per capita (PPP) (US$) 27,486 (1999)
Resources salt, hydroelectric power, forest
Population 7,386,000 (2000 est)
Population density (per sq km) 178 (1999 est)
Language German (65%), French (18%), Italian (10%), Romansch (1%) (all official)
Religion Roman Catholic 46%, Protestant 40%
Time difference GMT +1

Syria

Map page 114

National name al-Jumhuriyya al-Arabiyya as-Suriyya/Syrian Arab Republic
Area 185,200 sq km/ 71,505 sq mi
Capital Damascus
Major towns/cities Aleppo, Homs, Al Lādhiqīyah, Hamāh, Ar Raqqah, Dayr az Zawr
Major ports Al Lādhiqīyah
Physical features mountains alternate with fertile plains and desert areas; Euphrates River
Currency Syrian pound
GNP per capita (PPP) (US$) 2,761 (1999)
Resources petroleum, natural gas, iron ore, phosphates, salt, gypsum, sodium chloride, bitumen
Population 16,125,000 (2000 est)
Population density (per sq km) 85 (1999 est)
Language Arabic (89%) (official), Kurdish (6%), Armenian (3%), French, English, Aramaic, Circassian
Religion Sunni Muslim 74%; other Islamic sects 16%, Christian 10%
Time difference GMT +2

Taiwan

Map page 104

National name Chung-hua Min-kuo/Republic of China
Area 36,179 sq km/13,968 sq mi
Capital T'aipei
Major towns/cities Kaohsiung, T'aichung, T'ainan, Panch'iao, Chungho, Sanch'ung

Major ports Kaohsiung, Chilung
Physical features island (formerly Formosa) off People's Republic of China; mountainous, with lowlands in west; Penghu (Pescadores), Jinmen (Quemoy), Mazu (Matsu) islands
Currency New Taiwan dollar
GNP per capita (PPP) (US$) 18,950 (1998 est)
Resources coal, copper, marble, dolomite; small reserves of petroleum and natural gas
Population 22,113,000 (1999 est)
Population density (per sq km) 685 (1999 est)
Language Chinese (dialects include Mandarin (official), Min, and Hakka)
Religion officially atheist; Buddhist 23%, Taoist 18%, I-Kuan Tao 4%, Christian 3%, Confucian and other 3%
Time difference GMT +8

Tajikistan

Map page 100

National name Jumhurii Tojikston/Republic of Tajikistan
Area 143,100 sq km/ 55,250 sq mi
Capital Dushanbe
Major towns/cities Khŭjand, Qŭrghonteppa, Kŭlob, Ŭroteppa, Kofarnihon

Physical features mountainous, more than half of its territory lying above 3,000 m/10,000 ft; huge mountain glaciers, which are the source of many rapid rivers
Currency Tajik rouble
GNP per capita (PPP) (US$) 981 (1999)
Resources coal, aluminium, lead, zinc, iron, tin, uranium, radium, arsenic, bismuth, gold, mica, asbestos, lapis lazuli; small reserves of petroleum and natural gas
Population 6,188,000 (2000 est)
Population density (per sq km) 43 (1999 est)
Language Tajik (related to Farsi; official), Russian
Religion Sunni Muslim; small Russian Orthodox and Jewish communities
Time difference GMT +5

Tanzania

Map page 128

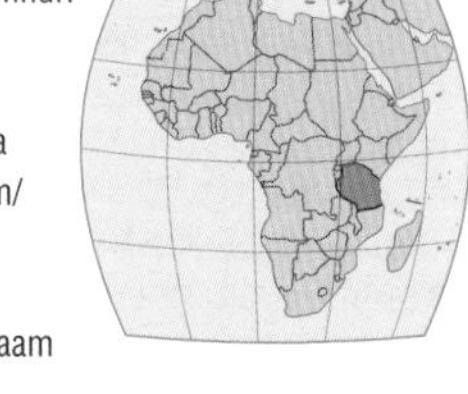

National name Jamhuri ya Muungano wa Tanzania/United Republic of Tanzania
Area 945,000 sq km/ 364,864 sq mi
Capital Dodoma (official), Dar es Salaam (administrative)
Major towns/cities Zanzibar, Mwanza, Mbeya, Tanga, Morogoro
Major ports Dar es Salaam
Physical features central plateau; lakes in north and west; coastal plains; lakes Victoria, Tanganyika, and Nyasa; half the country is forested; comprises islands of Zanzibar and Pemba; Mount Kilimanjaro, 5,895 m/ 19,340 ft, the highest peak in Africa; Olduvai Gorge; Ngorongoro Crater, 14.5 km/9 mi across, 762 m/ 2,500 ft deep
Currency Tanzanian shilling
GNP per capita (PPP) (US$) 478 (1999)
Resources diamonds, other gemstones, gold, salt, phosphates, coal, gypsum, tin, kaolin (exploration for petroleum in progress)
Population 33,517,000 (2000 est)
Population density (per sq km) 35 (1999 est)
Language Kiswahili, English (both official), Arabic (in Zanzibar), many local languages
Religion Muslim, Christian, traditional religions
Time difference GMT +3

Thailand

Map page 108

National name Ratcha Anachak Thai/Kingdom of Thailand
Area 513,115 sq km/198,113 sq mi
Capital Bangkok (and chief port)

Major towns/cities Chiang Mai, Hat Yai, Khon Kaen, Songkhla, Nakhon Ratchasima, Nonthaburi, Udon Thani
Major ports Nakhon Sawan
Physical features mountainous, semi-arid plateau in northeast, fertile central region, tropical isthmus in south; rivers Chao Phraya, Mekong, and Salween
Currency baht
GNP per capita (PPP) (US$) 5,599 (1999)
Resources tin ore, lignite, gypsum, antimony, manganese, copper, tungsten, lead, gold, zinc, silver, rubies, sapphires, natural gas, petroleum, fish
Population 61,399,000 (2000 est)
Population density (per sq km) 119 (1999 est)
Language Thai, Chinese (both official), English, Lao, Malay, Khmer
Religion Buddhist 95%; Muslim 5%
Time difference GMT +7

Togo

Map page 126

National name République Togolaise/ Togolese Republic
Area 56,800 sq km/ 21,930 sq mi
Capital Lomé
Major towns/cities Sokodé, Kpalimé, Kara, Atakpamé, Bassar, Tsévié
Physical features two savannah plains, divided by range of hills northeast-southwest; coastal lagoons and marsh; Mono Tableland, Oti Plateau, Oti River
Currency franc CFA
GNP per capita (PPP) (US$) 1,346 (1999 est)
Resources phosphates, limestone, marble, deposits of iron ore, manganese, chromite, peat; exploration for petroleum and uranium was under way in the early 1990s
Population 4,629,000 (2000 est)
Population density (per sq km) 79 (1999 est)
Language French (official), Ewe, Kabre, Gurma, other local languages
Religion animist about 50%, Catholic and Protestant 35%, Muslim 15%
Time difference GMT +/-0

Tonga

Map page 132

National name Pule'anga Fakatu'i 'o Tonga/Kingdom of Tonga
Area 750 sq km/ 290 sq mi
Capital Nuku'alofa (on Tongatapu island)
Major towns/cities Neiafu, Vaini
Physical features three groups of islands in southwest Pacific, mostly coral formations, but actively volcanic in west; of the 170 islands in the Tonga group, 36 are inhabited
Currency pa'anga, or Tongan dollar
GNP per capita (PPP) (US$) 4,281 (1999)
Population 99,000 (2000 est)
Population density (per sq km) 131 (1999 est)
Language Tongan (official), English
Religion mainly Free Wesleyan Church; Roman Catholic, Anglican
Time difference GMT +13

Trinidad and Tobago

Map page 152

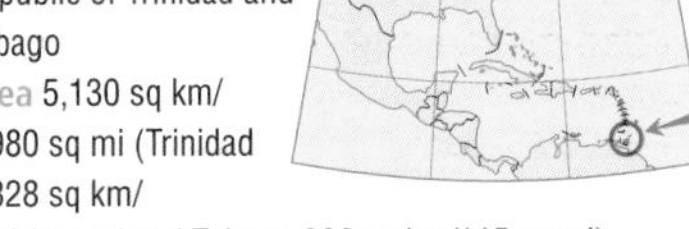

National name Republic of Trinidad and Tobago
Area 5,130 sq km/ 1,980 sq mi (Trinidad 4,828 sq km/ 1,864 sq mi and Tobago 300 sq km/115 sq mi)
Capital Port of Spain (and chief port)
Major towns/cities San Fernando, Arima, Point Fortin
Major ports Scarborough
Physical features comprises two main islands and

some smaller ones in Caribbean Sea; coastal swamps and hills east-west
Currency Trinidad and Tobago dollar
GNP per capita (PPP) (US$) 7,262 (1999)
Resources petroleum, natural gas, asphalt (world's largest deposits of natural asphalt)
Population 1,295,000 (2000 est)
Population density (per sq km) 251 (1999 est)
Language English (official), Hindi, French, Spanish
Religion Roman Catholic 33%, Hindu 25%, Anglican 15%, Muslim 6%, Presbyterian 4%
Time difference GMT -4

Tunisia

Map page 124

National name Al-Jumhuriyya at-Tunisiyya/Tunisian Republic
Area 164,150 sq km/ 63,378 sq mi
Capital Tunis (and chief port)
Major towns/cities Sfax, L'Ariana, Bizerte, Gabès, Sousse, Kairouan
Major ports Sfax, Sousse, Bizerte
Physical features arable and forested land in north graduates towards desert in south; fertile island of Jerba, linked to mainland by causeway (identified with island of lotus-eaters); Shott el Jerid salt lakes
Currency Tunisian dinar
GNP per capita (PPP) (US$) 5,478 (1999)
Resources petroleum, natural gas, phosphates, iron, zinc, lead, aluminium fluoride, fluorspar, sea salt
Population 9,586,000 (2000 est)
Population density (per sq km) 58 (1999 est est)
Language Arabic (official), French
Religion Sunni Muslim (state religion); Jewish and Christian minorities
Time difference GMT +1

Turkey

Map page 116

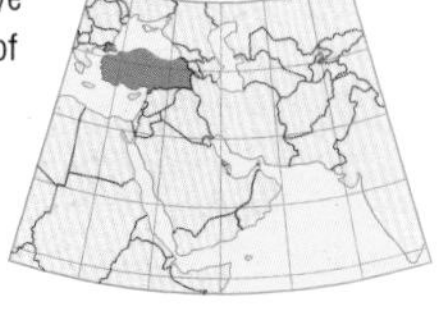

National name Türkiye Cumhuriyeti/Republic of Turkey
Area 779,500 sq km/ 300,964 sq mi
Capital Ankara
Major towns/cities İstanbul, İzmir, Adana, Bursa, Gaziantep, Konya, Mersin, Antalya, Diyarbakduringr
Major ports İstanbul and İzmir
Physical features central plateau surrounded by mountains, partly in Europe (Thrace) and partly in Asia (Anatolia); Bosporus and Dardanelles; Mount Ararat (highest peak Great Ararat, 5,137 m/16,854 ft); Taurus Mountains in southwest (highest peak Kaldi Dag, 3,734 m/12,255 ft); sources of rivers Euphrates and Tigris in east
Currency Turkish lira
GNP per capita (PPP) (US$) 6,126 (1999)
Resources chromium, copper, mercury, antimony, borax, coal, petroleum, natural gas, iron ore, salt
Population 66,591,000 (2000 est)
Population density (per sq km) 84 (1999 est)
Language Turkish (official), Kurdish, Arabic
Religion Sunni Muslim 99%; Orthodox, Armenian churches
Time difference GMT +3

Turkmenistan

Map page 100

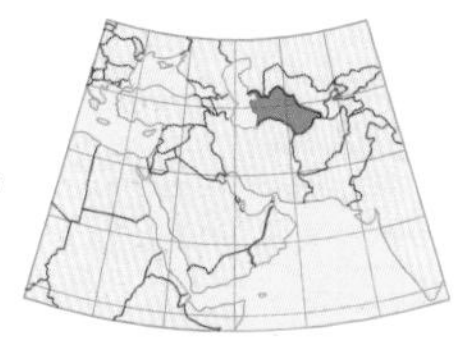

National name Türkmenistan/ Turkmenistan
Area 488,100 sq km/ 188,455 sq mi
Capital Ashkhabad
Major towns/cities Chardzhev, Mary, Nebitdag, Dashkhovuz, Turkmenbashi
Major ports Turkmenbashi
Physical features about 90% of land is desert including the Kara Kum 'Black Sands' desert (area 310,800 sq km/120,000 sq mi)

Currency manat
GNP per capita (PPP) (US$) 3,099 (1999)
Resources petroleum, natural gas, coal, sulphur, magnesium, iodine-bromine, sodium sulphate and different types of salt
Population 4,459,000 (2000 est)
Population density (per sq km) 9 (1999 est)
Language Turkmen (a Turkic language; official), Russian, Uzbek, other regional languages
Religion Sunni Muslim
Time difference GMT +5

Tuvalu

Map page 132

National name Fakavae Aliki-Malo i Tuvalu/Constitutional Monarchy of Tuvalu
Area 25 sq km/ 9.6 sq mi
Capital Fongafale (on Funafuti atoll)
Physical features nine low coral atolls forming a chain of 579 km/650 mi in the Southwest Pacific
Currency Australian dollar
GNP per capita (PPP) (US$) 970 (1998 est)
Population 12,000 (2000 est)
Population density (per sq km) 423 (1999 est)
Language Tuvaluan, English (both official), a Gilbertese dialect (on Nui)
Religion Protestant 96% (Church of Tuvalu)
Time difference GMT +12

Uganda

Map page 128

National name Republic of Uganda
Area 236,600 sq km/ 91,351 sq mi
Capital Kampala
Major towns/cities Jinja, Mbale, Entebbe, Masaka, Mbarara, Soroti
Physical features plateau with mountains in west (Ruwenzori Range, with Mount Margherita, 5,110 m/ 16,765 ft); forest and grassland; 18% is lakes, rivers, and wetlands (Owen Falls on White Nile where it leaves Lake Victoria; Lake Albert in west); arid in northwest
Currency Ugandan new shilling
GNP per capita (PPP) (US$) 1,136 (1999 est)
Resources copper, apatite, limestone; believed to possess the world's second-largest deposit of gold (hitherto unexploited); also reserves of magnetite, tin, tungsten, beryllium, bismuth, asbestos, graphite
Population 21,778,000 (2000 est)
Population density (per sq km) 89
Language English (official), Kiswahili, other Bantu and Nilotic languages
Religion Christian 65%, animist 20%, Muslim 15%
Time difference GMT +3

Ukraine

Map page 96

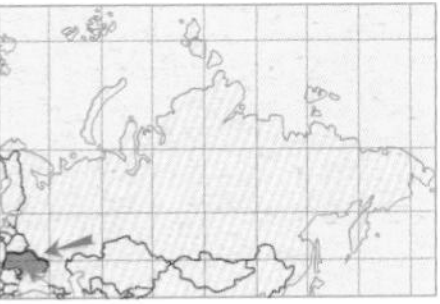

National name Ukrayina/Ukraine
Area 603,700 sq km/ 233,088 sq mi
Capital Kiev
Major towns/cities Kharkiv, Donets'k, Dnipropetrovs'k, L'viv, Kryvyy Rih, Zaporizhzhya, Odessa
Physical features Russian plain; Carpathian and Crimean Mountains; rivers: Dnieper (with the Dnieper dam 1932), Donetz, Bug
Currency hryvna
GNP per capita (PPP) (US$) 3,142 (1999)
Resources coal, iron ore (world's fifth-largest producer), crude oil, natural gas, salt, chemicals, brown coal, alabaster, gypsum
Population 50,456,000 (2000 est)
Population density (per sq km) 84 (1999 est)
Language Ukrainian (a Slavonic language; official), Russian (also official in Crimea), other regional languages
Religion traditionally Ukrainian Orthodox; also Ukrainian Catholic; small Protestant, Jewish, and Muslim communities
Time difference GMT +2

United Arab Emirates

Map page 119

National name Dawlat Imarat al-'Arabiyya al Muttahida/State of the Arab Emirates (UAE)
Area 83,657 sq km/ 32,299 sq mi
Capital Abu Dhabi
Major towns/cities Dubai, Sharjah, Ra's al Khaymah, Ajmān, Al 'Ayn
Major ports Dubai
Physical features desert and flat coastal plain; mountains in east
Currency UAE dirham
GNP per capita (PPP) (US$) 18,825 (1999 est)
Resources petroleum and natural gas
Population 2,441,000 (2000 est)
Population density (per sq km) 29 (1999 est)
Language Arabic (official), Farsi, Hindi, Urdu, English
Religion Muslim 96% (of which 80% Sunni); Christian, Hindu
Time difference GMT +4

United Kingdom

Map page 82

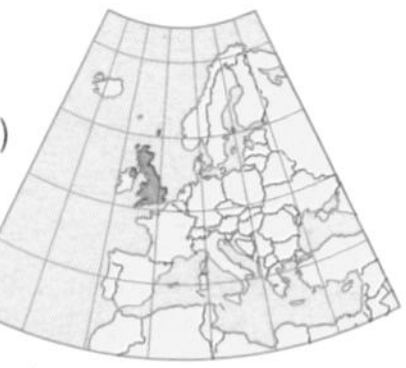

National name United Kingdom of Great Britain and Northern Ireland (UK)
Area 244,100 sq km/ 94,247 sq mi
Capital London
Major towns/cities Birmingham, Glasgow, Leeds, Sheffield, Liverpool, Manchester, Edinburgh, Bradford, Bristol, Coventry, Belfast, Cardiff
Major ports London, Grimsby, Southampton, Liverpool
Physical features became separated from European continent in about 6000 BC; rolling landscape, increasingly mountainous towards the north, with Grampian Mountains in Scotland, Pennines in northern England, Cambrian Mountains in Wales; rivers include Thames, Severn, and Spey
Territories Anguilla, Bermuda, British Antarctic Territory, British Indian Ocean Territory, British Virgin Islands, Cayman Islands, Falkland Islands, Gibraltar, Montserrat, Pitcairn Islands, St. Helena and Dependencies (Ascension, Tristan da Cunha), South Georgia, South Sandwich Islands, Turks and Caicos Islands; the Channel Islands and the Isle of Man are not part of the UK but are direct dependencies of the crown
Currency pound sterling
GNP per capita (PPP) (US$) 20,883 (1999)
Resources coal, limestone, crude petroleum, natural gas, tin, iron, salt, sand and gravel
Population 58,830,000 (2000 est)
Population density (per sq km) 240 (1999 est)
Language English (official), Welsh (also official in Wales), Gaelic
Religion about 46% Church of England (established church); other Protestant denominations, Roman Catholic, Muslim, Jewish, Hindu, Sikh
Time difference GMT +/-0

United States of America

Map page 142

National name United States of America (USA)
Area 9,372,615 sq km/ 3,618,766 sq mi
Capital Washington D.C.
Major towns/cities New York, Los Angeles, Chicago, Philadelphia, Detroit, San Francisco, Dallas, San Diego, San Antonio, Houston, Boston, Phoenix, Indianapolis, Honolulu, San José
Physical features topography and vegetation from tropical (Hawaii) to arctic (Alaska); mountain ranges parallel with east and west coasts; the Rocky Mountains separate rivers emptying into the Pacific from those flowing into the Gulf of Mexico; Great Lakes in north; rivers include Hudson, Mississippi, Missouri, Colorado, Columbia, Snake, Rio Grande, Ohio
Territories the commonwealths of Puerto Rico and Northern Marianas; Guam, the US Virgin Islands, American Samoa, Wake Island, Midway Islands, Johnston Atoll, Baker Island, Howland Island, Jarvis

Island, Kingman Reef, Navassa Island, Palmyra Island
Currency US dollar
GNP per capita (PPP) (US$) 30,600 (1999)
Resources coal, copper (world's second-largest producer), iron, bauxite, mercury, silver, gold, nickel, zinc (world's fifth-largest producer), tungsten, uranium, phosphate, petroleum, natural gas, timber
Population 278,357,000 (2000 est)
Population density (per sq km) 29 (1999 est)
Language English, Spanish
Religion Protestant 58%; Roman Catholic 28%; atheist 10%; Jewish 2%; other 4% (1998)
Time difference GMT -5-11

Uruguay

Map page 158

National name República Oriental del Uruguay/Eastern Republic of Uruguay
Area 176,200 sq km/ 68,030 sq mi
Capital Montevideo
Major towns/cities Salto, Paysandú, Las Piedras, Rivera, Tacuarembó
Physical features grassy plains (pampas) and low hills; rivers Negro, Uruguay, Río de la Plata
Currency Uruguayan peso
GNP per capita (PPP) (US$) 8,280 (1999)
Resources small-scale extraction of building materials, industrial minerals, semi-precious stones; gold deposits are being developed
Population 3,337,000 (2000 est)
Population density (per sq km) 19 (1999 est)
Language Spanish (official), Brazilero (a mixture of Spanish and Portuguese)
Religion mainly Roman Catholic
Time difference GMT -3

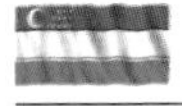

Uzbekistan

Map page 100

National name Özbekiston Respublikasi/Republic of Uzbekistan

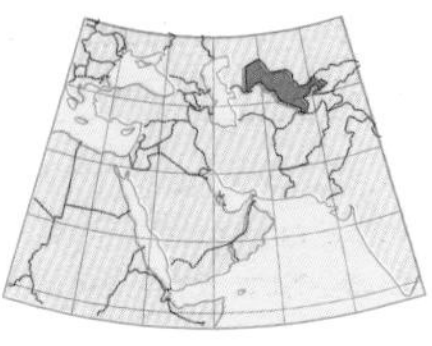

Area 447,400 sq km/ 172,741 sq mi
Capital Tashkent
Major towns/cities Samarkand, Bukhara, Namangan, Andijon, Nukus, Karshi
Physical features oases in deserts; rivers: Amu Darya, Syr Darya; Fergana Valley; rich in mineral deposits
Currency som
GNP per capita (PPP) (US$) 2,092 (1999)
Resources petroleum, natural gas, coal, gold (world's seventh-largest producer), silver, uranium (world's fourth-largest producer), copper, lead, zinc, tungsten
Population 24,318,000 (2000 est)
Population density (per sq km) 54 (1999 est)
Language Uzbek (a Turkic language; official), Russian, Tajik
Religion predominantly Sunni Muslim; small Wahhabi, Sufi, and Orthodox Christian communities
Time difference GMT +5

Vanuatu

Map page 132

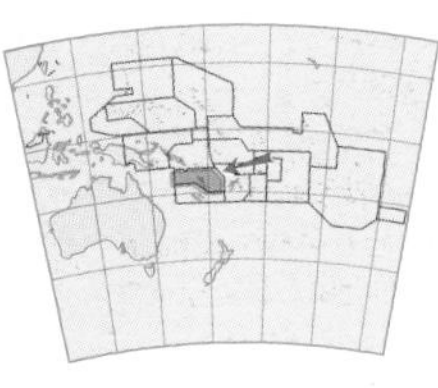

National name Ripablik blong Vanuatu/République de Vanuatu/Republic of Vanuatu
Area 14,800 sq km/ 5,714 sq mi
Capital Port-Vila (on Efate island) (and chief port)
Major towns/cities Luganville (on Espíritu Santo)
Physical features comprises around 70 inhabited islands, including Espíritu Santo, Malekula, and Efate; densely forested, mountainous; three active volcanoes; cyclones on average twice a year
Currency vatu
GNP per capita (PPP) (US$) 2,771 (1999 est)
Resources manganese; gold, copper, and large deposits of petroleum have been discovered but have hitherto remained unexploited
Population 190,000 (2000 est)
Population density (per sq km) 13 (1999 est)
Language Bislama (82%), English, French (all official)

Religion Christian 80%, animist about 8%
Time difference GMT +11

Vatican City

Map page 90

National name Stato della Città del Vaticano/Vatican City State
Area 0.4 sq km/ 0.2 sq mi
Physical features forms an enclave in the heart of Rome, Italy
Currency Vatican City lira and Italian lira
GNP per capita (PPP) see Italy
Population 1,000 (2000 est)
Population density (per sq km) 2,500 (2000 est)
Language Latin (official), Italian
Religion Roman Catholic
Time difference GMT +1

Venezuela

Map page 156

National name República de Venezuela/ Republic of Venezuala
Area 912,100 sq km/ 352,161 sq mi
Capital Caracas
Major towns/cities Maracaibo, Maracay, Barquisimeto, Valencia, Ciudad Guayana, Petare
Major ports Maracaibo
Physical features Andes Mountains and Lake Maracaibo in northwest; central plains (llanos); delta of River Orinoco in east; Guiana Highlands in southeast

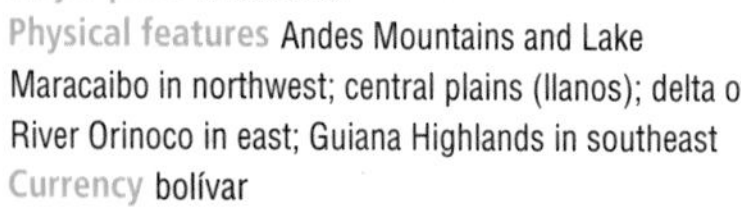

Currency bolívar
GNP per capita (PPP) (US$) 5,268 (1999)
Resources petroleum, natural gas, aluminium, iron ore, coal, diamonds, gold, zinc, copper, silver, lead, phosphates, manganese, titanium
Population 24,170,000 (2000 est)
Population density (per sq km) 26 (1999 est)
Language Spanish (official), Indian languages (2%)
Religion Roman Catholic 92%
Time difference GMT -4

Vietnam

Map page 108

National name Công-hòa xã-hôi chu-nghia Viêt Nam/ Socialist Republic of Vietnam
Area 329,600 sq km/ 127,258 sq mi
Capital Hanoi
Major towns/cities Ho Chi Minh (formerly Saigon), Hai Phong, Da Năng, Cân Tho, Nha Trang, Biên Hoa, Huê
Major ports Ho Chi Minh (formerly Saigon), Da Năng, Hai Phong
Physical features Red River and Mekong deltas, centre of cultivation and population; tropical rainforest; mountainous in north and northwest
Currency dong
GNP per capita (PPP) (US$) 1,755 (1999)
Resources petroleum, coal, tin, zinc, iron, antimony, chromium, phosphate, apatite, bauxite
Population 79,832,000 (2000 est)
Population density (per sq km) 237 (1999 est)
Language Vietnamese (official), French, English, Khmer, Chinese, local languages
Religion mainly Buddhist; Christian, mainly Roman Catholic (8-10%); Taoist, Confucian, Hos Hoa, and Cao Dai sects
Time difference GMT +7

Yemen

Map page 114

National name Al-Jumhuriyya al Yamaniyya/ Republic of Yemen
Area 531,900 sq km/205,366 sq mi
Capital Şan'ā
Major towns/cities Aden, Ta'izz, Al Mukallā, Al Ḩudaydah, Ibb, Dhamār
Major ports Aden
Physical features hot, moist coastal plain, rising to

plateau and desert
Currency riyal
GNP per capita (PPP) (US$) 688 (1999)
Resources petroleum, natural gas, gypsum, salt; deposits of copper, gold, lead, zinc, molybdenum
Population 18,112,000 (2000 est)
Population density (per sq km) 33 (1999 est)
Language Arabic (official)
Religion Sunni Muslim 63%, Shiite Muslim 37%
Time difference GMT +3

Yugoslavia

Map page 92

National name Savezna Republika Jugoslavija/ Federal Republic of Yugoslavia
Area 58,300 sq km/22,509 sq mi
Capital Belgrade
Major towns/cities Priština, Novi Sad, Niš, Kragujevac, Podgorica (formerly Titograd), Subotica
Physical features federation of republics of Serbia and Montenegro and two former autonomous provinces, Kosovo and Vojvodina
Currency new Yugoslav dinar
GNP per capita (PPP) (US$) 5,880 (1997 est)
Resources petroleum, natural gas, coal, copper ore, bauxite, iron ore, lead, zinc
Population 10,640,000 (2000 est)
Population density (per sq km) 182 (1999 est)
Language Serbo-Croat (official), Albanian (in Kosovo)
Religion Serbian and Montenegrin Orthodox; Muslim in southern Serbia
Time difference GMT +1

Zambia

Map page 130

National name Republic of Zambia
Area 752,600 sq km/290,578 sq mi
Capital Lusaka
Major towns/cities Kitwe, Ndola, Kabwe, Mufulira, Chingola, Luanshya, Livingstone
Physical features forested plateau cut through by rivers; Zambezi River, Victoria Falls, Kariba Dam
Currency Zambian kwacha
GNP per capita (PPP) (US$) 686 (1999)
Resources copper (world's fourth-largest producer), cobalt, zinc, lead, coal, gold, emeralds, amethysts and other gemstones, limestone, selenium
Population 9,169,000 (2000 est)
Population density (per sq km) 12 (1999 est)
Language English (official), Bantu languages
Religion about 64% Christian, animist, Hindu, Muslim
Time difference GMT +2

Zimbabwe

Map page 130

National name Republic of Zimbabwe
Area 390,300 sq km/ 150,694 sq mi
Capital Harare
Major towns/cities Bulawayo, Gweru, Kwekwe, Mutare, Kadoma, Chitungwiza
Physical features high plateau with central high veld and mountains in east; rivers Zambezi, Limpopo; Victoria Falls
Currency Zimbabwe dollar
GNP per capita (PPP) (US$) 2,470 (1999)
Resources gold, nickel, asbestos, coal, chromium, copper, silver, emeralds, lithium, tin, iron ore, cobalt
Population 11,669,000 (2000 est)
Population density (per sq km) 30 (1999 est)
Language English, Shona, Ndebele (all official)
Religion 50% follow a syncretic (part Christian, part indigenous beliefs) type of religion, Christian 25%, animist 24%, small Muslim minority
Time difference GMT +2

Equatorial Scale 1 : 180 400 000

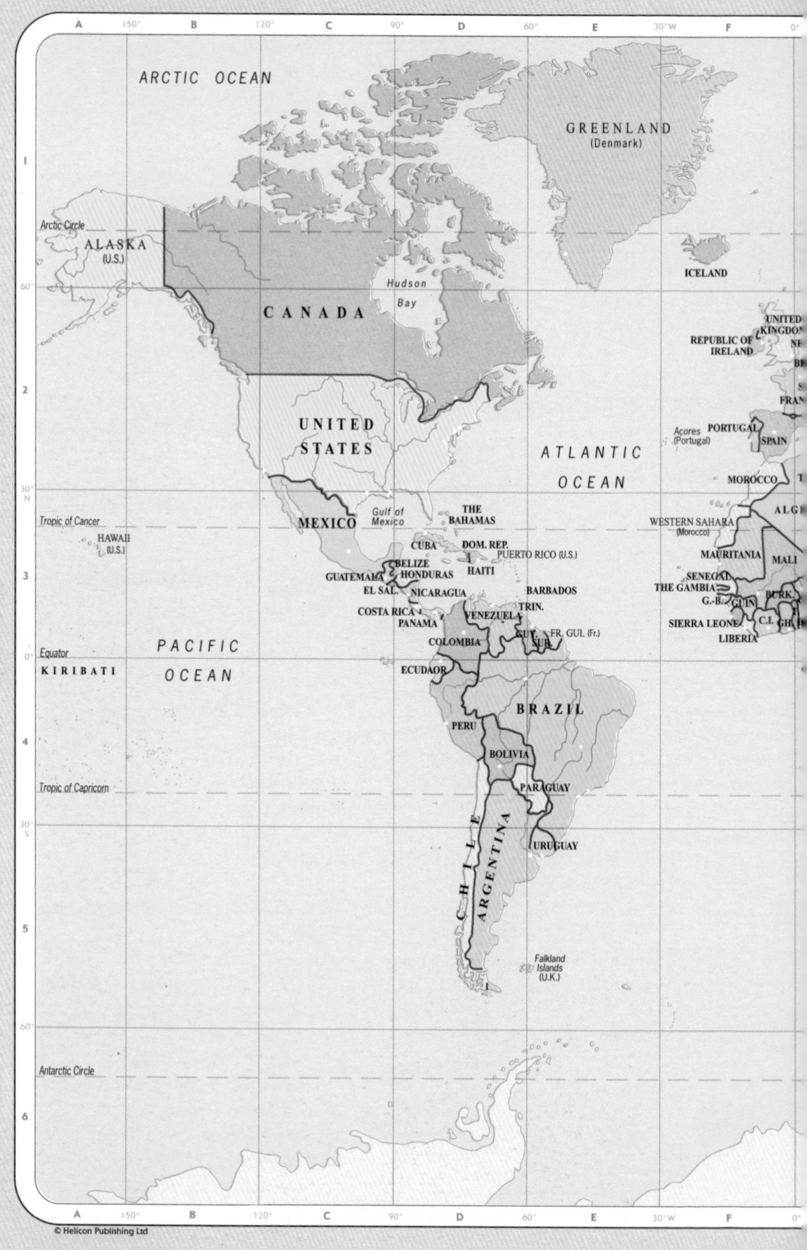

ARCTIC OCEAN
Severnaya Zemlya
Novaya Zemlya
Barents Sea
RUSSIA
Arctic Circle
Bering Sea
Sea of Okhotsk
ESTONIA
LATVIA
LITH.
POLAND
BELARUS
UKRAINE
MOL.
SLOVA.
HUNG.
ROM.
BUL.
BOS.
ALB.
MAC.
GEORGIA
ARM.
AZER.
TURKEY
GREECE
SYRIA
LEBANON
ISRAEL
JORDAN
IRAQ
KUWAIT
IRAN
TURK.
UZBEKISTAN
KYRGYZSTAN
TAJIKISTAN
AFGHANISTAN
PAKISTAN
KAZAKHSTAN
MONGOLIA
CHINA
N. KOREA
S. KOREA
JAPAN
PACIFIC OCEAN
Tropic of Cancer
TAIWAN
NEPAL
BHUTAN
BANG.
MYAN.
LAOS
THAILAND
VIETNAM
CAMBODIA
PHILIPPINES
INDIA
EGYPT
SAUDI ARABIA
U.A.E.
OMAN
YEMEN
Arabian Sea
SRI LANKA
MALDIVES
MALAYSIA
BRUNEI
MARSHALL ISLANDS
FEDERATED STATES OF MICRONESIA
Equator
INDONESIA
PAPUA NEW GUINEA
SOLOMON ISLANDS
VANUATU
FIJI
CHAD
SUDAN
ERITREA
DJIBOUTI
SOMALIA
ETHIOPIA
C.A.R.
UGANDA
RW.
KENYA
DEM. REP. OF CONGO
BURUNDI
TANZANIA
SEYCHELLES
COMOROS
ZAMBIA
MALAWI
MOZAMBIQUE
MADAGASCAR
ZIMBABWE
BOTSWANA
MAURITIUS
INDIAN OCEAN
AUSTRALIA
Tropic of Capricorn
SWAZILAND
SOUTH AFRICA
LESOTHO
NEW ZEALAND
SOUTHERN OCEAN
Antarctic Circle
ANTARCTICA
G
30°E
H
60°
J
90°
K
120°
L
150°
M
180° N
1
2
3
4
5
6
60°
30° N
0°
30° S
60°
Country Abbreviations
ALB. ALBANIA
ARM. ARMENIA
AUS. AUSTRALIA
AZER. AZERBAIJAN
BANG. BANGLADESH
BEL. BELGIUM
BOS. BOSNIA-HERZEGOVINA
BUL. BULGARIA
BURK. BURKINA FASO
CAM. CAMEROON
C.A.R. CENTRAL AFRICAN REPUBLIC
C.I. CÔTE D'IVOIRE
CRO. CROATIA
CZECH. CZECH REPUBLIC
DEN. DENMARK
DOM. REP. DOMINICAN REPUBLIC
E.G. EQUATORIAL GUINEA
EL SAL. EL SALVADOR
FR. GUI. FRENCH GUIANA
GH. GHANA
GUIN. GUINEA
G.-B. GUINEA-BISSAU
GUY. GUYANA
HUNG. HUNGARY
LITH. LITHUANIA
MAC. MACEDONIA
MOL. MOLDOVA
MYAN. MYANMAR (BURMA)
NETH. NETHERLANDS
ROM. ROMANIA
RW. RWANDA
SLOVA. SLOVAK REPUBLIC
SL. SLOVENIA
SUR. SURINAME
SWITZ. SWITZERLAND
T. TOGO
TRIN. TRINDAD AND TOBAGO
U.A.E. UNITED ARAB EMIRATES
YUG. YUGOSLAVIA

1 : 32 400 000

0 500 1000 1500 km

0 250 500 750 miles

Barents Sea
Vadsø
O. Kolguyev
Murmansk
White Sea
Arkhangel'sk
Severnaya Dvina
Pechora
Ural'skiy Khrebet (Ural Mountains)
Arctic Circle
Surgut
Ob'
NOVOSIBIRSK
Irtysh
OMSK
Kama
Onezhskoye Ozero (Lake Onega)
Ladozhskoye Ozero (Lake Ladoga)
Vologda
Kirov
PERM'
YEKATERINBURG
CHELYABINSK
Astana
RUSSIA
SANKT-PETERBURG (ST. PETERSBURG)
KAZAN'
UFA
NIZHNIY NOVGOROD
Volga
Dvina
MOSKVA (MOSCOW)
SAMARA
MINSK
Don
Aral Sea
Ural
VOLGOGRAD
KYYIV (KIEV)
KHARKIV
Donets
UKRAINE
DONETS'K
DNIPROPETROVS'K
Astrakhan'
ROSTOV-NA-DONU
MOLDOVA
Chişinău
Dnieper
ODESA (ODESSA)
Sea of Azov
Stavropol'
Caspian Sea
Aktau
Krym'
Elbrus 5642
Groznyy
Ashgabat (Ashkhabad)
BUCUREŞTI (BUCHAREST)
Sevastopol'
Caucasus
Black Sea
T'BILISI
BAKI (BAKU)
MASHHAD
Burgas
Samsun
YEREVAN
İSTANBUL
Bursa
ANKARA
TEHRĀN (TEHERAN)
İZMIR
Gaziantep
ASIA
Antalya
Rodos (Rhodes) (Greece)
Lefkosia (Nicosia)
BAGHDĀD
DIMASHQ (DAMASCUS)
BAYROUTH (BEIRUT)
Al Kuwayt (Kuwait)
AMMĀN
Yerushalayim (Jerusalem)
The Gulf
EL QÂHIRA (CAIRO)
Nile

1 : 9 300 000
0
200
400
600 km
0
100
200
300 miles
Barents Sea
Greenland Sea
NORWEGIAN SEA
ICELAND
FINLAND
SWEDEN
NORWAY
RUSSIA
KARELIYA
Lappland
Gulf of Bothnia
Murmansk
Severomorsk
Monchegorsk
Apatity
Kandalaksha
Umba
Kovdor
Zelenoborskiy
Kuolayarvi
Loukhi
Kalevala
Kostomuksha
Muyezerskiy
Sortavala
Vardø
Vadsø
Varangerfjorden
Nordkapp
Nordkinn
Magerøya
Kåfjord
Hammerfest
Porsanger
Utsjoki
Inarijärvi
Ivalo
Vuotso
Sodankylä
Kemijärvi
Rovaniemi
Kittilä
Muonio
Pello
Övertorneå
Tornio
Kemi
Haparanda
Oulu
Hailuoto
Raahe
Kajaani
Kuhmo
Nurmes
Joensuu
Kuopio
Iisalmi
Ylivieska
Kokkola
Jakobstad
Vaasa
Seinäjoki
Lapua
Jyväskylä
Savonlinna
Kuusamo
Pudasjärvi
Kalixälven
Luleå
Piteå
Skellefteå
Umeå
Kiruna
Gällivare
Jokkmokk
Arvidsjaur
Karesuando
Kebnekaise 2123
Torneträsk
Storuman
Vilhelmina
Åsele
Lycksele
Örnsköldsvik
Kramfors
Sollefteå
Strömsund
Östersund
Storsjön
Gäddede
Tärnaby
Mo i Rana
Bodø
Narvik
Tromsø
Senja
Vesterålen
Lofoten
Vestfjorden
Svolvær
Snøtinden 1599
Oktinden 1916
Mosjøen
Sandnessjøen
Namsos
Trondheim
Trondheimsfjorden
Storlien
1796
Kristiansund
Smøla
Hitra
Arctic Circle
Reykjavík
Keflavík
Hafnarfjörður
Selfoss
Hekla 1491
Vatnajökull
Hvannadalshnúkur 2119
Snæfell 1833
Grímsvötn 1719
Hofsjökull
Langjökull
Akureyri
Húsavík
Ísafjörður
Siglufjörður
Sauðárkrókur
Höfn
Vík
Vestmannaeyjar
Heimaey
Surtsey
Faxaflói
Breiðafjörður
Húnaflói
Seyðisfjörður
Egilsstaðir
Kirkjubæjarklaustur
Borgarnes
Mývatn
Grímsey
Reykjanestá

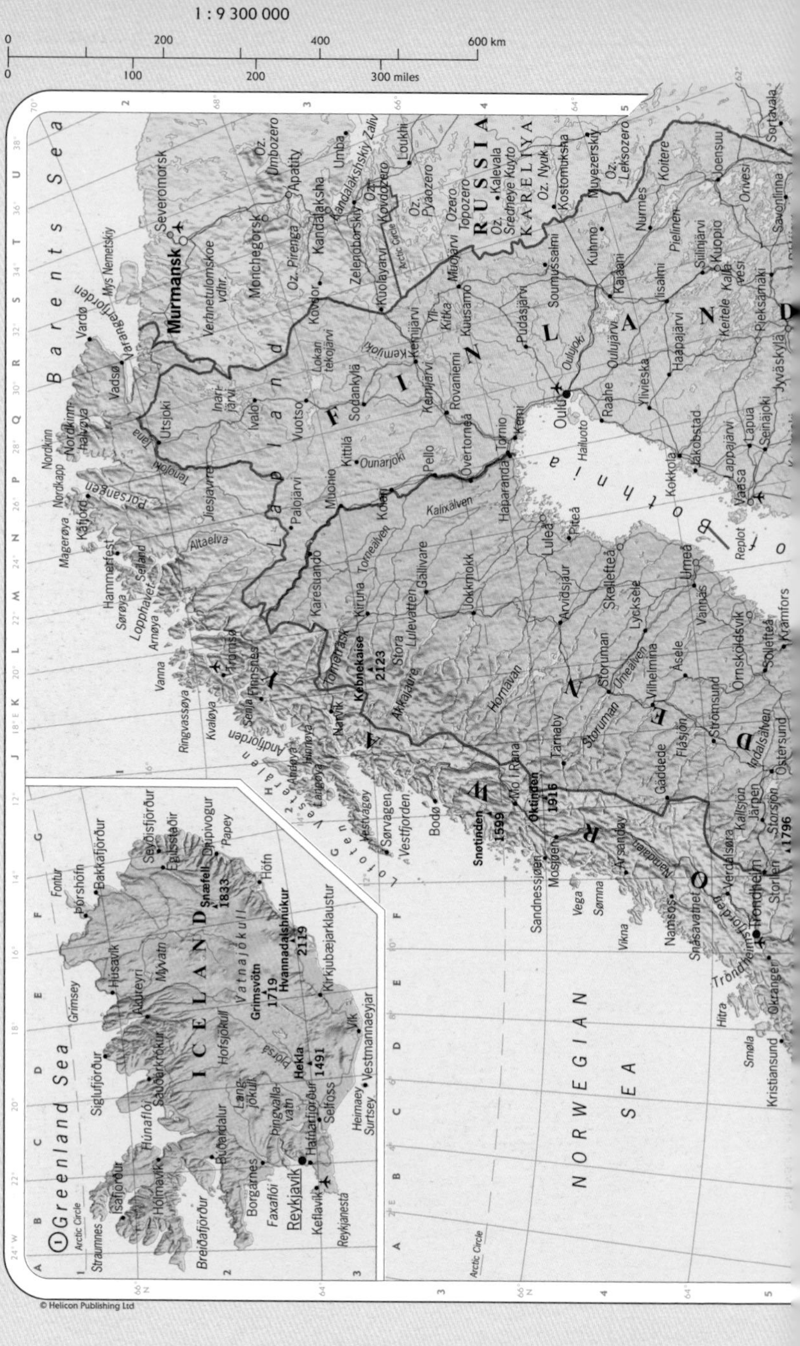

NORTH SEA
BALTIC SEA
Skagerrak
Kattegat
Gulf of Finland
Gulf of Riga
Gulf of Gdansk
Pomeranian Bay
Hanöbukten
Courland Lagoon
ESTONIA
LATVIA
LITHUANIA
RUSSIA
BELARUS
POLAND
GERMANY
DENMARK
NETHERLANDS
Oslo
Stockholm
Helsinki
Tallinn
Riga
Vilnius
København (Copenhagen)
SANKT-PETERBURG
Kaliningrad
HAMBURG
Bremen
Göteborg
Malmö
Gdańsk
Gdynia
Szczecin
Bydgoszcz
Kaunas
Tartu
Turku
Tampere
Bergen
Stavanger
Kristiansand
Uppsala
Västerås
Örebro
Linköping
Norrköping
Jönköping
Gotland
Öland
Saaremaa
Hiiumaa
Bornholm
Fyn
Jylland
Sjælland
Lolland
Åland
Vänern
Vättern
Hardangervidda
Galdhøpiggen 2470
2286
96 97
78 79
76 77

1 : 5 600 000
0
100
200
300 km
0
50
100
150 miles
74 75
78 79
© Helicon Publishing Ltd
Kattegat
SWEDEN
DENMARK
LATVIA
LITHUANIA
RUSSIA
BELARUS
POLAND
GERMANY
BALTIC SEA
Halmstad
Ängelholm
Helsingborg
Helsingør
Hässleholm
Markaryd
Kristianstad
Ivösjön
Åsnen
Tingsryd
Karlshamn
Ronneby
Karlskrona
Kalmar
Öland
Hanö
Hanöbukten
Landskrona
København (Copenhagen)
Malmö
Trelleborg
Ystad
Køge Bugt
Køge
Fakse Bugt
Roskilde
Holbæk
Frederiksværk
Sjælland
Næstved
Vordingborg
Møn
Falster
Nykøbing
Bornholm
Rønne
Kap Arkona
Rügen
Sassnitz
Stralsund
Greifswald
Pomeranian Bay
Rostock
Güstrow
Demmin
Neubrandenburg
Anklam
Peene
Waren
Müritz
Neustrelitz
Prenzlau
Wittstock
Kyritz
Rathenow
Oranienburg
Eberswalde
Schwedt
Havel
Premnitz
Falkensee
Brandenburg
Potsdam
BERLIN
Fürstenwalde
Frankfurt
Spree
Eisenhüttenstadt
Cottbus
Finsterwalde
Senftenberg
Spremberg
Hoyerswerda
Lutherstadt Wittenberg
Dessau
Elbe
Torgau
Wurzen
Halle
Świnoujście
Goleniów
Szczecin
Gryfino
Odra
Dębno
Kostrzyn
Warta
Słubice
Świebodzin
Gubin
Żary
Zielona Góra
Głogów
Leszno
Grodzisk Wielkopolski
Luboń
Poznań
Szamotuły
Gorzów Wielkopolski
Choszczno
Stargard Szczeciński
Drawsko Pomorskie
Gryfice
Kołobrzeg
Świdwin
Koszalin
Wałcz
Szczecinek
Słupsk
Bytów
Chojnice
Złotów
Piła
Noteć
Czarnków
Września
Gniezno
Bydgoszcz
Inowrocław
Toruń
Chełmno
Grudziądz
Kościerzyna
Lębork
Wejherowo
Puck
Gdynia
Gdańsk
Gulf of Gdansk
Tczew
Malbork
Elbląg
Iława
Brodnica
Działdowo
Olsztyn
Lidzbark Warmiński
Braniewo
Bartoszyce
Kętrzyn
Mrągowo
Szczytno
Mława
Ciechanów
Płock
Sierpc
Lipno
Włocławek
Konin
Turek
Kalisz
Prosna
Ostrów Wielkopolski
Rawicz
Śrem
Kutno
Łęczyca
Zgierz
Łódź
Pabianice
Piotrków Trybunalski
Tomaszów Mazowiecki
WARSZAWA (WARSAW)
Pruszków
Legionowo
Wołomin
Warka
Dęblin
Puławy
Ostrołęka
Ostrów Mazowiecka
Łomża
Narew
Bug
Pisa
Jezioro Śniardwy
Ełk
Grajewo
Augustów
Suwałki
Gołdap
Siemiatycze
Siedlce
Łuków
Biała Podlaska
Włodawa
Białystok
Łapy
Hajnówka
Bielsk Podlaski
Brest
Malaryta
Shats'k
Vawkavysk
Hrodna
Druskininkai
Kaliningrad (Königsberg)
Svetlogorsk
Baltiysk
Mamonovo
Gvardeysk
Chernyakhovsk
Gusev
Sovetsk
Neman
Courland Lagoon
Klaipėda
Liepāja
Kretinga
Skuodas
Mažeikiai
Plungė
Telšiai
Šilalė
Tauragė
Jurbarkas
Kelmė
Kuršėnai
Šiauliai
Bauska
Biržai
Panevėžys
Ukmergė
Jonava
Kaunas
Prienai
Alytus
Marijampolė
Nemunas
Venta

Central Europe

96 97
92 93
90 91
88 89

1 : 4 100 000
0
100
200 km
0
50
100 miles
76 77
74 75
84 85
NORTH SEA
BALTIC SEA
SWEDEN
DENMARK
POLAND
NETHERLANDS
Bornholm
Trelleborg
Sjælland
Fyn
Lolland
Falster
Møn
Als
Ærø
Langeland
Rügen
Usedom
Fehmarn
Poel
Nordfriesische Inseln
Frisian Islands
Ostfriesische Inseln
Waddeneilanden
Waddenzee
Sylt
Føhr
Amrum
Pellworm
Rømø
Fanø
Fanø Bugt
Helgoland
Helgoländer Bucht
Wangerooge
Spiekeroog
Langeoog
Norderney
Juist
Borkum
Schiermonnikoog
Ameland
Terschelling
Store Bælt
Smålandsfarvandet
Fakse Bugt
Kieler Bucht
Mecklenburger Bucht
Pomeranian Bay
Stettiner Haff
Greifswalder Bodden
Kap Arkona
Hiddensee
Darß
Lüneburger Heide
Uckermark
Harz
Odense
Esbjerg
Ribe
Vojens
Haderslev
Åbenrå
Tinglev
Tønder
Skaerbaek
Assens
Fåborg
Nyborg
Svendborg
Slagelse
Sorø
Ringsted
Næstved
Præstø
Vordingborg
Nykøbing
Sakskøbing
Rødby Havn
Gedser
Flensburg
Flensburg Fjorde
Angeln
Schleswig
Eckernförde
Kiel
Preetz
Plön
Rendsburg
Neumünster
Husum
Tönning
Heide
Leck
Eider
Dithmarschen
Itzehoe
Brunsbüttel
Cuxhaven
Elbe
Weser
Nord-Ostsee-Kanal
Puttgarden
Oldenburg
Neustadt
Bad Schwartau
Lübeck
Ratzeburg
Schweriner See
Schwerin
Wismar
Bad Doberan
Rostock
Bützow
Güstrow
Teterow
Barth
Stralsund
Sassnitz
Bergen
Grimmen
Greifswald
Wolgast
Anklam
Demmin
Kummerower See
Peene
Recknitz
Torgelow
Neubrandenburg
Neustrelitz
Waren
Müritz
Prenzlau
Schwedt
Szczecin
Swinoujscie
Eberswalde
Strausberg
BERLIN
Rüdersdorf
Frankfurt
Slubice
Fürstenwalde
Eisenhüttenstadt
Gubin
Odra
Cottbus
Spremberg
Lübben
Finsterwalde
Luckenwalde
Potsdam
B-Spandau
Falkensee
Hennigsdorf
Oranienburg
Neuruppin
Havel
Wittstock
Kyritz
Perleberg
Wittenberge
Parchim
Ludwigslust
Rathenow
Premnitz
Brandenburg
Genthin
Burg
Belzig
Lutherstadt Wittenberg
Coswig
Dessau
Roßlau
Mulde
Köthen
Bernburg
Schönebeck
Magdeburg
Stendal
Gardelegen
Salzwedel
Uelzen
Dannenberg
Lauenburg
Geesthacht
HAMBURG
Norderstedt
Pinneberg
Bergedorf
Harburg
Stade
Lüneburg
Soltau
Buchholz
Rotenburg
Visselhövede
Walsrode
Celle
Gifhorn
Wolfsburg
Aller
Helmstedt
Braunschweig
Wolfenbüttel
Oschersleben
Halberstadt
Quedlinburg
Blankenburg
Bode
Salzgitter
Peine
Hildesheim
Goslar
Bad Harzburg
Hannover
Langenhagen
Garbsen
Wunstorf
Nienburg
Springe
Hameln
Alfeld
Einbeck
Leine
Höxter
Verden
Bremen
Bremerhaven
Bremervörde
Zeven
Brake
Delmenhorst
Syke
Sulingen
Westerstede
Varel
Jadebusen
Wilhelmshaven
Wittmund
Norden
Emden
Leer
Papenburg
Cloppenburg
Vechta
Löningen
Meppen
Lingen
Nordhorn
Rheine
Ems
Osnabrück
Bramsche
Espelkamp
Minden
Bückeburg
Herford
Bad Salzuflen
Detmold
Bielefeld
Gütersloh
Rheda-Wiedenbrück
Paderborn
Lippstadt
Münster
Greven
Coesfeld
Ahlen
Haltern
Recklinghausen
Bocholt
Ahaus
Gronau
Mittellandkanal
Groningen
Delfzijl
Veendam
Emmen
Assen
Hoogeveen
Dokkum
Leeuwarden
Harlingen
Sneek
Heerenveen
Lemmer
Noord-Oost-Polder
Kampen
Zwolle
Hardenberg
Almelo
Hengelo
Enschede
Deventer
Apeldoorn
Amersfoort
Ede
Arnhem
Nijmegen
Doetinchem
Goch
Lelystad
Oostelijk Flevoland
IJssel
Rhine (Rhein)
Waal
Dollard

Germany

GERMANY
CZECH REPUBLIC
AUSTRIA
SWITZERLAND
FRANCE
BELGIUM
LUXEMBOURG
Dresden
Leipzig
Chemnitz
PRAHA (PRAGUE)
Erfurt
Kassel
Köln
Bonn
Düsseldorf
Wuppertal
Frankfurt
Wiesbaden
Mainz
Mannheim
Heidelberg
Karlsruhe
Stuttgart
Nürnberg
Regensburg
MÜNCHEN (MUNICH)
Augsburg
Ulm
Würzburg
Strasbourg
Zürich
Basel
Salzburg
Rhine (Rhein)
Danube (Donau)
Main
Neckar
Moselle

1 : 3 700 000
0 100 200 km
0 50 100 miles
UNITED KINGDOM
ENGLAND
NORTH SEA
English Channel
LONDON
BIRMINGHAM
Nottingham
Leicester
Coventry
PARIS
Strait of Dover
The Wash
The Fens
The Broads
South Downs
The Weald
Isle of Wight
Baie de la Seine
Baie de la Somme
Thames
Seine
Somme
Oise
Eure
Lys
Aisne
Great Ouse
Little Ouse
Welland
Nene
Trent
Yare
Stour
Norwich
Ipswich
Cambridge
Oxford
Reading
Southampton
Portsmouth
Brighton
Dover
Calais
Boulogne-sur-Mer
Dunkerque
Lille
Amiens
Rouen
Le Havre
Caen
Cherbourg
Dieppe
Beauvais
Versailles
82 83
84 85
© Helicon Publishing Ltd

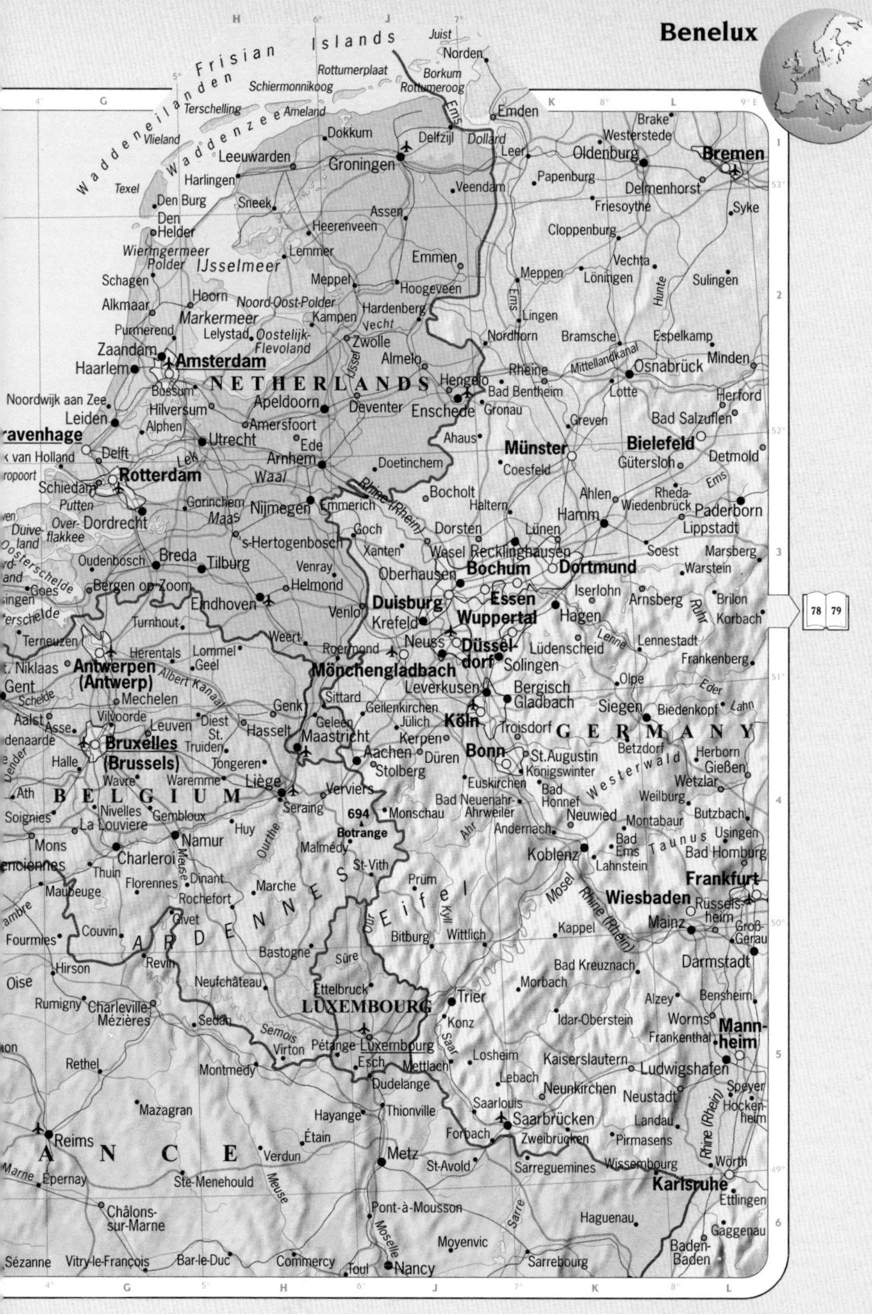

Benelux
Frisian Islands
Waddeneilanden
Waddenzee
Juist
Norden
Borkum
Rottumerplaat
Rottumeroog
Schiermonnikoog
Terschelling
Ameland
Vlieland
Texel
Emden
Ems
Dollard
Delfzijl
Dokkum
Leeuwarden
Groningen
Harlingen
Leer
Brake
Westerstede
Oldenburg
Bremen
Papenburg
Veendam
Delmenhorst
Den Burg
Den Helder
Sneek
Assen
Friesoythe
Syke
Heerenveen
Cloppenburg
Wieringermeer Polder
IJsselmeer
Lemmer
Emmen
Vechta
Schagen
Meppel
Hoogeveen
Meppen
Löningen
Hunte
Sulingen
Alkmaar
Hoorn
Noord-Oost-Polder
Hardenberg
Kampen
Vecht
Lingen
Markermeer
Purmerend
Lelystad
Oostelijk-Flevoland
Zwolle
Nordhorn
Bramsche
Espelkamp
Zaandam
Amsterdam
Haarlem
IJssel
Almelo
Mittellandkanal
Osnabrück
Minden
Bussum
NETHERLANDS
Hengelo
Rheine
Bad Bentheim
Lotte
Herford
Noordwijk aan Zee
Hilversum
Apeldoorn
Deventer
Enschede
Gronau
Leiden
Alphen
Amersfoort
Greven
Bad Salzuflen
's-Gravenhage
Utrecht
Ede
Ahaus
Münster
Bielefeld
Hoek van Holland
Delft
Lek
Arnhem
Doetinchem
Coesfeld
Gütersloh
Detmold
Europoort
Rotterdam
Waal
Schiedam
Rhine (Rhein)
Bocholt
Ahlen
Rheda-Wiedenbrück
Ems
Putten
Gorinchem
Nijmegen
Emmerich
Haltern
Hamm
Paderborn
Dordrecht
Maas
Goch
Dorsten
Lünen
Lippstadt
Duiveland
Overflakkee
's-Hertogenbosch
Xanten
Wesel
Recklinghausen
Soest
Marsberg
Oosterschelde
Oudenbosch
Breda
Tilburg
Venray
Oberhausen
Bochum
Dortmund
Warstein
Goes
Bergen op Zoom
Helmond
Iserlohn
Arnsberg
Ruhr
Brilon
Westerschelde
Eindhoven
Venlo
Duisburg
Essen
Hagen
Krefeld
Wuppertal
Korbach
Turnhout
Terneuzen
Weert
Neuss
Düsseldorf
Lüdenscheid
Lenne
Lennestadt
Herentals
Lommel
Roermond
Frankenberg
St. Niklaas
Antwerpen (Antwerp)
Geel
Mönchengladbach
Solingen
Albert Kanaal
Leverkusen
Bergisch Gladbach
Olpe
Eder
Gent
Schelde
Mechelen
Genk
Sittard
Geilenkirchen
Siegen
Biedenkopf
Lahn
Aalst
Asse
Vilvoorde
Leuven
Diest
Geleen
Jülich
Köln
Troisdorf
Oudenaarde
Bruxelles (Brussels)
St. Truiden
Hasselt
Maastricht
Kerpen
GERMANY
Dender
Halle
Tongeren
Aachen
Düren
Bonn
St. Augustin
Betzdorf
Herborn
Stolberg
Königswinter
Westerwald
Gießen
Wavre
Waremme
Liège
Euskirchen
Wetzlar
Ath
BELGIUM
Verviers
Bad Honnef
Bad Neuenahr-Ahrweiler
Weilburg
Seraing
Nivelles
Gembloux
694 Botrange
Monschau
Neuwied
Montabaur
Butzbach
Soignies
La Louvière
Huy
Andernach
Ahr
Usingen
Mons
Namur
Ourthe
Malmédy
Bad Ems
Taunus
Charleroi
Koblenz
Bad Homburg
Valenciennes
Thuin
Meuse
Dinant
St-Vith
Lahnstein
Frankfurt
Maubeuge
Florennes
Marche
Prüm
Mosel
Wiesbaden
Rüsselsheim
Sambre
Rochefort
ARDENNES
Eifel
Kyll
Rhine (Rhein)
Mainz
Givet
Our
Groß-Gerau
Fourmies
Couvin
Bitburg
Wittlich
Kappel
Bastogne
Darmstadt
Revin
Sûre
Bad Kreuznach
Hirson
Oise
Neufchâteau
Ettelbruck
Morbach
Bensheim
LUXEMBOURG
Trier
Alzey
Rumigny
Charleville-Mézières
Konz
Idar-Oberstein
Worms
Mannheim
Sedan
Semois
Saar
Frankenthal
Virton
Pétange
Luxembourg
Losheim
Kaiserslautern
Rethel
Montmedy
Esch
Mettlach
Ludwigshafen
Lebach
Dudelange
Neunkirchen
Speyer
Neustadt
Saarlouis
Hockenheim
Mazagran
Thionville
Hayange
Saarbrücken
Landau
Étain
Forbach
Zweibrücken
Pirmasens
Rhine (Rhein)
Reims
FRANCE
Verdun
Metz
St-Avold
Sarreguemines
Wissembourg
Wörth
Marne
Épernay
Ste-Menehould
Meuse
Karlsruhe
Ettlingen
Châlons-sur-Marne
Pont-à-Mousson
Sarre
Haguenau
Moselle
Moyenvic
Gaggenau
Baden-Baden
Sézanne
Vitry-le-François
Bar-le-Duc
Commercy
Toul
Nancy
Sarrebourg
78 79

1 : 5 600 000
0
100
200
300 km
0
50
100
150 miles
ATLANTIC
OCEAN
NORTH
SEA
Herma Ness
Unst
Yell
Out Skerries
Shetland Islands
Hillswick
Papa Stour
Whalsay
Foula
Mainland
Lerwick
North Ronaldsay
Fair Isle
Westray
Sanday
Rousay
Stronsay
Mainland
Kirkwall
Orkney Islands
Hoy
Rona
Dunnet Head
South Ronaldsay
John o' Groats
Cape Wrath
Thurso
Wick
Flannan Islands
Stornoway
Lewis
The Minch
998
Ben More Assynt
Lochinver
Helmsdale
Tarbert
South Harris
St. Kilda
Ullapool
Outer Hebrides
North Uist
Moray Firth
Dingwall
Elgin
Fraserburgh
Nairn
Peterhead
Benbecula
Portree
Kyle of Lochalsh
Inverness
South Uist
Little Minch
Northwest Highlands
Loch Ness
Aviemore
Spey
Grampian Mountains
Skye
Aberdeen
Inner Hebrides
Barra
Sea of the Hebrides
Rum
Mallaig
Eigg
Fort William
Dee
Stonehaven
Mingulay
Ben Nevis
1343
Coll
Tiree
Arbroath
SCOTLAND
Tay
Perth
Dundee
Mull
Firth of Lorn
Oban
Iona
Loch Lomond
Kirkcaldy
St Andrews
Colonsay
Jura
Argyll
Forth
Firth of Forth
Clyde
Greenock
Glasgow
Edinburgh
Berwick-upon-Tweed
Islay
Paisley
Motherwell
Holy Island
Port Ellen
Irvine
Galashiels
Tweed
Kintyre
Arran
Kilmarnock
Malin Head
Campbeltown
Firth of Clyde
Ayr
Moffat
Alnwick
Rathlin I.

80 81

84 85

IRELAND
REPUBLIC OF IRELAND
DUBLIN (BAILE ÁTHA CLIATH)
ENGLAND
WALES
FRANCE
LONDON
BIRMINGHAM
MANCHESTER
Belfast
Bangor
Lisburn
Antrim
Armagh
Lough Neagh
Omagh
Enniskillen
Lower Lough Erne
Upper Lough Erne
Donegal
Donegal Bay
Sligo
Ballina
Belmullet
Achill I.
Castlebar
Lough Mask
Connemara
Roscommon
Lough Corrib
Galway
Galway Bay
Aran Islands
Athlone
Ballinasloe
Longford
Lough Ree
Mullingar
Dundalk
Drogheda
Dun Laoghaire
Wicklow Mts
Port Laoise
Lough Derg
Limerick
Kilkenny
Slaney
Arklow
Wexford
Carnsore Point
Waterford
Dungarvan
Clonmel
Suir
Tipperary
Blackwater
Cork
Kinsale
Old Head of Kinsale
Bantry
Killarney
Tralee
Tralee Bay
Dingle Bay
Kilrush
Mouth of the Shannon
Liscannor Bay
C. Clear
Mizen Head
Channel
ISLE OF MAN (U.K.)
Douglas
IRISH SEA
St. George's Channel
Cardigan Bay
Bristol Channel
Celtic Sea
English Channel
ATLANTIC OCEAN
Strait of Dover
Solway
Workington
Penrith
Lake District
978
Scafell Pike
Barrow-in-Furness
Stockton-on-Tees
Middlesbrough
Darlington
Tees
Wharfe
Harrogate
York
Scarborough
Lancaster
Blackpool
Preston
Wigan
St. Helens
Liverpool
Mersey
Warrington
Bradford
Leeds
Castleford
Huddersfield
Doncaster
Sheffield
Kingston-upon-Hull
Grimsby
Scunthorpe
Lincoln
Trent
Skegness
The Wash
Boston
Nottingham
Stoke-on-Trent
Crewe
Chester
Wrexham
Bangor
Holyhead
Anglesey
Caernarfon
1085
Snowdon
Dee
Shrewsbury
Telford
Wolverhampton
Walsall
Derby
Loughborough
Leicester
Coventry
Rugby
Northampton
Peterborough
King's Lynn
Norwich
Cromer
Great Yarmouth
Ely
Ouse
Little Ouse
Bury St. Edmunds
Ipswich
Harwich
Colchester
Chelmsford
Cambridge
Stevenage
St. Albans
Watford
Luton
Aylesbury
Oxford
Cheltenham
Gloucester
Stratford-upon-Avon
Avon
Worcester
Hereford
Wye
Builth Wells
Usk
Severn
Cambrian Mountains
Aberystwyth
Aberaeron
Fishguard
Carmarthen
St David's
Haverfordwest
Pembroke
Swansea
Port Talbot
Merthyr Tydfil
Cardiff
Newport
Severn Estuary
Bristol
Bath
Thames
Reading
Slough
Basingstoke
Salisbury
Winchester
Guildford
Reigate
Crawley
Maidstone
Gravesend
Southend-on-Sea
Canterbury
Ramsgate
Dover
Folkestone
Hastings
Brighton
Beachy Head
Worthing
Portsmouth
Southampton
Isle of Wight
Newport
Bournemouth
Poole
Bill of Portland
Bridgwater
Taunton
Ilfracombe
Bideford
Exeter
Teignmouth
Torquay
Plymouth
Start Point
Launceston
Bodmin
St. Austell
Newquay
Penzance
Land's End
Lizard Point
Isles of Scilly
Alderney
Guernsey
St. Peter Port
Jersey
St. Helier
Channel Islands (U.K.)
Cap de la Hague
Cherbourg
Coutances
St-Lô
Caen
Baie de la Seine
Cap d'Antifer
Le Havre
Lisieux
Evreux
Elbeuf
Yvetot
Seine
Rouen
Neufchâtel-en-Bray
Dieppe
Beauvais
Versailles
Amiens
Abbeville
Somme
Berck
Boulogne-sur-Mer
Calais
St-Omer

82 83
78 79
1 : 5 600 000
0 100 200 km
0 50 100 miles
UNITED KINGDOM
ENGLAND
WALES
NETHERLANDS
BELGIUM
GERMANY
LUXEMBOURG
North Sea
English Channel
Bristol Channel
Strait of Dover
Channel Islands (U.K.)
Golfe de Saint-Malo
Baie de la Seine
Ardennes
Eifel
LONDON
BIRMINGHAM
Coventry
Bristol
Cardiff
Amsterdam
's-Gravenhage
Rotterdam
Antwerpen (Antwerp)
Bruxelles (Brussels)
Duisburg
Düsseldorf
Essen
Mönchen-gladbach
Köln
Bonn
PARIS
Strasbourg
Grand Ballon 1424
Botrange 694

France

FRANCE
SPAIN
ITALY
SWITZERLAND
ANDORRA
MONACO
ATLANTIC OCEAN
Bay of Biscay
MEDITERRANEAN SEA
Golfe du Lion
Massif Central
PYRENEES
Plateau du Limousin
Alpes Maritimes
Pertuis Breton
Île de Ré
Île d'Oléron
Île d'Yeu
Îles d'Hyères
Camargue
Étang de Berre
Lake Geneva
Lac du Bourget
Massif des Écrins
Cap d'Agde
Loire
Vienne
Creuse
Cher
Allier
Dordogne
Isle
Garonne
Gironde
Lot
Tarn
Aude
Adour
Ariège
Rhône
Saône
Isère
Drôme
Durance
Drac
Dora
Po
Ebro
Tet
Mont Blanc 4808
Matterhorn 4478
Gran Paradiso 4061
Monte Viso 3841
Mont Pelat 3053
Puy de Dôme 1464
Puy de Sancy 1885
Mont Mézenc 1753
Aneto 3404
Monte Perdino 3355
Bordeaux
Toulouse
Marseille
Lyon
Nice
Montpellier
Limoges
Grenoble
Clermont-Ferrand
St-Étienne
Perpignan
Nîmes
Toulon
Poitiers
La Rochelle
Rochefort
Niort
Angoulême
Périgueux
Bergerac
Libourne
Pessac
Agen
Montauban
Albi
Castres
Rodez
Carcassonne
Narbonne
Béziers
Sète
Pau
Tarbes
Lourdes
Bayonne
Biarritz
Dax
Mont-de-Marsan
Avignon
Aix-en-Provence
Arles
Valence
Chambéry
Annecy
Genève
Lausanne
Torino
Monaco
Cannes
Zaragoza
Bilbao
Donostia (San Sebastián)
Pamplona
Vitoria-Gasteiz
Logroño
Huesca
Girona
Figueres
Andorra la Vella
Les Sables-d'Olonne
La Roche-sur-Yon
Châtellerault
Royan
Soulac-sur-Mer
La Teste
Mimizan-Plage
Brive-la-Gaillarde
Aurillac
Le Puy
Mende
Millau
Cahors
Montluçon
Moulins
Vichy
Roanne
Mâcon

Costa Verde
Bay of Biscay
Cabo Ortegal
Ortigueira
Ferrol
Viveiro
A Coruña
Luarca
Cabo Peñas
Gijón
Santander
Ribadeo
Avilés
Villaviciosa
Carballo
Villalba
Oviedo
Langreo
Torrelavega
Laredo
Baraka
Camariñas
Betanzos
Cangas de Narcea
Mieres
Cabañaquinta (Aller)
Bilbao
Lugo
Cabo Fisterra (Cape Finisterre)
Santiago
Villablino
Cordillera Cantábrica
Embalse del Ebro
Muros
Noia
Sarria
Bererreá
Reinosa
A Estrada
Lalín
Cistierna
Ebro
Miranda de Ebro
Villagarcia
Monforte de Lemos
Ponferrada
Sta. Eugenia (Ribeira)
Pontevedra
León
Sedano
Miño
Sil
Astorga
Marín
Briviesca
Vigo
Redondela
Ourense
O Barco (Barco de Valdeorras)
La Bañeza
Sahagún
Burgos
Porriño
Tui
A Gudiña
Benavente
Hortiguela
Caminha
Verín
Palencia
Esla
Bragança
Viana do Castelo
Emb. de Ricobayo
Valladolid
Aranda de Duer
Braga
Miranda do Douro
Mirandela
Peñafiel
Póvoa de Varzim
Guimarães
Zamora
Toro
Duero
Sabor
Matosinhos
Vila Real
Medina de Campo
Porto
Vila Nova de Gaia
Emb. de Almendra
Douro
Torre de Moncorvo
Fuentesauco
Espinho
Lumbrales
Salamanca
Peñaranda de Bracamonte
Segovia
Puerto de Navacerrada
Aveiro
Pinhel
Ciudad-Rodrigo
Colmenar Viejo
Viseu
Ávila
Emb. de Sta. Teresa
Guarda
Alcobendas
Guadala
Santa Comba Dão
Sierra de Gata
MADRID
Alcala Henare
Serra da Estrela
Sistema Central
Cabo Mondego
Béjar
Alcorcón
Getafe
Estrela 1993
Covilhã
Emb. de Gabriel y Galán
2592 Pico Almanzor
Figueira da Foz
Coimbra
Parla
Tiétar
Talavera de la Reina
Aranjuez
Tagus
Pombal
Plasencia
Tarancón
Toledo
Merinha Grande
Castelo Branco
Bgem. do Castelo de Bode
Emb. de Alcántara Uno
SPAI
Nazaré
Abrantes
Navahermosa
Belmo
Peniche
Entroncamento
PORTUGAL
Valencia de Alcántara
Cáceres
Trujillo
Emb. de García Sola
Santarém
Portalegre
Alcazar de S. Juan
Tagus (Tejo)
Alburquerque
Guadiana
Tomelloso
Torres Vedras
Coruche
Mora
Don Benito
Manzana
Elvas
Ciudad Real
Estoril
Lisboa (Lisbon)
Badajoz
Mérida
Emb. de la Serena
Almadén
Almada
Barreiro
Estremoz
Valdepeñ
Costa do Sol
Setúbal
Évora
Almendralejo
Castuera
Puertollano
Cabo de Espichel
Jerez de los Caballeros
Zafra
Sierra Morena
Sado
Pozoblanco
La Carolina
Grândola
R. Ardila
Azuaga
Peñarroya-Pueblonuevo
Linares
Villaca
Ferreira do Alentejo
Beja
Moura
Andújar
Sines
Serpa
Cortegana
Córdoba
Montoro
Úbeda
Aljustrel
Guadiana
Jaén
Jódar
Emb. Negratí
Odemira
Lora del Río
Palma del Río
Baena
Martos
Valverde del Camino
Genil
Écija
Lucena
Alcalá la Real
Sevilla
Marchena
Cordiller
Huelva
Almonte
Puente-Genil
Rute
Lagos
Portimão
Ayamonte
Dos Hermanas
Utrera
Osuna
Granada
Cabo de S. Vicente
Albufeira
Faro
Olhão
Golfo de Cádiz
Morón de la Frontera
Loja
Sierra
3482 Mulhac
Lebrija
Olvera
Antequera
Sanlúcar de Barrameda
Ronda
Vélez-Málaga
Motril
Jerez de la Frontera
Ubrique
Málaga
Adra
Cádiz
Puerto Real
Torremolinos
ATLANTIC OCEAN
San Fernando
Medina Sidonia
Marbella
Costa del Sol
Estepona
Vejer de la Frontera
La Línea
Cabo de Trafalgar
Algeciras
Gibraltar (U.K.)
Strait of Gibraltar
Isla de Alborán (Spain)
Ceuta (Spain)
Tanger
Cap Negro
Tétouan
Cap des Fourches
Asilah
MOROCCO
Bou Ahmed
© Helicon Publishing Ltd

1 : 5 600 000
0
100
200 km
0
50
100 miles
84 85
FRANCE
Bayonne
Orthez
Biarritz
Pau
Tarbes
Lourdes
Oloron-Ste-Marie
Donostia (San Sebastián)
Tolosa
Roncesvalles
Alsasua
Pamplona
Tafalla
Logroño
Calahorra
Tudela
Tarazona
Alagón
Soria
Jaca
Huesca
Ejea de los Caballeros
Aínsa
Barbastro
Monzón
PYRENEES
3355 Monte Perdino
Aneto 3404
ANDORRA
Andorra la Vella
La Seu d'Urgell
Tremp
Balaguer
Lleida
Fraga
Cinca
Zaragoza
Muret
Garonne
St-Gaudens
St-Girons
Pamiers
Ariège
Aude
Carcassonne
Limoux
Béziers
Agde
Cap d'Agde
Narbonne
Golfe du Lion
Rivesaltes
Perpignan
Port-Vendres
Ax-les-Thermes
Têt
Figueres
Ripoll
Olot
Banyoles
Manlleu
Vic
Girona
Palamós
Sant Celoni
Sant Feliu de Guíxols
Costa Brava
Manresa
Terrassa
Sabadell
Mataró
Igualada
BARCELONA
El Prat de Llobregat
Montblanc
Vilanova y la Geltrú
Sitges
Reus
Tarragona
Costa Dorada
Caspe
Azaila
Alcañiz
Calatayud
Medinaceli
Daroca
Calamocha
Montalbán
Tortosa
Amposta
Morella
Vinaròs
Teruel
Sierra de Gúdar
Cuenca
Islas Baleares (Balearic Islands)
Menorca
Ciutadella
Mahón
Pollença
Cap de Formentor
Sóller
Inca
Arta
Manacor
Palma de Mallorca
Llucmajor
Mallorca
Cabrera
Cap de ses Salines
Castelló de la Plana
Vila-real
Borriana
Islas Columbretes
La Vall d'Uixo
Sagunto
Golfo de Valencia
Emb. de Contreras
Utiel
Paterna
Valencia
Torrent
Cofrents
Júcar
Algemes
Cullera
Alzira
Gandia
Dénia
Cabo de la Nao
Eivissa (Ibiza)
San Antonia Abad
Formentera
La Roda
Albacete
Almansa
Chincilla de Monte-Aragón
Alcoi
Alcaraz
Hellín
Jumilla
Elda
Benidorm
Novelda
Alicante
Cieza
Elch
Santa Pola
Orihuela
Alcantarilla
Murcia
Costa Blanca
Zarzadilla de Totana
Lorca
La Union
Cartagena
Albox
Águilas
Golfo de Mazarrón
Vera
Nijar
Almería
Cabo de Gata
Mediterranean Sea
ALGER (ALGIERS)
Dellys
Tizi Ouzou
Ain Taya
Thenia
Bou Ismail
Cherchell
Larba
Lakhdaria
Blida
Bouira
Ténès
Médéa
Bouzghaia
Miliana
Khemis Miliana
Beni Slimane
Sour el Ghozlane
Berrouaghia
Atlas Mountains
Ech Chélif
Chélif
Aïn-Tédélès
Mostaganem
Bou Kadir
Theniet el Had
ALGERIA
Ksar el Boukhari
Aïn el Hadjel
Mers el Kébir
Gdyel
Relizane
Oran
Mohammadia
El Amria
Sig
Mascara
Beni Saf
124 125
laura Velasco

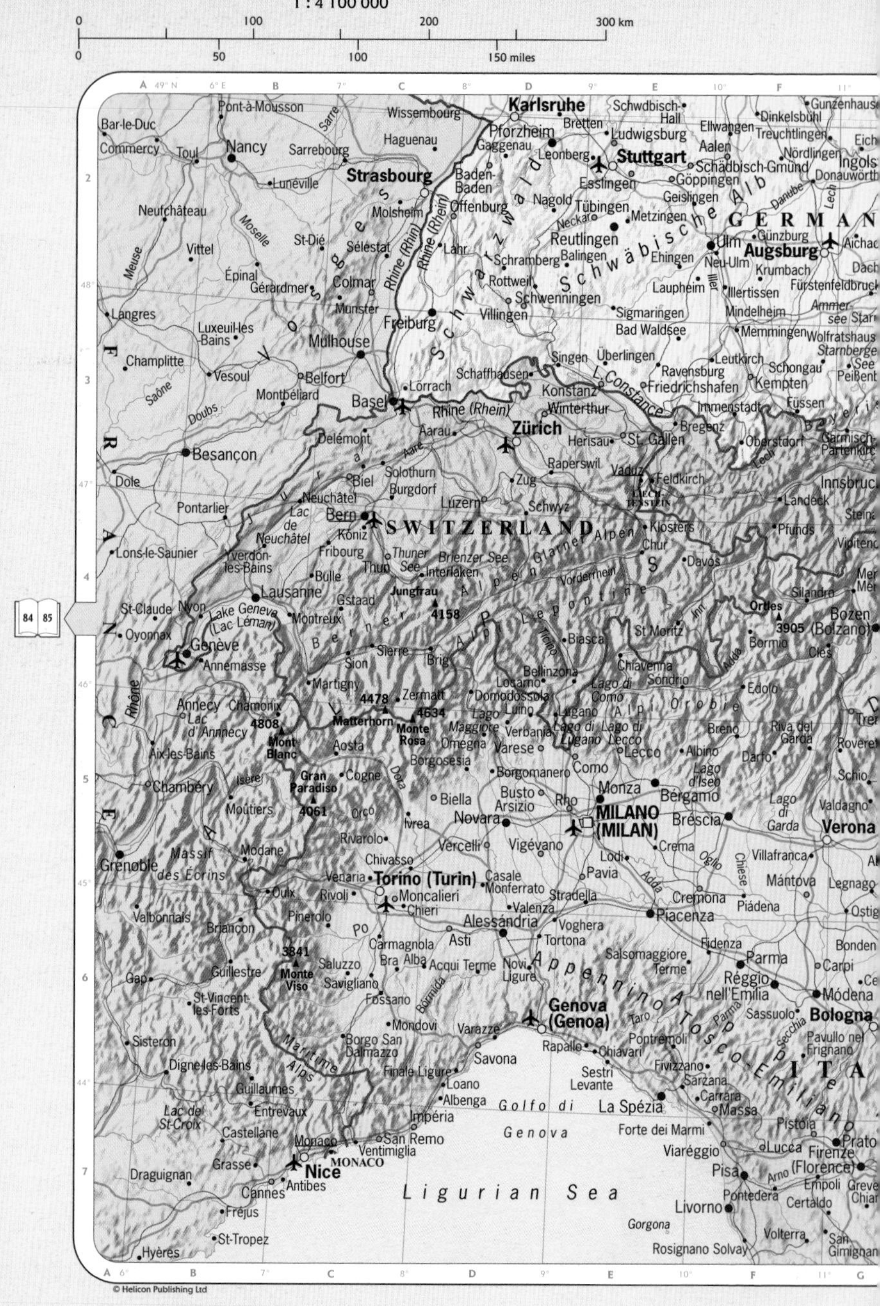
1 : 4 100 000
0
100
200
300 km
0
50
100
150 miles
84 85
Karlsruhe
Pforzheim
Bretten
Gaggenau
Leonberg
Stuttgart
Esslingen
Schwdbisch-Hall
Ludwigsburg
Ellwangen
Aalen
Schädbisch-Gmünd
Göppingen
Geislingen
Dinkelsbühl
Treuchtlingen
Nördlingen
Donauwörth
Gunzenhausen
Wissembourg
Haguenau
Pont-à-Mousson
Bar-le-Duc
Commercy
Toul
Nancy
Sarrebourg
Sarre
Lunéville
Strasbourg
Baden-Baden
Offenburg
Nagold
Tübingen
Metzingen
Reutlingen
Balingen
Neckar
Ulm
Neu-Ulm
Günzburg
Augsburg
Ehingen
Krumbach
Laupheim
Illertissen
Iller
Danube
Lech
G E R M A N
Neufchâteau
Moselle
St-Dié
Molsheim
Sélestat
Colmar
Gérardmer
Épinal
Vittel
Meuse
Munster
Lahr
Schramberg
Rottweil
Schwenningen
Villingen
Sigmaringen
Bad Waldsee
Mindelheim
Memmingen
Fürstenfeldbruck
Wolfratshausen
Starnberger See
Ammer see
Langres
Luxeuil-les-Bains
Freiburg
Mulhouse
Rhine (Rhin)
Rhine (Rhein)
Schwarzwald
Schwäbische Alb
Vosges
Champlitte
Vesoul
Belfort
Saône
Montbéliard
Doubs
Basel
Lörrach
Schaffhausen
Singen
Überlingen
Konstanz
L. Constance
Ravensburg
Friedrichshafen
Leutkirch
Kempten
Schongau
Peißenberg
Immenstadt
Füssen
Winterthur
Rhine (Rhein)
Zürich
Aarau
Aare
Delémont
Herisau
St. Gallen
Bregenz
Oberstdorf
Garmisch-Partenkirchen
Besançon
Dole
Biel
Solothurn
Burgdorf
Raperswil
Zug
Vaduz
Feldkirch
LIECHTENSTEIN
Innsbruck
Landeck
Pontarlier
Neuchâtel
Lac de Neuchâtel
Bern
Luzern
Schwyz
SWITZERLAND
Klosters
Pfunds
Lons-le-Saunier
Köniz
Fribourg
Yverdon-les-Bains
Thun
Thuner See
Brienzer See
Interlaken
Glarner Alpen
Chur
Davos
Bulle
Lausanne
Gstaad
Jungfrau
4158
Vorderrhein
Berner Alpen
Lepontine
Inn
Ortles
3905
Bozen (Bolzano)
Silandro
St-Claude
Nyon
Oyonnax
Lake Geneva (Lac Léman)
Montreux
Genève
Annemasse
Sion
Sierre
Brig
Ticino
Biasca
St Moritz
Bormio
Cles
Chiavenna
Sondrio
Bellinzona
Locarno
Martigny
Domodossola
Lago di Como
Adda
Edolo
Rhône
Annecy
Lac d'Annecy
Chamonix
4808
Mont Blanc
4478
Matterhorn
Zermatt
4634
Monte Rosa
Lago Maggiore
Lugano
Lago di Lugano
Lago di Lecco
Orobie
Breno
Riva del Garda
Rovereto
Aix-les-Bains
Aosta
Omegna
Verbania
Varese
Lecco
Albino
Darfo
Borgosesia
Chambéry
Isère
Gran Paradiso
4061
Cogne
Dora
Borgomanero
Como
Lago d'Iseo
Schio
Moûtiers
Orco
Biella
Busto Arsizio
Rho
Monza
Bergamo
Lago di Garda
Valdagno
Ivrea
Novara
MILANO (MILAN)
Brescia
Verona
Rivarolo
Grenoble
Massif des Écrins
Modane
Vercelli
Vigévano
Crema
Oglio
Chiese
Villafranca
Chivasso
Lodi
Venaria
Torino (Turin)
Casale Monferrato
Pavia
Mántova
Legnago
Oulx
Rivoli
Moncalieri
Chieri
Stradella
Cremona
Piádena
Valbonnais
Briançon
Pinerolo
Po
Valenza
Alessándria
Voghera
Piacenza
Tortona
Carmagnola
Asti
3841
Monte Viso
Saluzzo
Bra
Alba
Acqui Terme
Novi Ligure
Fidenza
Salsomaggiore Terme
Parma
Carpi
Gap
Guillestre
Savigliano
Fossano
Réggio nell'Emilia
Módena
St-Vincent-les-Forts
Bormida
Appennino Tosco-Emiliano
Sassuolo
Bologna
Mondovì
Varazze
Genova (Genoa)
Taro
Secchia
Sisteron
Borgo San Dalmazzo
Maritime Alps
Rapallo
Chiavari
Pontrémoli
Pavullo nel Frignano
Savona
Digne-les-Bains
Finale Ligure
Loano
Sestri Levante
Fivizzano
Sarzana
I T A
Guillaumes
Albenga
Golfo di Genova
La Spézia
Carrara
Massa
Lac de St-Croix
Entrevaux
Impéria
Pistóia
Castellane
Monaco
San Remo
Ventimiglia
Forte dei Marmi
Viaréggio
Lucca
Prato
Firenze (Florence)
Arno
Grasse
Nice
MONACO
Draguignan
Cannes
Antibes
Ligurian Sea
Pisa
Pontedera
Empoli
Certaldo
Fréjus
Livorno
Gorgona
St-Tropez
Hyères
Volterra
Rosignano Solvay
San Gimignano
F R A N C E
A
B
C
D
E
F
G
2
3
4
5
6
7
49° N
6° E
7°
8°
9°
10°
11°
48°
47°
46°
45°
44°

78 79
92 93
90 91
CZECH REPUBLIC
AUSTRIA
SLOVAK REPUBLIC
HUNGARY
SLOVENIA
CROATIA
BOSNIA-HERZEGOVINA
SAN MARINO
Regensburg
Straubing
Deggendorf
Abensberg
Landau
Dingolfing
Vilshofen
Passau
Landshut
Vilsbiburg
Pfarrkirchen
Pocking
Schärding
Altötting
Burghausen
Haar
Traunreut
Chiemsee
Freilassing
Rosenheim
Berchtesgaden
Kufstein
Mittersill
Zwiesel
Prachatice
České Budějovice
Český Krumlov
Rohrbach
Gmünd
Zwettl
Horn
Thaya
Dyje
Hodonín
Břeclav
Veselí
Holíč
Nové Mesto
Myjava
Senica
Váh
Mistelbach
Hollabrunn
Stockerau
Krems
Klosterneuburg
Trnava
Pezinok
Sereď
WIEN (VIENNA)
Bratislava
Danube
Galanta
Malý Dunaj
Mödling
Baden
Bad Vöslau
Dunajská Streda
Danube (Dunaj)
Neusiedler See
Eisenstadt
Wiener Neustadt
Neunkirchen
Ternitz
Mürzzuschlag
Győr
Sopron
Kapuvár
Csorna
Rába
Aspang Markt
Kőszeg
Pápa
Sárvár
Celldömölk
Szombathely
Güssing
Vasvár
Körmend
Ajka
Tapolca
Zalaegerszeg
Keszthely
Balaton
Fonyód
Lenti
Nagykanizsa
Nagyatád
Linz
Danube (Donau)
Inn
Braunau
Ried
Wels
Traun
Enns
Steyr
Melk
St. Pölten
Amstetten
Scheibbs
Waidhofen
Mariazell
Vöcklabruck
Attersee
Gmunden
Bad Ischl
Salzach
Salzburg
Hallein
Bad Aussee
Liezen
Eisenerz
Bruck
Leoben
Bischofshofen
Zell am See
Niedere Tauern
Fohnsdorf
Knittelfeld
Raab
Feistritz
Graz
Tamsweg
Judenburg
Gleisdorf
Großglockner 3798
Badgastein
Lungau
Köflach
Voitsberg
Mur
Hohe Tauern
Gmünd
Friesach
Wolfsberg
St. Andrä
Leibnitz
Isel
Möll
Lienz
Bruneck
Spittal
Feldkirchen
Völkermarkt
Toblach
Mauthen
Drau
Villach
Klagenfurt
Dravograd
Maribor
Murska Sobota
Karnische Alpen
Tarvisio
Triglav 2864
Jesenice
Mozirje
Titovo Velenje
Ptuj
Čakovec
Varaždin
Koprivnica
Drava
Pieve di Cadore
Tolmezzo
Gemona del Friuli
Kranj
Trbovlje
Celje
Tolmin
Škofja Loka
Domžale
Ljubljana
Sava
Križevci
Bjelovar
Barcs
Belluno
Vittório Veneto
Pordenone
Codroipo
Udine
Gorizia
Nova Gorica
Brežice
Zabok
Zaprešić
Sesvete
Virovitica
Montebelluna
Monfalcone
Postojna
Novo Mesto
Samobor
Zagreb
Grubišno Polje
Treviso
Portogruaro
San Donà di Piave
Trieste
Snežnik 1796
Ribnica
Kočevje
Jastrebarsko
Cittadella
Golfo di Trieste
Koper
Karlovac
Sisak
Kutina
Pakrac
Mestre
Venézia (Venice)
Gulf of Venice
Rijeka
Delnice
Petrinja
Kostajnica
Nova Gradiška
Piove di Sacco
Istra
Poreč
Ogulin
Slunj
Velika Kladuša
Bosanska Dubica
Bosanska Gradiška
Monsélice
Chióggia
Labin
Porozina
Krk
Novi Vinodolski
Rovigo
Rovinj
Cres
Senj
Bosanski Novi
Prijedor
Banja Luka
Po
Adria
Porto Tolle
Pula
Prvić
Otočac
Bihać
Sanski Most
Codigoro
Rab
Valli di Comacchio
Unije
Lošinj
Pag
Gospić
Dinaric Alps
Susak
Bosanski Petrovac
Drvar
Jajce
Vrbas
Lugo
Ravenna
Silba
Maun
Olib
Premuda
Vaganski Vrh 1758
Gračac
Faenza
Forlì
Cervia
Vir
Molat
Sestrunj
Zadar
Donji Vakuf
Adriatic Sea
Cesena
Ugljan
Knin
Glamoč
Rímini
Mercato Saraceno
Riccione
Dugi Otok
Pašman
Biograd
Žut
Drniš
Livno
San Marino
Pésaro
Fano
Kornat
Murter
Šibenik
Urbino
Senigallia
Sinj
Buško jez.
Sansepolcro
Cessano
Ancona
Žirje
Trogir
Split
Imotski
Jesi
Città di Castello
Cagli
Supetar
Šolta
Brač
Arezzo
Gubbio
Fabriano
Aso
Macerata
Makarska
Alpen
Dolomiti
12°
13°
14°
15°
16°
17°
48°
47°
46°
45°
44°
H
J
K
L
M
N
2
3
4
5
6
7

1 : 5 600 000

0 100 200 300 km

0 50 100 150 miles

Tyrrhenian Sea
Ionian Sea
MEDITERRANEAN SEA
Golfo di Taranto
Sicilian Channel
Malta Channel
SARDEGNA (SARDINIA) (Italy)
SICILIA (SICILY)
TUNISIA
ALGERIA
MALTA
Appennino Lucano
Isole Ponziane
Isole Lipari
Isole Égadi
Anzio
Terracina
Fondi
Gaeta
Golfo di Gaeta
Capua
Caserta
Benevento
Cerignola
Andria
Molfetta
Bari
Monopoli
NAPOLI (NAPLES)
Nola
Avellino
Vesuvio 1281
Pompei
Salerno
Sorrento
Capri
Ischia
Ponza
Golfo di Salerno
Eboli
Sala Consilina
Melfi
Potenza
Gravina in Puglia
Altamura
Matera
Gioia del Colle
Martina Franca
Massafra
Taranto
Pisticci
Agri
Ostuni
Brindisi
Mesagne
Francavilla
Mandúria
Lecce
Nardò
Otranto
Casarano
Capo S. Maria di Leuca
Lauria
2248
Monte Pollino
Castrovillari
Golfo di Policastro
Capo Palinuro
Rossano
Acri
Páola
Cosenza
Cirò Marina
S. Giovanni in Fiore
Crotone
Cutro
Catanzaro
Catanzaro Marina
Nicastro
Golfo di Sant'Eufemia
Vibo Valéntia
Rosarno
Palmi
Polistena
Locri
Reggio di Calabria
Messina
Strómboli
Salina
Filicudi
Alicudi
Lipari
Milazzo
Patti
Ústica
Capo Gallo
Palermo
Bagheria
Términi Imerese
Cefalù
Gangi
Corleone
Belice
Capo S. Vito
Partinico
Alcamo
Trapani
Marsala
Favignana
Lévanzo
Marettimo
Castelvetrano
Mazara del Vallo
Sciacca
Agrigento
Favara
Canicattì
Caltanissetta
Licata
Enna
Piazza Armerina
Riesi
Gela
Golfo di Gela
Randazzo
Monte Etna 3323
Adrano
Paternò
Taormina
Acireale
Catánia
Golfo di Catánia
Lentini
Augusta
Siracusa
Caltagirone
Niscemi
Palazzolo Acrèide
Ragusa
Scicli
Ispica
Avola
Pachino
Capo Passero
Isola di Pantelleria (Italy)
Linosa (Italy)
Gwardex (Gozo)
Victoria
Valletta
Strait of Bonifacio
La Maddalena
Palau
Costa Smeralda
Olbia
Tempio Pausania
Monte Limbara 1359
Golfo dell' Asinara
Asinara
Porto Torres
Sassari
Alghero
Ozieri
Núoro
Orosei
Golfo di Orosei
Bosa
Macomer
Punta La Marmora 1834
Láconi
Tirso
Tortolì
Oristano
Golfo di Oristano
Villacidro
Iglésias
Carbónia
Sant' Antíoco
Teulada
Capo Spartivento
Cagliari
Quartu Sant'Elena
Villaputzu
Capo Carbonara
La Galite
Cap Serrat
Cap Blanc
Bizerte
Lac de Bizerte
Menzel Bourguiba
Mateur
Tabarka
Béja
Mejez El Bab
Medjerda
L'Ariana
Tunis
La Goulette
Golfe de Tunis
Île Zembra
Hammam Lif
Cap Bon
Kelibia
Menzel Temime
Korba
Nabeul
Golfe de Hammamet
El Fahs
Siliana
Jendouba
El Kef
El Kala
El Tarf
124 125

1 : 5 600 000
0
100
200
300 km
0
50
100
150 miles
76 77
88 89
94
SLOVAK REPUBLIC
AUSTRIA
HUNGARY
SLOVENIA
CROATIA
BOSNIA-
HERZEGOVINA
SRBIJA
(SERBIA)
YUGOSLAVI
CRNA GORA
(MONTENEGRO)
KOSOVO
VOJVODINA
ALBANIA
ITALY
MACE
ADRIATIC SEA
Alföld
Dinaric Alps
WIEN
(VIENNA)
Bratislava
BUDAPEST
Ljubljana
Zagreb
Sarajevo
BEOGRAD
(BELGRADE)
Tiranë
(Tirana)
Skopje
Podgorica
St. Pölten
Wels
Enns
Steyr
Amstetten
Mödling
Bad
Vöslau
Neunkirchen
Mariazell
Mürzzuschlag
Eisenerz
Bruck an der Mur
Leoben
Knittelfeld
Judenburg
Köflach
Graz
Mur
St Veit an der Glan
Wolfsberg
Villach
Klagenfurt
Triglav
2864
Jesenice
Dravograd
Velenje
Maribor
Ptuj
Kranj
Trbovlje
Celje
Nova Gorica
Trieste
Postojna
Novo Mesto
Snežnik
1796
Kočevje
Samobor
Karlovac
Istra
Poreč
Rovinj
Rijeka
Pula
Cres
Krk
Ogulin
Slunj
Senj
Rab
Lošinj
Pag
Gospić
Olib
Molat
Zadar
Gračac
Dugi Otok
Pašman
Kornat
Knin
Šibenik
Sinj
Split
Šolta
Brač
Makarska
Hvar
Vis
Svetac
Vela Luka
Korčula
Lastovo
Mljet
Palagruža
Dubrovnik
Cavtat
Metković
Imotski
Livno
Buško jez.
2228
Pločno
Mostar
Stolac
Gacko
Bileća
Trebinje
Nikšić
Cetinje
Durmitor
2522
Kolašin
Ivangrad
Bijelo Polje
Prijepolje
Sjenica Jez.
Priboj
Foča
Drina
Goražde
Nitra
Trnava
Danube (Donau)
Galanta
Malý Dunaj
Levice
Nové Zámky
Komárno
Velký Krtíš
Rimavská Sobota
Kazincbarcika
Hernád
Košice
Michalovc
Ózd
Salgótarján
Balassagyarmat
Kékes
1014
Eger
Miskolc
Szerencs
Nyíregyháza
Mezőkövesd
Tisza
Hajdúböszö
Gyöngyös
Hatvan
Heves
Esztergom
Vác
Gödöllő
Jászberény
Debrecen
Karcag
Neusiedler See
Eisenstadt
Moson-magyaróvár
Sopron
Kapuvár
Győr
Tata
Tatabánya
Kisbér
Rába
Pápa
Mór
Érd
Monor
Kőszeg
Szombathely
Székesfehérvár
Ráckeve
Cegléd
Szolnok
Berettyóújfalu
Mezőtúr
Ajka
Veszprém
Balatonfüred
Dunaújváros
Siófok
Zalaegerszeg
Keszthely
Balaton
Fonyód
Tab
Kecskemét
Gyomaendrőd
Békéscsaba
Gyula
Paks
Kiskunfélegyháza
Szentes
Nagykanizsa
Kalocsa
Kaposvár
Dombóvár
Kiskunhalas
Hódmezővásárhely
Nagyatád
Szekszárd
Szeged
Makó
Arad
Mureş
Komló
Pécs
Mohács
Danube (Duna)
Varaždin
Koprivnica
Zabok
Križevci
Zaprešić
Bjelovar
Virovitica
Barcs
Drava
Subotica
Senta
Sânnicolau Mare
Jimbolia
Timişoara
Sombor
Apatin
Tisa
Bečej
Novi Bečej
Vrbas
Bačka Palanka
Zrenjanin
Novi Sad
Vršac
Reşiţa
Podravska Slatina
Sisak
Kutina
Našice
Osijek
Vukovar
Slavonska Požega
Nova Gradiška
Slavonski Brod
Županja
Sava
Bosanska Gradiška
Bosanski Novi
Prijedor
Bihać
Derventa
Modriča
Brčko
Bijeljina
Stara Pazova
Pančevo
Bela Crkva
Smederevo
Požarevac
Morava
Kučevo
Banja Luka
Doboj
Bosna
Gračanica
Tuzla
Bosanski Petrovac
Jajce
Vrbas
Travnik
Zavidoviči
Zenica
Zvornik
Loznica
Valjevo
Mladenovac
Kragujevac
Užice
Čačak
Paraćin
Kraljevo
Kruševac
Raška
Novi Pazar
Ibar
Kuršumlija
Leskova
Kosovska Mitrovica
Priština
Vranje
Peć
Đakovica
Gnjilane
Uroševac
Prizren
Kuma
Tetovo
Gostivar
Veles
Kičevo
Kavada
Debar
Prilep
Struga
Ohrid
Bitola
L. Ohrid
L. Prespa
Lake Scutari
Bar
Shkodër
Liq. i Fierzës
Kukës
Pukë
Lezhë
Laç
Burrel
Krujë
Durrës
Kavajë
Elbasan
Isole Trémiti
Térmoli
Lago di Verano
Monte Calvo
1055
Vieste
San Sévero
Manfredonia
Fóggia
Cervaro
Cerignola
Barletta
Molfetta
Andria
Bari
Melfi
Gravina in Puglia
Altamura
Monópoli
© Helicon Publishing Ltd

The Balkans

UKRAINE
MOLDOVA
ROMANIA
BULGARIA
TURKEY
GREECE
BLACK SEA
Carpathian Mountains
Kam"yanets'-Podil's'kyy
Horodenka
Kolomyya
Nadvirna
Dniester (Dnister)
Prut
Chernivtsi
Hlyboka
Verkhovyna
2061
Rakhiv
Khust
Berehove
Svalyava
Mukacheve
Tysa
Mohyliv-Podil's'kyy
Yampil'
Briceni
Soroca
Darabani
Florești
Bălți
Răut
Rîbnița
Rezina
Kotovs'k
Balta
Novoselivka
Dubăsari
Grigoriopol
Siret
Botoșani
Rădăuți
Suceava
Câmpulung Moldovenesc
Fălești
Satu Mare
Sighetu Marmației
Vișeu de Sus
Someș
Baia Mare
Baia Sprie
Carei
Bistrița
Moldova
Pașcani
Târgu-Neamț
Piatra-Neamț
Iași
Ungheni
Strășeni
Chișinău
Tiraspol
Tighina
Rozdil'na
Hîncești
Dniester
ODESA (ODESSA)
Năsăud
Zalău
Dej
Bistrița
Toplița
Bicaz
Roman
Cluj-Napoca
Mureș
Gheorgheni
Vaslui
Bacău
Moinești
Turda
Luduș
Târgu Mureș
Miercurea-Ciuc
Olt
Târgu Ocna
Trotuș
Onești
Bârlad
Basarabeasca
Bilhorod-Dnistrovs'kyy
Ciadîr-Lunga
Aiud
Odorheiu Secuiesc
Sighișoara
Mediaș
Alba Iulia
Brad
Cahul
Artsyz
Tatarbunary
Sfântu Gheorghe
Tecuci
Mărășești
Deva
Sebeș
Făgăraș
Sibiu
Avrig
Codlea
Brașov
Focșani
Bolhrad
Kiliya
Ozero Yalpug
Lacul Brates
2544 Vârful Moldoveanu
Hațeg
Petrila
Petroșani
Râmnicu Sărat
Galați
Izmayil
Brăila
Tulcea
Mouths of the Danube
Brațul
Danube (Dunărea)
Câmpulung
Sinaia
Vălenii de Munte
Buzău
Curtea de Argeș
Râmnicu Vâlcea
Argeș
Câmpina
Mizil
Făurei
Pucioasa
Jiu
Târgu Jiu
Babadag
Lacul Razim
Târgoviște
Ploiești
Pitești
Găești
Urziceni
Hârșova
Lacul Sinoie
Strehaia
Drăgășani
Buftea
Ialomița
Titu
Slobozia
Filiași
BUCUREȘTI (BUCHAREST)
Drobeta-Turnu Severin
Fetești
Medgidia
Slatina
Videle
Călărași
Constanța
Craiova
Roșiori de Vede
Danube (Dunărea)
Oltenița
Silistra
Giurgiu
Negru Vodă
Mangalia
Cetate
Caracal
Vidin
Calafat
Alexandria
Turnu Măgurele
Dulovo
Corabia
Ruse
Ludogorie
Dobrič
Lom
Danube (Dunav)
Svištov
Kavarna
Iskăr
Razgrad
Nos Kaliakra
Bjala Slatina
Novi Pazar
Midzor 2169
Levski
Montana
Červen Brjag
Pleven
Tărgovište
Varna
Šumen
Provadija
Loveč
Veliko Tărnovo
Gorna Orjahovica
Vraca
Mezdra
Trojan
Gabrovo
Trjavna
Stara Planina
Kostinbrod
SOFIJA (SOFIA)
Sliven
Ajtos
Nos Emine
Pomorie
Pernik
Karlovo
Kazanlăk
Burgaski Zaliv
Burgas
Sozopol
Panagjurište
Nova Zagora
Jambol
Stanke Dimitrov
Samokov
Stara Zagora
Grudovo
Pazardžik
Elhovo
Kjustendil
Musala 2925
Peštera
Plovdiv
Dimitrovgrad
Gălăbovo
Rezovo
Blagoevgrad
Asenovgrad
Harmanli
Yıldız Dağları
İğneada
Razlog
Haskovo
Rodopi Planina
Svilengrad
Kırklareli
Kıyıköy
Edirne
Arda
Smoljan
Kărdžali
Vize
Saray
Karacaköy
İstanbul Boğazı (Bosporus)
Babaeski
Orestiada
Sandanski
Lüleburgaz
Petrič
Hayrabolu
Çorlu
İSTANBUL
Sidirokastro
Silivri
Xanthi
Komotini
Tekirdağ
Yeşilköy
Serres
Drama
Ipsala
Kilkis
Strimonas
Meriç
Malkara
Marmara Denizi (Sea of Marmara)
Kavala
Alexandroupoli
Keşan

1 : 5 600 000
0
100
200
300 km
0
50
100
150 miles
92 93
YUGOSLAVIA
SRBIJA (SERBIA)
CRNA GORA (MONTENEGRO)
Nikšić
Podgorica
Kosovska Mitrovica
Leskovac
Priština
KOSOVO
Peć
Đakovica
Gnjilane
Vranje
Bosilegrad
Dimitrovgrad
Kostinbrod
SOFIJA (SOFIA)
Pernik
Mezdra
Loveč
Veliko Tărnovo
Trojan
Gabrovo
Trjavna
Kazanlăk
Stara Planina
BULGARIA
Karlovo
Panagjurište
Samokov
Stara Zagora
Nova Zagora
Kjustendil
Stanke Dimitrov
Musala 2925
Pazardžik
Plovdiv
Dimitrovgrad
Gălăbovo
Harmanli
Haskovo
Svilengrad
Asenovgrad
Peštera
Rodopi Planina
Pirin
Razlog
Blagoevgrad
Smoljan
Arda
Kărdžali
Sandanski
Petrič
Lake Dojran
Sidirokastro
Prizren
Uroševac
Kumanovo
Skopje
Kratovo
Kočani
Štip
Tetovo
Gostivar
Vardar
Veles
MACEDONIA
Strumica
Kavadarci
Prilep
Kičevo
Debar
Struga
Ohrid
Bitola
Vitolište
L. Ohrid
L. Prespa
Lake Scutari
Bar
Shkodër
Liq. i Fierzës
Pukë
Kukës
Lezhë
Burrel
Krujë
Tiranë (Tirana)
Durrës
Kavajë
ALBANIA
Elbasan
Fier
Berat
Korçë
Vlorë
Përmet
Gjirokastër
Sarandë
Drama
Serres
Xanthi
Komotini
Kavala
Strimonas
Kilkis
Polykastro
Florina
Edessa
Giannitsa
L. Vegoritis
L. Volvi
Thessaloniki
Veroia
Kastoria
Argos Orestiko
Kozani
Aliakmonas
Epanomi
Katerini
Stratoni
Chalkidiki
Thasos
Thrakiko Pelagos
Alexandroupoli
Samothraki
Gelibolu Yarimadasi
Gökceada
Eceabat
Limnos
Moudros
Bozcaada
Thermaïkos Kolpos
Kolpos Kassandras
Kolpos Agiou Orous
2033
Sikea
2911 Olympos
Grevena
Pindos
Kalpakio
Metsovo
Paleokastritsa
Kerkyra
Kerkyra (Corfu)
Ioannina
Igoumenitsa
Parga
Paxoi
Tyrnavos
Larisa
Trikala
Karditsa
Volos
Agios Efstratios
Edremit Körfezi
Mithymna
Lesvos (Lesbos)
Polichnitos
Giroura
Alonnisos
Kyra Panagia
Skiathos
Skopelos
Aegean
Sea
Arta
GREECE
Almiros
Preveza
Lefkada
Amfilochia
Lamia
Istiaia
Vóreios Evvoïkos Kolpos
Skyros
Ionioi Nisoi
Ionian Sea
Agrinio
L. Trichonida
Kefallonia
Ithaki
Sami
Argostoli
Mesolongi
Amfissa
2457
Delfoi
Evvoia
Kymi
Chalkida
Psara
Chios
Patraikis Kolpos
Patra
Korinthiakos Kolpos
Thiva
Zakynthos
Kyllini
Kalavryta
Korinthos
Megara
Elefsina
Salamina
Athina (Athens)
Peiraias
Karystos
Andros
Lavrio
Aigina
Akra Sounio
Kea
Ikaria
Tinos
Mykonos
Peloponnisos
Pyrgos
Argos
Tripoli
Kyperissiakos Kolpos
Kyparissia
Argolikos Kolpos
Portocheli
Ydra
Kyklades (Cyclades)
Ermoupoli
Syros
Kythnos
Serifos
Mirtoö Pelagos
Naxos
Paros
Sifnos
Kimolos
Milos
Sikinos
Ios
Amorgos
Messini
Sparti
Kalamata
Pylos
Schiza
Messiniakos Kolpos
Lakonikos Kolpos
Neapoli
Vathia
Kythira
Thira
Anafi
Antikythira
Krytiko Pelagos
Steno Antikythiro
Akra Spatha
Chania
Kastelli
Rethymno
Irakleio (Iraklion)
Kolpos Mirampelou
2456
Sfakia
Ierapetra
Gavdos
Kriti (Crete)
MEDITERRANEAN SEA
© Helicon Publishing Ltd

BLACK SEA
MEDITERRANEAN SEA
TURKEY
ANATOLIA
İSTANBUL
ANKARA
İzmit
Bursa
Eskişehir
Konya
Antalya
İZMIR
Varna
Burgas
Zonguldak
Sakarya
Kütahya
Afyon
Uşak
Manisa
Balıkesir
Aydın
Denizli
Isparta
Marmara Denizi (Sea of Marmara)
Tuz Gölü
Antalya Körfezi
Toros Dağları
Köroğlu Dağları
Köroğlu Tepesi 2400
Rodos (Rhodes)
Karpathos
CYPRUS
Lefkosia (Nicosia)
Lemesos (Limassol)
Larnaka
Ammochostos (Famagusta)
Olympus 1952
İçel (Mersin)
116 117

1 : 16 700 000
0 400 800 1200 km
0 200 400 600 miles
Norwegian Sea
Barents Sea
Tärnaby
Jokkmokk
Arctic Circle
Sodankylä
Monchegorsk
Namsos
Molde
Trondheim
Gäddede
Storuman
Övertorneå
Salla
Kandalaksha
Kolskiy
Poluostrov
NORWAY
1796
Helagsfjället
2470
Galdhöpiggen
Dombås
Åsele
Piteå
Luleå
Tornio
Kemi
Rovaniemi
Kuusamo
Kemijoki
Skellefteå
Östersund
Umeälven
Oulu
Oulujoki
Kandalakshskiy Zaliv
Ozero Topozero
Kuzomen'
Fagernes
Glomma
SWEDEN
Ånge
Umeå
Gulf of Bothnia
Kokkola
Oulujärvi
Kalevala
Beloye More (White Sea)
Lillehammer
Särna
Kramfors
Vaasa
Kajaani
Kem'
Dvinskaya Guba
Severodvinsk
Hønefoss
Sundsvall
Seinäjoki
Iisalmi
Belomorsk
Oslo
Klarälven
Hudiksvall
FINLAND
KARELIYA
Arkhangel'sk
Borlänge
Pielinen
Segezha
Arvika
Gävle
Pori
Jyväskylä
Kuopio
Onega
Karlstad
Tampere
Joensuu
Oz. Vygozero
Samoded
Vänern
Örebro
Uppsala
Päijänne
Medvezh'yegorsk
Lahti
Saimaa
Suoyarvi
Plesetsk
Vättern
Norrköping
Stockholm
Turku
Kondopoga
Bereznik
Borås
Södertälje
Espoo
Imatra
Sortavala
Petrozavodsk
Jönköping
Linköping
Helsinki
Kotka
Ladozhskoye Ozero (Lake Ladoga)
Onezhskoye Ozero
Kargopol'
Shenkursk
Nyandoma
Gulf of Finland
Vyborg
Olonets
Vytegra
Bestuzhevo
Hiiumaa
Tallinn
Kohtla-Järve
Växjö
Saaremaa
SANKT-PETERBURG (ST. PETERSBURG)
Ozero Beloye
Vel'sk
Gotland
ESTONIA
Narva
Karlskrona
Öland
Pärnu
Viljandi
Lake Peipus
Gatchina
Tikhvin
Belozersk
Tot'ma
BALTIC SEA
Ventspils
Gulf of Riga
Tartu
L. Pskov
Luga
Malaya Vishera
Cherepovets
Sokol
Liepāja
Rīga
Võru
Novgorod
Oz. Il'men'
Borovichi
Vologda
Jūrmala
LATVIA
Gulbene
Pskov
Staraya Russa
Rybinskoye Vodokhranilishche
Gryazovets
Koszalin
Klaipėda
Šiauliai
Daugava
Jēkabpils
Ostrov
Dno
Buy
Galich
Gdynia
LITHUANIA
Vyshniy Volochek
Rybinsk
Kostroma
Gdańsk
Kaliningrad
Nemunas
Panevėžys
Daugavpils
Velikiye Luki
Ostashkov
Yaroslavl'
Tczew
RUSSIA
Tver'
Uglich
Elbląg
Zap. Dvina
Volga
Bydgoszcz
Kaunas
Ivanovo
Kineshma
Olsztyn
Suwałki
Polatsk
Rzhev
Kimry
Klin
Sergiyev Posad
NIZHNIY NOVGOROD
Włocławek
POLAND
Alytus
Vilnius
Vitsyebsk
MOSKVA (MOSCOW)
Noginsk
Vladimir
Płock
WARSZAWA (WARSAW)
Hrodna
Maladzyechna
Nyoman
Barysaw
Smolensk
Podol'sk
Dzerzhinsk
Kalisz
Białystok
MINSK
Orsha
Safonovo
Obninsk
Kolomna
Murom
Łódź
Slonim
Dnieper
Pochinok
Serpukhov
Arzamas
Częstochowa
Brest
Baranavichy
Mahilyow
Kirov
Kaluga
Stupino
Ryazan'
Radom
Bug
Babruysk
Roslavl'
Tula
Novomoskovsk
MORDOVIYA
Saransk
Pinsk
BELARUS
Bryansk
Katowice
Lublin
Homyel'
Klintsy
Ryazhsk
Shatsk
Ruzayevka
Kraków
Kovel'
Mazyr
Novozybkov
Orel
Mtsensk
Zamość
Zheleznogorsk
Yefremov
Michurinsk
Penza
Luts'k
Rzeszów
Yelets
Tambov
Rivne
Chornobyl'
Chernihiv
Desna
SLOVAK REP.
L'viv
Shostka
Kursk
Lipetsk
Kirsanov
Košice
Sambir
Zhytomyr
Ryl'sk
Voronezh
Zherdevka
Rtishchevo
Stryy
Ternopil'
Sumy
Staryy Oskol
Balashov
Uzhhorod
Carpathian Mts
KYYIV (KIEV)
Ivano-Frankivs'k
Romny
Belgorod
Borisoglebsk
Vinnytsya
Bila Tserkva
Okhtyrka
Liski
Povorino
HUNGARY
Kam'yanets'-Podil's'kyy
Don
239
Uryupinsk
Debrecen
Satu Mare
Chernivtsi
Cherkasy
Rossosh'
Kalach
Privolzhskaya
Oradea
UKRAINE
Poltava
KHARKIV
Mikhaylovka
Dniester
Cluj-Napoca
Suceava
Prut
MOLDOVA
Kirovohrad
Kremenchuk
Kamyshin
Mureș
Târgu Mureș
Bălţi
Dniprodzerzhyns'k
DNIPROPETROVS'K
Lysychans'k
Deva
Iaşi
Kotovsk
Kryvyy Rih
Kramators'k
Kalach-na-Donu
Volzhskiy
ROMANIA
Bacău
Chişinău
Zaporizhzhya
Makiyivka
Luhans'k
Petroşani
Sibiu
Braşov
Tighina
ODESA (ODESSA)
Dnieper
DONETS'K
Shakhty
VOLGOGRAD
Tsimlyanskoye Vodokhranilishche
Piteşti
Focşani
Melitopol'
Mariupol'
Taganrog
Volgodonsk
Ploieşti
Galaţi
Bilhorod-Dnistrovs'kyy
Kherson
ROSTOV-NA-DONU
Dubovskoye
Craiova
Berdyans'k
Azov
BUCUREŞTI (BUCHAREST)
Tulcea
Yeysk
Sal'sk
Pleven
Ruse
Danube (Dunav)
Silistra
Constanța
Yevpatoriya
Krym'
Sea of Azov
Stavropol'skaya Vozvyshennost'
Elista
Lovеč
BULGARIA
Sevastopol'
Kerch
Tikhoretsk
Yashkul'
Simferopol'
Krasnodar
Ipatovo
Balaklava
Yalta
Armavir
Svetlograd
Novorossiysk
Maykop
Stavropol'
ADYGEYA
KARACHAYEVO-CHERKESIYA
Budennovsk
Black Sea
Tuapse
Cherkessk
DAGESTAN
74 75
116 117
© Helicon Publishing Ltd

100 101

1 : 52 900 000

0 800 1600 2400 km

0 400 800 1200 miles

ALASKA (U.S.)
Bering Strait
St. Lawrence I.
O. Vrangelya
Vostochno-Sibirskoye More (East Siberian Sea)
Novosibirskiye Ostrova
More Laptevykh (Laptev Sea)
Bering Sea
Anadyr'
Aleutian Islands (U.S.)
Aleutian Trench
International Date Line
Khrebet Kolymskiy
Verkhoyanskiy Khrebet
Lena
Kamchatka
Petropavlovsk-Kamchatskiy
Yakutsk
Sea of Okhotsk
Kuril'skiye Ostrova (Kuril Islands)
Kuril Trench
Sakhalin
Stanovoy Khrebet
Tropic of Cancer
Amur
Ozero Baykal
PACIFIC
Hokkaidō
SAPPORO
HARBIN
Vladivostok
JAPAN
Honshū
Ulaanbaatar
Sea of Japan
TŌKYŌ
Wake I. (U.S.)
NORTH KOREA
3776
Fuji-san
SHENYANG
P'YŎNGYANG
Japan Trench
Izu-shotō
OCEAN
BEIJING (PEKING)
SŎUL (SEOUL)
SOUTH KOREA
ŌSAKA
Shikoku
Gobi Desert
QINGDAO
Yellow Sea
Nagasaki
Kyūshū
Ogasawara-shotō (Japan)
Kazan-rettō (Japan)
Huang He
East China Sea
Nansei-shotō (Ryukyu Islands)
Amami-Ōshima
Marianas Trench
SHANGHAI
Okinawa
Pohnpei
WUHAN
Northern Mariana Islands (U.S.)
Guam (U.S.)
FUZHOU
Chang Jiang
T'AIPEI
TAIWAN
Challenger Deep
11033
Caroline Islands
GUANGZHOU
XIANGGANG (HONG KONG)
Luzon Strait
Equator
HA NÔI (HANOI)
2929 Mt. Pulog
Luzon
Philippine Trench
Yap
OCEANIA
Mekong
Hainan
Viangchan (Vientiane)
PHILIPPINES
MANILA
VIETNAM
LAOS
South China Sea
Mindoro
Samar
Cebu
YANGON (RANGOON)
THAILAND
Panay
Mindanao
Bismarck Sea
CAMBODIA
Palawan
Negros
Davao
Phnum Penh
Sulu Sea
HÔ CHI MINH (SAIGON)
G. Kinabalu 4094
Biak
New Guinea
Gulf of Thailand
Sabah
Celebes Sea
Halmahera
Puncak Jaya 5030
Irian Jaya
Bandar Seri Begawan
BRUNEI
MALAYSIA
Molucca Sea
Aru
Dolak
Torres Strait
Sarawak
Selat Makassar
Seram
Arafura Sea
KUALA LUMPUR
Buru
Sulawesi (Celebes)
Banda Sea
Tanimbar
SINGAPORE
Borneo
Gulf of Carpentaria
Sumatera (Sumatra)
Banjarmasin
INDONESIA
Kepulauan Mentawai
Java Sea
Flores
Timor
SURABAYA
Sumba
JAKARTA
Jawa (Java)
Sumbawa
Bali
Lombok
Timor Sea

1 : 22 000 000
0 400 800 1200 km
0 200 400 600 miles
BARENTS SEA
Karskoye More (Kara Sea)
More Laptevykh (Laptev Sea)
Pechorskoye More
Beloye More (White Sea)
Zemlya Frantsa-Iosifa (Franz Josef Land)
Zemlya Alexsandry
Zemlya Vil'cheka
Novaya Zemlya
Severnaya Zemlya
Ostrov Komsomolets
Ostrov Bol'shevik
Ostrov Oktyabr'skoy
Ostrov Ushakova
Ostrov Vise
Ostrov Belyy
Ostrov Vaygach
Ostrov Kolguyev
Ostrov Bol. Begichev
Arkhipelag Nordenshel'da
Proliv Vil'kitskogo
Mys Zhelaniya
Mys Kanin Nos
Poluostrov Taymyr
Poluostrov Yamal
Gydanskiy Poluostrov
Tazovskiy Poluostrov
Kol'skiy Poluostrov
Yukorskiy Poluostrov
Obskaya Guba
Guba Buorkhaya
Ozero Taymyr
Sredne-sibirskoye Ploskogor'ye (Central Siberian Plateau)
Zapadno-Sibirskaya Ravnina (West Siberian Plain)
Yeniseyskiy Kryazh
Malozemel'skaya Tundra
Bol'shezemel'skaya Tundra
RUSSIA
SAKHA
KOMI
NORWAY
Nordkapp
Vadsø
Varangerfjorden
Murmansk
Arkhangel'sk
Severodvinsk
Onega
Mezen'
Vorkuta
Inta
Pechora
Ukhta
Sosnogorsk
Syktyvkar
Kotlas
Kirov
PERM'
Solikamsk
Berezniki
Serov
Nizhniy Tagil
Yoshkar-Ola
Cheboksary
Glazov
Salekhard
Nadym
Novyy Urengoy
Surgut
Nizhnevartovsk
Khanty-Mansiysk
Noril'sk
Dikson
Igarka
Khatanga
Tiksi
Bratsk
Ust'-Ilimsk
Lesosibirsk
Tura
2037 Gora Kamen
1883
1292
1104 Gora Yenashimskiy Polkan
Arctic Circle
102 103
96 97
© Helicon Publishing Ltd

Northwest Asia

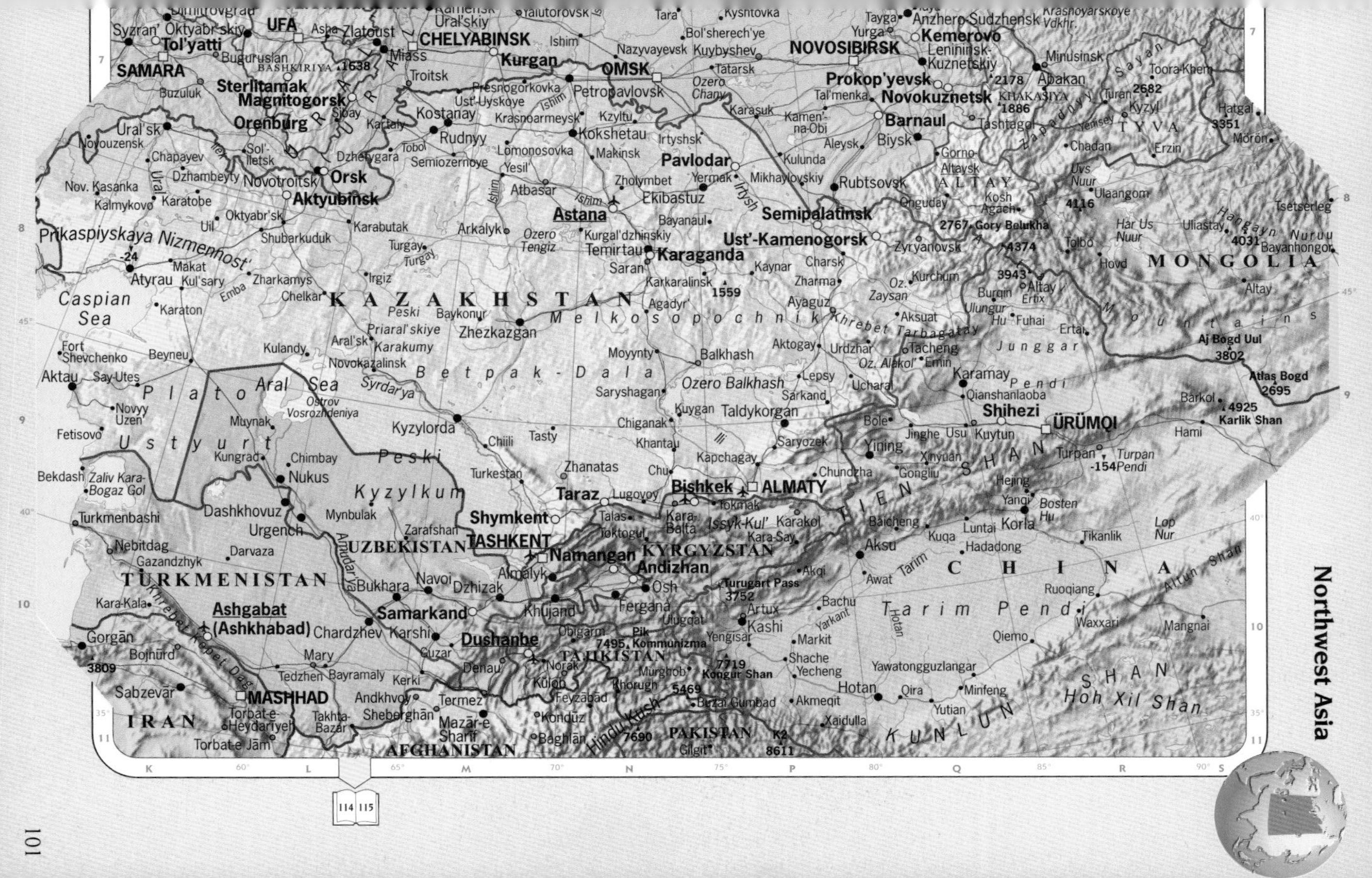

114 115

1 : 22 100 000
0
400
800
1200 km
0
200
400
600 miles
More Laptevykh (Laptev Sea)
Ostrov Bol'shoy Begichev
Tarko-Sale
Khantayka
Noril'sk
Dolgany
Kheta
Novorybnoye
Sidorovsk
Chasel'ka
Krasnosel'kup
Igarka
Boyarka
Khatanga
Arctic Circle
Raduznny
Tol'ka
2037 Gora Kamen
Saskylakh
Taymylyr
Ratta
Turukhansk
Anabar
Yenisey
Bykovskiy
Vereshchagino
Korliki
Tunguska
Yessey
Olenek
Tiksi
Verkhneimbatsk
Srednesibirskoye
Kyusyur
Napas
Vakh
Bakhta
Siktyakh
Yano-Ind
Tutonchany
Olenek
Sym
Ploskogor'ye
Lena
Dzhardzhan
Sym
Tura
Ust' Ozernoye
Yartsevo
Yeniseyskiy Kryazh
Udachnyy
Baykit
Kystatyam
Novonazimovo
1104 Gora Yenashimskiy Polkan
(Central Siberian
Zhigansk
Verkhoyansk
Yukta
Morkoka
Syalakh
Verkhoyanskiy
Lesosibirsk
Mutoray
Plateau)
Achinsk
Motygino
Chernyshevskiy
Nazarovo
Boguchany
Vilyuysk
Aryta
Mirnyy
Kezhma
Nyurba
Sangar
Yerbogachen
Krasnoyarsk
Suntar
Kansk
Ilbenge
Batamay
Uyar
Ust'-Ilimsk
RUSSIA
Lensk
Yakutsk
Vostochnyy Sayan
Nepa
Tayshet
Khamra
Turukta
Bratsk
Chuya
Olekminsk
Pokrovsk
Mayya
Uda
Lena
Kachikattsy
Nizhneudinsk
Ust'-Kut
Bratskoye Vodokhranilishche
Mama
Olekma
Toora-Khem
Tulun
Vitim
Lena
Bodaybo
Verkhnyaya Amga
Zima
Stanovoye
Oka
Zhigalovo
Aldan
TYVA
Severobaykal'sk
Aldan
Cheremkhovo
Nagor'ye
2287
Kachug
Usol'ye Sibirskoye
Chara
2100
Hovsgol Nuur
Angarsk
2484
Ozero Baykal
Stanovoy
3351
Kurumkan
Irkutsk
BURYATIYA
Kalakan
Khrebet
Neryungri
Hatgal
Slyudyanka
Ust'-Barguzin
Bagdarin
Vitim
Tungir
Khrebet
Babushkin
Ulan-Ude
Moron
Zakamensk
Yablonovyy
Tynda
Zeyskoye Vodokhranilishche
Petrovsk-Zabaykal'skiy
Bukachacha
Mogocha
Hutag
Kyakhta
Chita
Never
Altanbulag
Khilok
Ulety
Shilka
Zeya
Bulgan
Krasnyy Chikoy
Shilka
Sretensk
Mohe
Tsetserleg
Yamarovka
Karymskoye
Khrebet
Magdagachi
Darhan
Bol'shoy Khingan
Baley
Zhangling
Dul'durga
Olovyannaya
Mayskiy
Ekimchan
Ulaanbaatar
Borzya
Aleksandrovskiy Zavod
Huma
Kumara
Norsk
Bayandelger
Onon
Arvayheer
Onon
Yituline
Orogen Zizhiqi
Svobodnyy
Solov'yevsk
MONGOLIA
Krasnokamensk
Aihui
Blagoveshchensk
Manzhouli
Hailar
Gobi Desert
Kerulen
Hulun Nur
Zavitinsk
Mandalgovĭ
Choyr
Choybalsan
Nen
Nenjiang
Amur
Birobidzhan
Dalandzadgad
Baruun Urt
Bei'an
Saynshand
Tamsagbulag
Hongor
QIQIHAR
Yichun
Leninskoye
Dong Ujimqin Qi
CHINA
Hegang
Erenhot
Sonid Zuoqi
Horqin Youyi Qianqi
Daqing
Suihua
Jiamusi
Baicheng
Anda
Bayan Obo
Sonid Yuoqi
NEI MONGGOL (INNER MONGOLIA)
Tao'an
Yilan
Shuangyashan
Linhe
Wuyuan
Bairin Yuoqi
Tongyu
Fuyu
HARBIN
Fangzheng
Jixi
Huang
Yushu
Wuhai
Habirag
Tongliao
CHANGCHUN
Mudanjiang
Xar Moron
Yabuli
Baotou
Shangdu
Chifeng
JILIN
Ozero Khanka
Shizuishan
Hohhot
Jining
Siping
Liaoyuan
Dunhua
Ussuriysk
Dongsheng
Fengning
Beipiao
Zhangwu
Tumen
Datong
Zhangjiakou
Chengde
Tieling
Hailong
Yanji
Vladivostok
N. KOREA
Ch'ŏngjin
Sea
© Helicon Publishing Ltd
100 101
104 105

Northeast Asia

1 : 18 600 000
0
400
800
1200 km
0
200
400
600 miles
102 103
A
95° E
B
100°
C
105°
D
110°
E
115°
F
Altai Mts.
Altay
Ulaanbaatar
(Ulan Bator)
Bayandelger
Choybalsan
Herlen Gol
Bayanhongor
Arvayheer
Tamsagbulag
Aj Bogd Uul
3802
3951
Choyr
Baruun Urt
Mandalgovĭ
GOBI
Barkol
4925
Karlik Shan
Atlas Bogd
2695
Yandun
MONGOLIA
Hongor
Dong Ujimqi
Saynshand
Urt
2825
Dalandzadgad
DESERT
Sonid Zuoqi
Xilinhot
Erenhot
Gongpoquan
Ejin Qi
Sonid Youqi
NEI MONGGOL
(INNER MONGOLIA)
Nart
Anxi
Qiaowan
Ruo Shui
Habirag
Dunhuang
Bayan Obo
Yumen
Jinta
Wuyuan
Shangdu
Fengning
6209
Jiayuguan
Linhe
Wuchuan
Jining
Zhangjiakou
Great Wall
Hohhot
Xuanhua
Qilian Shan
Baotou
Datong
6194
Zhangye
Wuhai
BEIJING
(PEKING)
Da Qaidam
Dongsheng
Yanqing
Qilian
Shizuishan
Hunyuan
TANG-SHAN
Jinchang
Otog Qi
Shanyin
Zhuo Xian
Yinchuan
Baode
3058
TIANJIN
Qinghai Hu
Wuwei
Yulin
Yellow River
Baoding
Qinghai Nanshan
Menyuan
Wuzhong
Yuanping
SHIJIAZHUANG
Dulan
Xining
Suide
Cangzhou
Gonghe
Huang He (Yellow River)
Wubu
TAIYUAN
Yangquan
Binzhou
LANZHOU
Gyaring Hu
Madoi
Guyuan
Yan'an
Fenyang
Xingtai
Dezhou
Handan
Liaocheng
Huang He
Linxia
Qingyang
Changzhi
Bayan Har Shan
Pingliang
Anyang
JINAN
Hancheng
Linfen
Houma
Jincheng
Tai'an
Tongchuan
Tianshui
Jiaozou
Xinxiang
Yushu
Darlag
Min Xian
Xianyang
Sanmenxia
Jining
Sêrxü
Weinan
Kaifeng
Baoji
Luoyang
ZHENGZHOU
Xuzhou
CHINA
XI'AN
Wudu
Shangqiu
Hanzhong
Pingdingshan
Xuchang
Huaibei
Songpan
Xi Xiang
Ankang
Neixiang
Luohe
Qamdo
Guangyuan
Nanyang
Fuyang
Bengbu
Garzê
Barkam
Han Shui
Jun Xian
Shiyan
Wanyuan
Zhumadian
Huainan
Mianyang
Jialing Jiang
Jinsha
Deyang
Xinyang
Dawu
Danba
Daxian
Xiangfan
NANJING
Nanchong
Huangchuan
CHENGDU
Suizhou
Guangshui
Lu'an
HEFEI
Markam
Litang
Chang Jiang (Yangtze)
Jingmen
7514
Ya'an
Wanxian
Macheng
Gongga Shan
Enshi
Yichang
Tianmen
WUHAN
Anqing
Leshan
Neijiang
Fuling
Jiangling
Dêqên
Shashi
Huangshi
Zigong
CHONGQING
Gongshan
Puqi
Jiujiang
Jinsha
Jinshi
Zhongdian
Yibin
Luzhou
Dayong
Yueyang
Xichang
Changde
Xiushui
Yongxiu
Poyang Hu
Jishou
Yiyang
Lijiang
Zunyi
Boyang
Salween
Dukou
CHANGSHA
NANCHANG
Shangrao
Bijie
Huaihua
Xiangtan
Xinyu
Lushui
Liupanshui
GUIYANG
Pingxiang
Yichun
Linchuan
Dali
Yuanmou
Shaoyang
Baoshan
Qujing
Anshun
Duyun
Hengyang
Ji'an
Nanping
Leiyang
Chuxiong
KUNMING
Xingyi
Ganzhou
Changting
Lincang
Chenzhou
Jinggu
Guilin
Tropic of Cancer
Kaiyuan
Hechi
Shaoguan
Longyan
Bose
Pingle
Lipu
Lian Xian
Zhangzhou
Yanshan
Lancang
Simao
Gejiu
Yuan
Heshan
Liuzhou
Meizhou
Xiamen
Jingxi
Chaozhou
Jinghong
Wuzhou
Binyang
Zhaoqing
GUANGZHOU
Shantou
Lai Chau
Lao Cai
Cao Bang
Nanning
Huizhou
Wuxu
Jiangmen
Lufeng
MYANMAR
LAOS
VIETNAM
Pingxiang
Yulin
Zhongshan
Shenzhen
Qinzhou
Hepu
Yangjiang
Macau
XIANGGANG
(HONG KONG)
Maoming
Beihai
Zhanjiang
B
100°
C
105°
D
110°
E
115°
F
© Helicon Publishing Ltd
108 109
112 113
1
45° N
2
40°
3
35°
4
30°
5
25°
6

SEA OF JAPAN
YELLOW SEA
EAST CHINA SEA
PACIFIC OCEAN
JAPAN
NORTH KOREA
SOUTH KOREA
TAIWAN
HARBIN
SHENYANG
P'YŎNGYANG
SŎUL (SEOUL)
PUSAN
TŌKYŌ
YOKOHAMA
ŌSAKA
KYŌTO
NAGOYA
SAPPORO
SHANGHAI
T'AIPEI
Vladivostok
HONSHŪ
HOKKAIDŌ
SHIKOKU
KYŪSHŪ
Nansei-shotō (Ryukyu Islands)
Sakhalin
Tropic of Cancer
La Pérouse Strait
Korea Strait
Korea Bay

1 : 9 300 000
0 200 400 600 km
0 100 200 300 miles
102 103
104 105
108 109
CHINA
RUSSIA
NORTH KOREA
SOUTH KOREA
Korea Bay
Yellow Sea
East China Sea
SEA OF JAPAN
Korea Strait
Tsushima
Higashi-suidō
KYŪSHŪ
SHIKOKU
Tongyu
Fuyu
Sanchahe
Shangzhi
Zhangguangcai Ling
Jixi
Linkou
Turiy Rog
Ozero Khanka
Yushu
Songhua
Nong'an
Yabuli
Mudanjiang
Spassk-Dal'niy
Shulan
Ning'an
Grodekovo
Suifenhe
Poltavka
Tongliao
CHANGCHUN
JILIN
Naizishan
Shuangliao
Ussuriysk
Dunhua
Tianqiaoling
Artem
Siping
Huadian
Songhua Hu
Liaoyuan
Yanji
Tumen
Hunchun
Vladivostok
Zhangwu
Faku
Slavyanka
Partizansk
Tieling
Hailong
Antu
Helong
Nakhodka
Xinmin
Liao
Fusong
Hoeryong
SHENYANG
FUSHUN
Hunjiang
Najin
Linjiang
Paekdu San 2750
2541
Liaoyang
Benxi
Tonghua
Kambo Ho
Ch'ŏngjin
ANSHAN
Yalu
Huanren
Hyesan
Haicheng
Kuandian
Manp'o
Mt.Tuun 2487
Kapsan
Yingkou
Kilchu
Gai Xian
Ch'osan
Dandong
Sakchu
Kimch'aek
Huich'ŏn
Zhuanghe
Donggou
Sinŭiju
Hamhŭng
Sinanju
Hŭngnam
Chŏngp'yŏng
P'YŎNGYANG
Wŏnsan
Yangdŏk
Songnim
Namp'o
Kosŏng
Sariwŏn
Haeju
Sokch'o
Kaesŏng
1708
Ongjin
Ch'unch'ŏn
SŎUL (SEOUL)
Kangnŭng
Songnam
Ullŭng do
INCH'ŎN
Wŏnju
Suwŏn
Ch'ŏngju
Ulchin
Taech'ŏn
Andong
Kar
TAEJŎN
P'ohang
Dōgo
Kunsan
Oki-shotō
Ch'ŏnju
TAEGU
Fu
KWANGJU
Namwŏn
Ulsan
Masan
PUSAN
Matsue
Tottori
Mokp'o
Sunch'ŏn
Izumo
Fukuchiyama
Chinju
Chin do
Hamada
Miyoshi
KYOTO
Haenam
Yŏsu
Okayama
Himeji
HIROSHIMA
Kurashiki
ŌSAKA
Yamaguchi
Fukuyama
Takamatsu
Shimonoseki
Tokuyama
Tokushima
KITA-KYŪSHŪ
Ube
Imabari
Wakay
Cheju
Iki
Matsuyama
Tanabe
Cheju do (South Korea)
FUKUOKA
Shikoku-sanchi
Sasebo
Kurume
Kōchi
Gotō-rettō
1788
Ōita
Kushim
Nagasaki
Omuta
Saiki
Tosa-wan
Muroto
Fukue
Kumamoto
Nakamura
Yatsushiro
Nobeoka
Hyūga
Akune
Miyazaki
Kagoshima
Miyakonojō
Makurazaki
Kanoya
Ōsumi-kaikyō
Ōsumi-shotō
Nishinoomote
Tanega-shima
Yaku-shima
© Helicon Publishing Ltd

Sea of Okhotsk
Ostrov Iturup
Ostrov Kunashir
Shikotan-tō
Shibotsu-jima
Wakkanai
Rebun-tō
Rishiri-tō
Teshio
Hamatonbetsu
Esashi
Otoineppu
Ōmū
Nayoro
Monbetsu
Shibetsu
Shiretoko-misaki
Abashiri
Yuzhno Kuril'sk
Shibetsu
Rumoi
Asahikawa
Asahi-dake 2290
Kitami
Nemuro
Takikawa
Ishikari-wan
Shakotan-misaki
Iwamizawa
Otaru
SAPPORO
Obihiro
Kushiro
Kutchan
Tomakomai
Oshamambe
Date
Monbetsu
Hiroo
HOKKAIDŌ
Muroran
Okushiri-tō
Mori
Urakawa
Erimo-misaki
Kamiiso
Esashi
Hakodate
Ō-shima
Ōma
Shiriya-zaki
Matsumae
Tsugaru-kaikyō
Mutsu
Aomori
Noheji
Ajigasawa
Hachinohe
Hirosaki
Ninohoe
Noshiro
Ōdate
Fudai
Morioka
Akita
Miyako
Hanamaki
Kamaishi
Yokote
Kitakami
2230
Ichinoseki
Kesennuma
Sakata
Shinjō
Furukawa
Tsuruoka
Ishinomaki
Yamagata
Sendai
Sado-shima
Ryōtsu
Shibata
Yonezawa
Niigata
Haramachi
Nagaoka
Fukushima
Kōriyama
Aizu-wakamatsu
HONSHŪ
Jōetsu
Shirakawa
Nanao
Mikuni-sammyaku
Iwaki
Nagano
Utsunomiya
Hitachi
Toyama
Maebashi
Mito
Ueda
Oyama
JAPAN
Matsumoto
Okaya
TŌKYŌ
PACIFIC
Funabashi
Hachiōji
Chiba
Gifu
YOKOHAMA
KAWASAKI
NAGOYA
3776
Fuji-san
Yokosuka
Shizuoka
Tateyama
Suzuka
Hamamatsu
Nojima-zaki
OCEAN
Toyohashi
Izu-shotō
Miyake-jima
Hachijō-jima
Aoga-shima
Sumisu-jima
Tori-shima
J
K
L
M
N
P
Q
R
138°
140°
142°
144°
146°
148°
150°
44°
42°
40°
38°
36°
34°
32°
30°
1
2
3
4
5
6
7
8

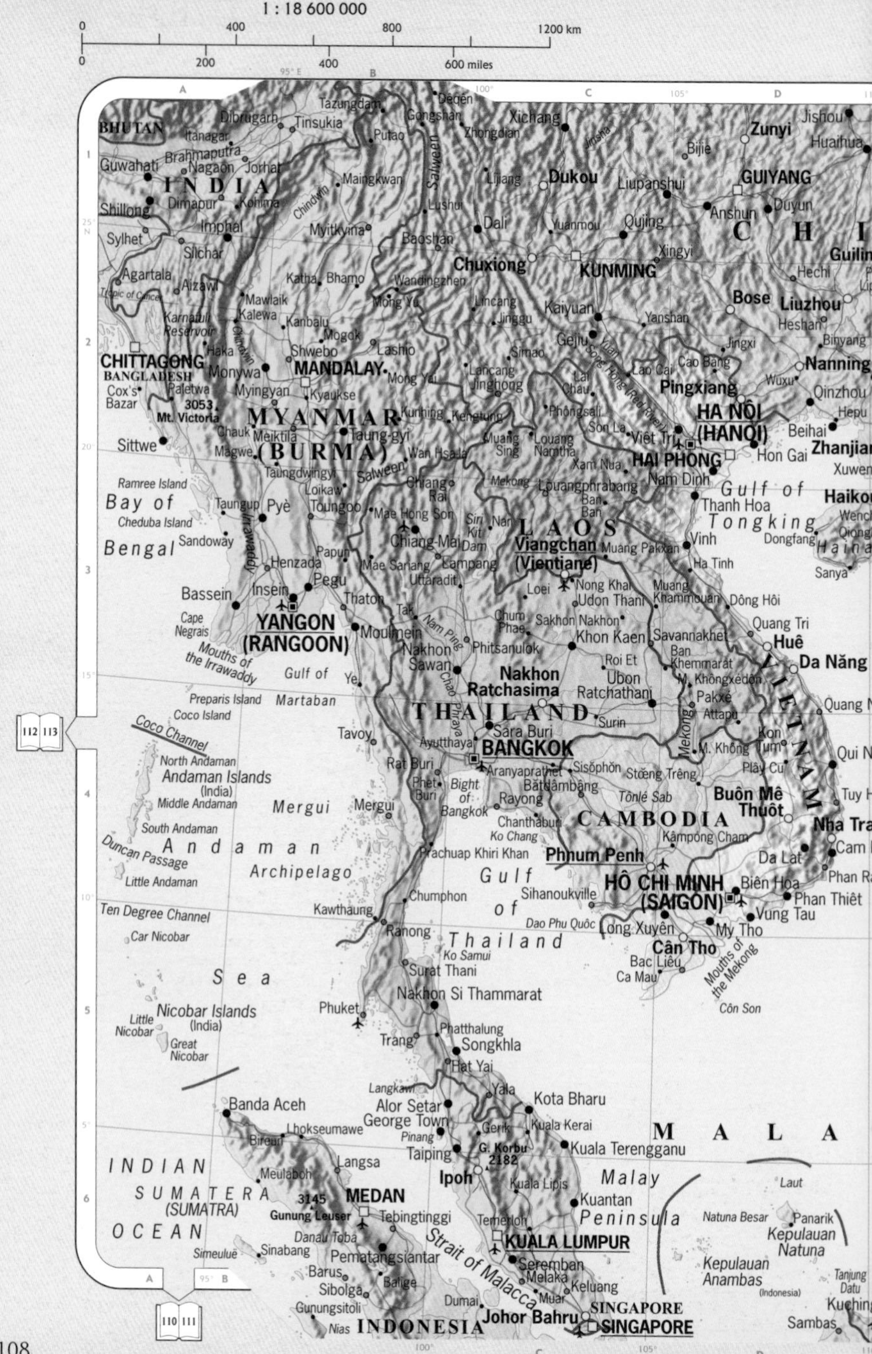

1 : 18 600 000
0
400
800
1200 km
0
200
400
600 miles
BHUTAN
Dibrugarh
Tinsukia
Tazungdam
Dêqên
Gongshan
Zhongdian
Xichang
Jishou
Zunyi
Huaihua
Itanagar
Putao
Bijie
Guwahati
Brahmaputra
Nagaon
Jorhat
I N D I A
Maingkwan
Lijiang
Dukou
Liupanshui
GUIYANG
Shillong
Dimapur
Kohima
Chindwin
Salween
Lushui
Anshun
Duyun
Imphal
Myitkyina
Dali
Yuanmou
Qujing
C H I
Sylhet
Silchar
Baoshan
Xingyi
Guilin
Chuxiong
KUNMING
Hechi
Agartala
Aizawl
Katha
Bhamo
Wandingzhen
Tropic of Cancer
Mawlaik
Kalewa
Mong Yu
Lincang
Jinggu
Kaiyuan
Yanshan
Bose
Liuzhou
Heshan
Karnafuli Reservoir
Kanbalu
Mogok
Shwebo
Lashio
Simao
Gejiu
Jingxi
Binyang
Haka
CHITTAGONG
BANGLADESH
Monywa
MANDALAY
Mong Yai
Lancang
Jinghong
Lai Chau
Lao Cai
Cao Bang
Wuxu
Nanning
Cox's Bazar
Paletwa
3053
Mt. Victoria
Myingyan
Kyaukse
Pingxiang
Qinzhou
Hepu
M Y A N M A R
(B U R M A)
Kunhing
Kengtung
Phôngsali
Son La
Viêt Tri
HA NÔI (HANOI)
Beihai
Zhanjiang
Chauk
Meiktila
Taung-gyi
Sittwe
Magwe
Wan Hsala
Muang Sing
Louang Namtha
Xam Nua
HAI PHONG
Hon Gai
Xuwen
Taungdwingyi
Salween
Ramree Island
Loikaw
Chiang Rai
Mekong
Louangphrabang
Nam Dinh
Gulf of Tongking
Haikou
Bay of Bengal
Taungup
Pyè
Toungoo
Mae Hong Son
Ban Ban
Thanh Hoa
Cheduba Island
Irrawaddy
Siri Kit Dam
Nan
L A O S
Sandoway
Chiang-Mai
Viangchan (Vientiane)
Muang Pakxan
Vinh
Dongfang
Hainan
Papun
Henzada
Mae Sariang
Lampang
Uttaradit
Ha Tinh
Sanya
Pegu
Loei
Nong Khai
Udon Thani
Muang Khammouan
Dông Hôi
Bassein
Insein
Thaton
Tak
YANGON (RANGOON)
Moulmein
Nam Ping
Chum Phae
Sakhon Nakhon
Quang Tri
Cape Negrais
Phitsanulok
Khon Kaen
Savannakhet
Huê
Mouths of the Irrawaddy
Nakhon Sawan
Roi Et
Ban Khemmarat
Da Năng
Gulf of Martaban
Ye
Chao Phraya
Nakhon Ratchasima
Ubon Ratchathani
M. Khôngxédôn
Pakxe
Preparis Island
T H A I L A N D
Surin
Attapu
Quang Ngai
Coco Island
Sara Buri
Tavoy
Ayutthaya
Mekong
V I E T N A M
Coco Channel
BANGKOK
Kon Tum
M. Không
Qui Nhon
North Andaman
Rat Buri
Andaman Islands (India)
Aranyaprathet
Sisôphôn
Stœng Trêng
Plây Cu
Phet Buri
Bight of Bangkok
Bătdâmbâng
Tuy Hoa
Middle Andaman
Mergui
Mergui
Rayong
Tônlé Sab
Buôn Mê Thuôt
South Andaman
Chanthaburi
C A M B O D I A
Nha Trang
Ko Chang
Kâmpong Cham
Andaman Sea
Duncan Passage
Prachuap Khiri Khan
Phnum Penh
Da Lat
Cam Ranh
Archipelago
Gulf of Thailand
Little Andaman
Sihanoukville
HÔ CHI MINH (SAIGON)
Biên Hoa
Phan Rang
Chumphon
Phan Thiêt
Ten Degree Channel
Kawthaung
Dao Phu Quôc
Long Xuyên
My Tho
Vung Tau
Car Nicobar
Ranong
Cân Tho
Ko Samui
Bac Liêu
Ca Mau
Mouths of the Mekong
Surat Thani
Nakhon Si Thammarat
Côn Son
Nicobar Islands (India)
Little Nicobar
Phuket
Great Nicobar
Phatthalung
Trang
Songkhla
Hat Yai
Langkawi
Yala
Kota Bharu
Banda Aceh
Alor Setar
George Town
Gerik
Kuala Kerai
M A L A
Lhokseumawe
Bireun
Pinang
Taiping
G. Korbu
2182
Kuala Terengganu
Langsa
INDIAN OCEAN
Meulaboh
Ipoh
Malay Peninsula
Laut
SUMATERA (SUMATRA)
3145
Gunung Leuser
MEDAN
Kuala Lipis
Kuantan
Tebingtinggi
Temerloh
Natuna Besar
Panarik
Kepulauan Natuna
Danau Toba
KUALA LUMPUR
Simeulue
Sinabang
Pematangsiantar
Strait of Malacca
Seremban
Kepulauan Anambas
(Indonesia)
Tanjung Datu
Barus
Melaka
Keluang
Sibolga
Balige
Muar
Dumai
Kuching
Gunungsitoli
SINGAPORE
Johor Bahru
SINGAPORE
Sambas
Nias
INDONESIA
112 113
110 111

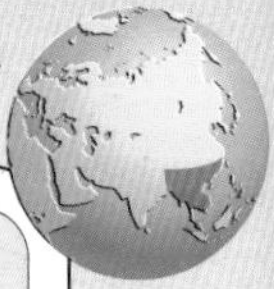

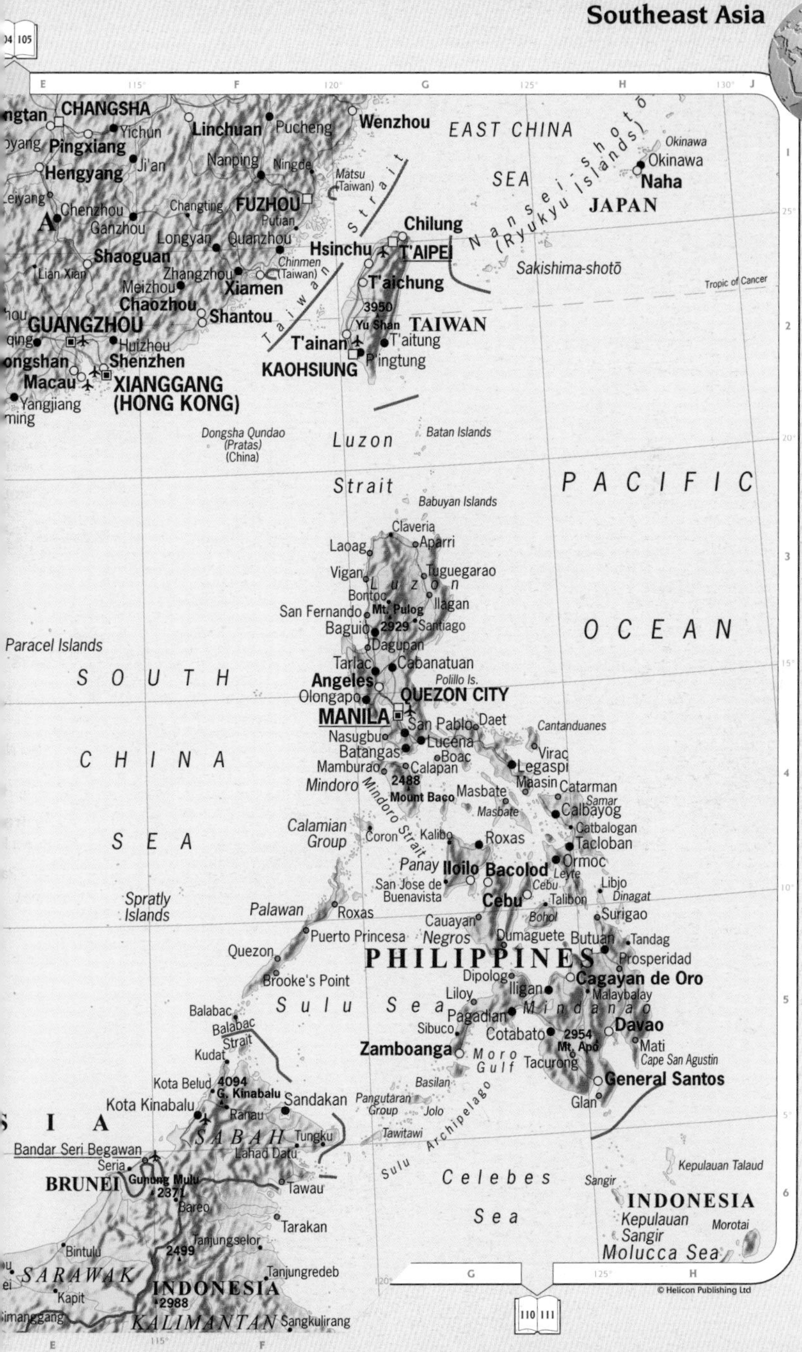

104 105
E
115°
F
120°
G
125°
H
130°
J
Xiangtan
CHANGSHA
Yichun
Pingxiang
Hengyang
Ji'an
Leiyang
Chenzhou
Ganzhou
Linchuan
Pucheng
Nanping
Ningde
Wenzhou
Matsu (Taiwan)
FUZHOU
Putian
Changting
Longyan
Quanzhou
Shaoguan
Lian Xian
Zhangzhou
Chinmen (Taiwan)
Meizhou
Xiamen
Chaozhou
Shantou
GUANGZHOU
Huizhou
Shenzhen
Zhongshan
Macau
XIANGGANG (HONG KONG)
Yangjiang
Taiwan Strait
Chilung
Hsinchu
T'AIPEI
T'aichung
3950
Yu Shan
TAIWAN
T'ainan
T'aitung
KAOHSIUNG
P'ingtung
EAST CHINA SEA
Nansei-shotō (Ryukyu Islands)
Okinawa
Naha
JAPAN
Sakishima-shotō
Tropic of Cancer
25°
20°
15°
10°
5°
1
2
3
4
5
6
Dongsha Qundao (Pratas) (China)
Luzon Strait
Batan Islands
Babuyan Islands
PACIFIC OCEAN
Claveria
Aparri
Laoag
Vigan
Tuguegarao
Luzon
Bontoc
Mt. Pulog
Ilagan
San Fernando
2929
Santiago
Baguio
Dagupan
Paracel Islands
SOUTH CHINA SEA
Tarlac
Cabanatuan
Angeles
Polillo Is.
Olongapo
QUEZON CITY
MANILA
San Pablo
Daet
Cantanduanes
Nasugbu
Lucena
Batangas
Boac
Virac
Mamburao
Calapan
Legaspi
2488
Mount Baco
Masbate
Maasin
Catarman
Samar
Mindoro
Mindoro Strait
Calbayog
Calamian Group
Catbalogan
Coron
Kalibo
Roxas
Tacloban
Panay
Ormoc
Leyte
Iloilo
Bacolod
San Jose de Buenavista
Cebu
Libjo
Dinagat
Talibon
Spratly Islands
Palawan
Roxas
Surigao
Cauayan
Bohol
Puerto Princesa
Negros
Dumaguete
Butuan
Tandag
Quezon
PHILIPPINES
Prosperidad
Dipolog
Cagayan de Oro
Brooke's Point
Iligan
Malaybalay
Liloy
Mindanao
Balabac
Sulu Sea
Pagadian
Davao
Balabac Strait
Sibuco
Cotabato
2954
Mt. Apo
Mati
Kudat
Zamboanga
Moro Gulf
Tacurong
Cape San Agustin
4094
G. Kinabalu
Kota Belud
Basilan
General Santos
Kota Kinabalu
Sandakan
Pangutaran Group
Jolo
Glan
Ranau
Tawitawi
Sulu Archipelago
MALAYSIA
SABAH
Tungku
Bandar Seri Begawan
Lahad Datu
Seria
Kepulauan Talaud
BRUNEI
Gunung Mulu
2371
Tawau
Celebes Sea
Sangir
Bareo
INDONESIA
Kepulauan Sangir
Tarakan
Morotai
Tanjungselor
Bintulu
2499
Molucca Sea
SARAWAK
Tanjungredeb
INDONESIA
Kapit
2988
KALIMANTAN
Sangkulirang
Simanggang
110 111
© Helicon Publishing Ltd

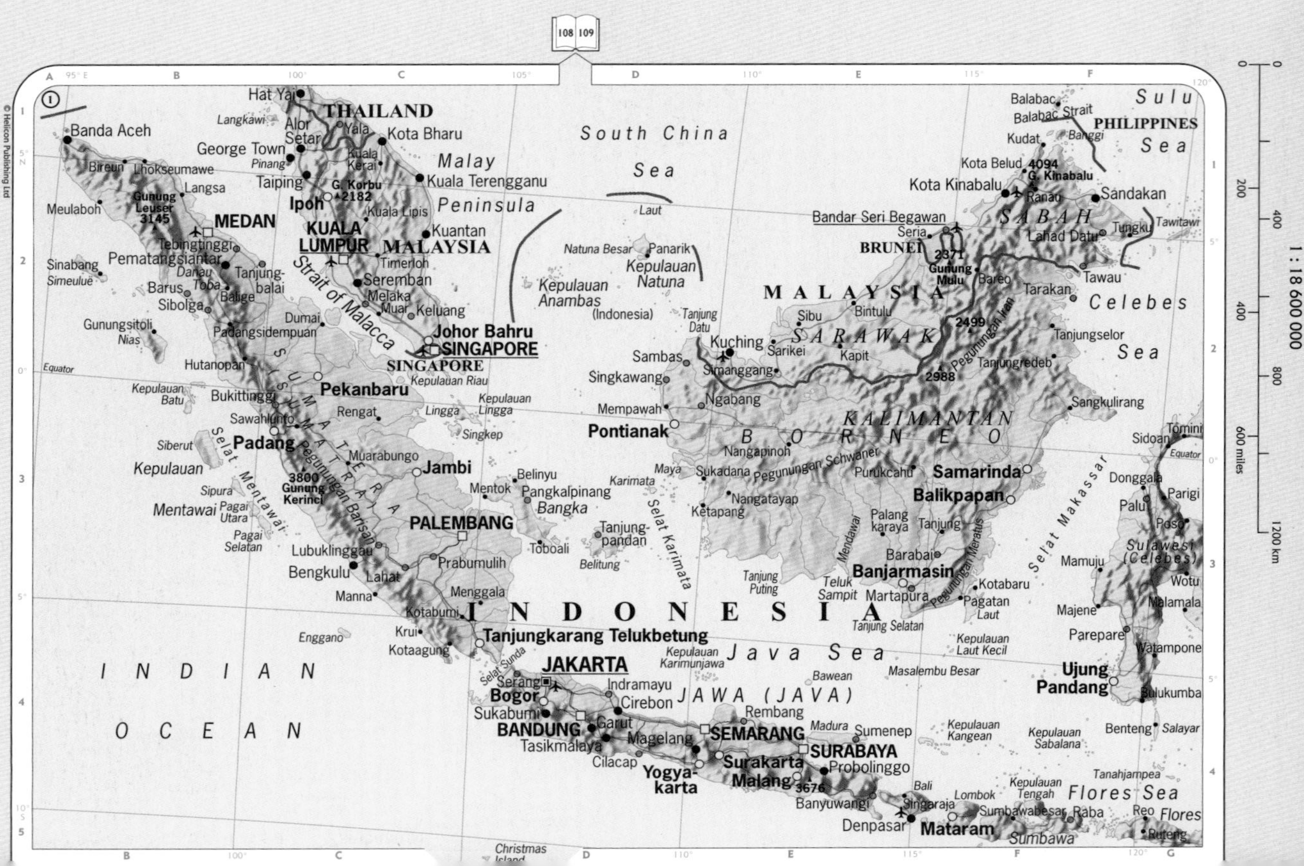

1 : 18 600 000
0 400 800 1200 km
0 200 400 600 miles
108 109
South China Sea
Sulu Sea
Celebes Sea
Java Sea
Flores Sea
Strait of Malacca
Selat Makassar
Selat Karimata
Selat Mentawai
Selat Sunda
INDIAN OCEAN
THAILAND
PHILIPPINES
MALAYSIA
BRUNEI
SINGAPORE
INDONESIA
Malay Peninsula
SABAH
SARAWAK
BORNEO
KALIMANTAN
SUMATERA
JAWA (JAVA)
Sulawesi (Celebes)
Equator
Hat Yai
Alor Setar
George Town
Pinang
Langkawi
Taiping
Ipoh
Yala
Kota Bharu
Kuala Kerai
Kuala Terengganu
Kuantan
Kuala Lipis
G. Korbu 2182
KUALA LUMPUR
Seremban
Melaka
Muar
Keluang
Timerloh
Johor Bahru
SINGAPORE
Banda Aceh
Lhokseumawe
Langsa
MEDAN
Tebingtinggi
Pematangsiantar
Gunung Leuser 3145
Sibolga
Barus
Danau Toba
Balige
Tanjungbalai
Padangsidempuan
Hutanopan
Dumai
Pekanbaru
Bukittinggi
Sawahlunto
Padang
Gunung Kerinci 3800
Jambi
PALEMBANG
Bengkulu
Lubuklinggau
Lahat
Prabumulih
Muarabungo
Rengat
Menggala
Kotabumi
Krui
Kotaagung
Manna
Tanjungkarang Telukbetung
Enggano
Pegunungan Barisan
Meulaboh
Bireun
Sinabang
Simeulue
Nias
Gunungsitoli
Kepulauan Batu
Siberut
Kepulauan Mentawai
Sipura
Pagai Utara
Pagai Selatan
Bangka
Pangkalpinang
Belinyu
Mentok
Toboali
Belitung
Tanjungpandan
Kepulauan Riau
Kepulauan Lingga
Lingga
Singkep
Kepulauan Anambas
(Indonesia)
Kepulauan Natuna
Natuna Besar
Laut
Panarik
Kota Kinabalu
Kota Belud
G. Kinabalu 4094
Kudat
Balabac
Balabac Strait
Banggi
Sandakan
Lahad Datu
Tawau
Tungku
Tawitawi
Ranau
Bandar Seri Begawan
Seria
Gunung Mulu 2371
Bareo
Bintulu
Sibu
Sarikei
Kapit
Kuching
Simanggang
Tanjung Datu
Sambas
Singkawang
Mempawah
Pontianak
Ngabang
Sukadana
Ketapang
Nangatayap
Nangapinoh
Pegunungan Schwaner
Purukcahu
Palang karaya
Banjarmasin
Martapura
Barabai
Tanjung
Balikpapan
Samarinda
Tanjungredeb
Tarakan
Tanjungselor
Sangkulirang
Pegunungan Iran
Pegunungan Meratus
Kotabaru
Pagatan
Laut
Sampit
Teluk Sampit
Tanjung Puting
Tanjung Selatan
Mendawai
Karimata
Maya
2499
2988
Kepulauan Laut Kecil
Masalembu Besar
Kepulauan Karimunjawa
Bawean
Madura
Kepulauan Kangean
JAKARTA
Serang
Bogor
Sukabumi
BANDUNG
Tasikmalaya
Garut
Cirebon
Indramayu
Cilacap
Magelang
Yogyakarta
SEMARANG
Surakarta
Rembang
Malang
SURABAYA
Sumenep
Probolinggo
Banyuwangi
3676
Bali
Denpasar
Singaraja
Lombok
Mataram
Sumbawa
Sumbawabesar
Raba
Reo
Flores
Ruteng
Christmas Island
Tomini
Sidoan
Donggala
Palu
Parigi
Poso
Wotu
Malamala
Watampone
Bulukumba
Mamuju
Majene
Parepare
Ujung Pandang
Benteng
Salayar
Kepulauan Sabalana
Kepulauan Tengah
Tanahjampea
© Helicon Publishing Ltd

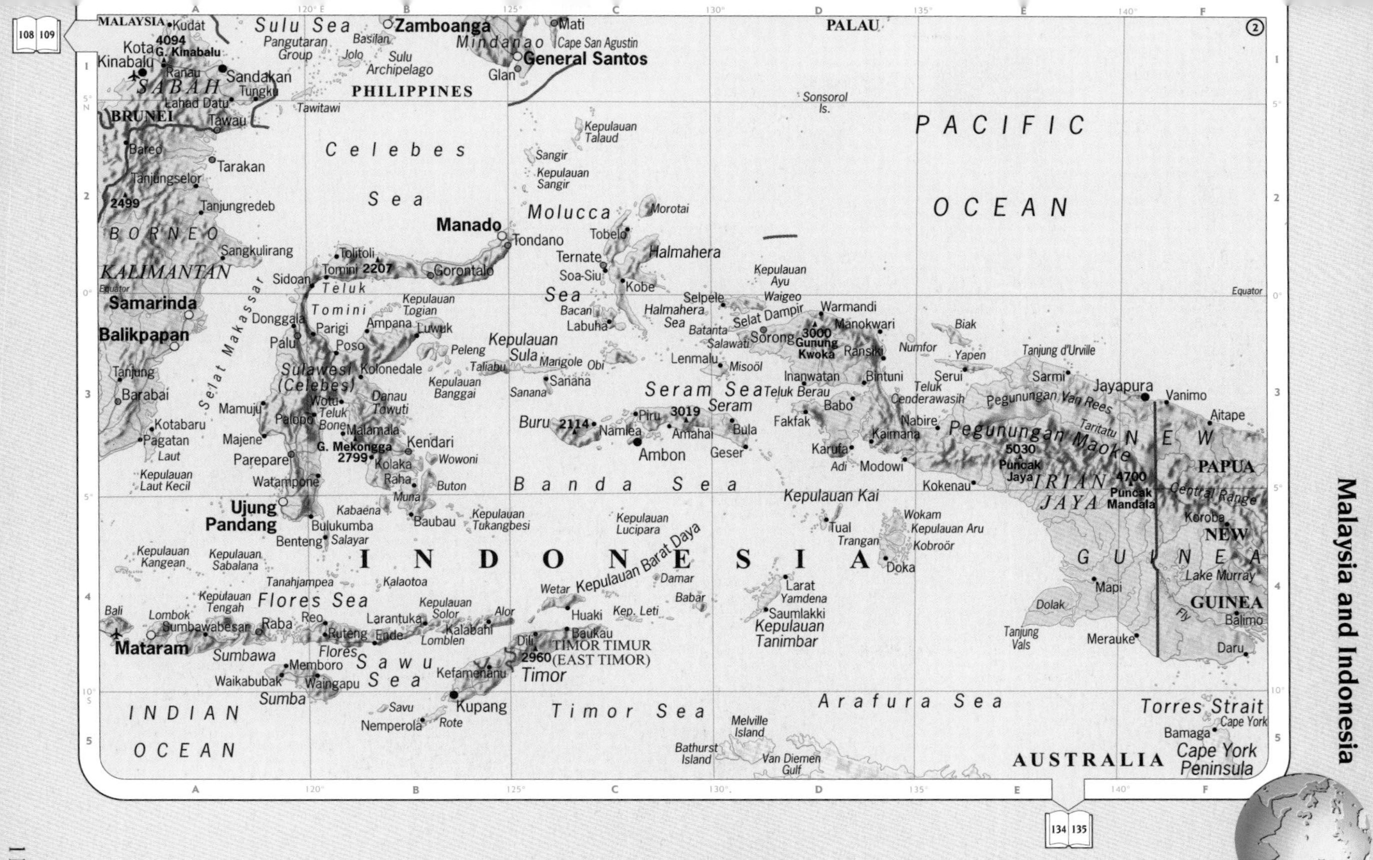

108 109

134 135

1 : 18 600 000
0
400
800
1200 km
0
200
400
600 miles
100 101
108 109
114 115
A
B
C
D
E
F
G
1
2
3
4
CHINA
Xizang Gaoyuan (Plateau of Tibet)
Kunlun Shan
Hoh Xil Shan
Bayan Har Shan
Gangdisê Shan
Karakoram
Hindu Kush
HIMALAYAS
Thar Desert
PAKISTAN
INDIA
NEPAL
BHUTAN
BANGLADESH
MYANMAR (BURMA)
AFGHANISTAN
JAMMU & KASHMIR
KĀBUL
Peshawar
Islamabad
Rawalpindi
LAHORE
FAISALABAD
Multan
Sargodha
Hyderabad
Sukkur
Srinagar
Amritsar
LUDHIANA
Chandigarh
Dehra Dun
DELHI
New Delhi
Meerut
Ghaziabad
Moradabad
Bareilly
Aligarh
Agra
JAIPUR
Jodhpur
Bikaner
Ajmer
Kota
Udaipur
AHMADABAD
Rajkot
Bhavnagar
Jamnagar
SURAT
VADODARA
Nasik
Dhule
Aurangābād
Akola
INDORE
Ujjain
BHOPAL
Sagar
Jabalpur
NAGPUR
Raipur
Gwalior
Jhansi
KANPUR
LUCKNOW
Faizabad
Allahabad
VARANASI
PATNA
Gaya
Gorakhpur
Kathmandu
Thimphu
Lhasa
Rajshahi
DHAKA
CHITTAGONG
KOLKATA (CALCUTTA)
Hāora
Khulna
Jamshedpur
Ranchi
Dhanbad
Asansol
Bhagalpur
Cuttack
Bhubaneshwar
Sambalpur
Ruarkela
Kharagpur
Shillong
Guwahati
Imphal
MANDALAY
Sittwe
Mount Everest 8848
Kangchenjunga 8586
K2 8611
Annapurna 8091
Nanda Devi 7816
Kamet 7756
Ganges
Indus
Brahmaputra
Tropic of Cancer
Mouths of the Ganges
Sundarbans
© Helicon Publishing Ltd

BAY OF BENGAL
INDIAN OCEAN
ARABIAN SEA
Coromandel Coast
Malabar Coast
Eastern Ghats
Western Ghats
Vizianagaram
VISHAKHAPATNAM
Rajahmundry
Kākināda
Vijayawada
Machilipatnam
Mouths of the Krishna
Warangal
Kottagudem
Eluru
Guntur
Ongole
Krishna
Nellore
CHENNAI (MADRAS)
Kanchipuram
Tirupati
Cuddapah
Pondicherry
Cuddalore
Kumbakonam
Tiruchchirāppalli
MADURAI
Jaffna
Palk Strait
Rameswaram
Tuticorin
Gulf of Mannar
Nagercoil
Cape Comorin
Tirunelveli
Rajapalaiyam
Dindigul
Salem
Vellore
Chittoor
Tiruvannamalai
Anantapur
Kurnool
Adoni
Bellary
HYDERABAD
Zahirabad
Mahbubnagar
Bidar
Medak
Gulbarga
Yadgir
Ilkal
Solapur
Kurduvadi
Sangli
Kolhapur
Satara
Ratnagiri
Ichalkaranji
Dharwad
Hubli
Panaji
Karwar
Kumta
Davangere
Chitradurga
Shimoga
Mangalore
BANGALORE
Mandya
Mysore
Madikeri
Cannanore
Kozhikode (Calicut)
COIMBATORE
Tiruppur
Valparai
Trichur
Kochi (Cochin)
Thiruvananthapuram (Trivandrum)
Laccadive Islands
Kavaratti
Kadamat
Androtti
Nine Degree Channel
Minicoy
Eight Degree Channel
Thiladhunmathee Atoll
Maalhosmadulu Atoll
Faadhippolhu Atoll
Male Atoll
Male
Ari Atoll
Mulaku Atoll
Huvadu Atoll
MALDIVES
One and Half Degree Channel
SRI LANKA
Vavuniya
Trincomalee
Anuradhapura
Puttalam
Kandy
2359
Pottuvil
Sri Jayawardenapura-Kotte
Negombo
Colombo
Galle
Matara
Dondra Head
Henzada
Bassein
Cape Negrais
Mouths of the Irrawaddy
Preparis Island
Coco Island
Coco Channel
North Andaman
Middle Andaman
South Andaman
Andaman Islands (India)
Duncan Passage
Little Andaman
Ten Degree Channel
Car Nicobar
Nicobar Islands (India)
Little Nicobar
Great Nicobar

1 : 20 400 000
0
400
800
1200 km
0
200
400
600 miles
A
B
C
D
E
F
30° E
35°
40°
45°
50°
40° N
35°
30°
25°
20°
15°
1
2
3
4
5
6
7
İSTANBUL
Zonguldak
Sinop
Black Sea
Zugdidi
K'ut'aisi
Izberbash
Fetisovo
RUSSIA
Derbent
Caspian
Bursa
İzmit
Kastamonu
Karabük
Samsun
Bat'umi
GEORGIA
T'BILISI
Caucasus
Quba
Bolu
Çorum
Trabzon
Rize
Rust'avi
Eskişehir
ANKARA
Amasya
Anadolu Dağları
Gyumri
Gäncä
BAKI
(BAKU)
Kütahya
Polatlı
Kırıkkale
Tokat
Sivas
3549
Keşiş Dağları
Kars
ARMENIA
YEREVAN
AZERBAIJAN
Afyon
TURKEY
Erzurum
Mt. Ararat
5165
Xankändi
Äli Bayramlı
Turkmen
Salyan
Denizli
Akşehir
Aksaray
Kayseri
Elazığ
Muş
Khvoy
Naxçıvan
Burdur
Isparta
Konya
Niğde
Malatya
Diyarbakır
Van
Marand
Astara
Sea
Antalya
Toros Dağları
ADANA
Gaziantep
Mardin
Siirt
TABRĪZ
Ardabīl
Fethiye
Alanya
Silifke
İçel
Sanlıurfa
Orūmīyeh
Rasht
Bandar-e Anzalī
Lāhījān
Amol
İskenderun
Dahuk
Marāgheh
Zanjān
Lefkosia
(Nicosia)
CYPRUS
HALAB
(ALEPPO)
Al Ḥasakah
Sinjār
Al Mawṣil
Mahābād
Saqqez
Qazvīn
Reshteh-ye Kūhhā
Lemesos
(Limassol)
Trâblous
(Tripoli)
Ḥimṣ
(Homs)
As Sulaymānīyah
Bījār
Karaj
Dayr az Zawr
Kirkūk
Sanandaj
Mediterranean
LEBANON
SYRIA
Tikrīt
Hamadān
Qom
BAYROUTH (BEIRUT)
DIMASHQ
(DAMASCUS)
Kermānshāh
Arāk
Kāshān
EL
Sea
Ar Ramādī
Īlām
Borūjerd
ISKANDARÎYA
(ALEXANDRIA)
ISRAEL
Irbid
Zarqā'
Ar Rutba
IRAQ
BAGHDĀD
Khorramābād
EṢFAH
Karbalā'
Dehlonān
Jerusalem
'AMMĀN
An Nukhayb
Al Ḥillah
Tigris
Al Kūt
Dezfūl
Dead Sea
An Najaf
Euphrates
Al 'Amārah
EL GÎZA
EL QÂHIRA
(CAIRO)
JORDAN
Al Jalāmīd
'Ar'ar
Ahvāz
Helwan
Ma'ān
An Nāṣirīyah
Khorramshahr
El Suweis
Elat
Al Baṣrah
Ābādān
Beni Suef
Sinai
Aqaba
Al Jawf
Rafḥā
KUWAIT
Al Kuwayt
(Kuwait)
Kāzerūn
Khalig el Suweis
Gulf of Aqaba
Al Jahrah
El Minya
Tabūk
An Nafud
Asyût
Sharm el Sheikh
Taymā'
Hafar al Bāṭin
Būshehr
(Bushire)
EGYPT
Ḥā'il
Ad Dahnā
The
Kangān
Sohâg
Qena
Bûr Safâga
SAUDI
Al Jubayl
El Khârga
Luxor
Al Wajh
Al Hijaz
Buraydah
Ad Dammām
Idfu
'Unayzah
Al Manāmah
BAHRAIN
Nile
Kom Ombo
Al Hufūf
QATAR
Aswân Dam
Aswân
ARABIA
Tropic of Cancer
Râs Banâs
Yanbu'al Bahr
Al Madīnah
(Medina)
AR RIYĀD
(RIYADH)
Ad Dawhah
(Doha)
Lake Nasser
'Afīf
Al Kharj
Ḥaraḍ
Abu Simbel
ADMINISTERED BY SUDAN
Rābigh
UNIT
Wadi Halfa
Halaib
JIDDAH
(JEDDA)
Makkah
(Mecca)
Zalim
Laylā
Al 'Ubayla
Nubian
Desert
Ras Abu Shagara
Aṭ Ṭā'if
RED SEA
Abu Hamed
Bur Sudan
(Port Sudan)
Qal'at Bīshah
As Sulayyil
Rub' al Khālī
(Empty Quarter)
Merowe
Suakin
Al Qunfudhah
Berber
Atbara
Haiya
Ras Kasar
Abhā
SUDAN
Zahrān
Najrān
Sanāw
Algena
Shendi
Jīzān
Sa'dah
Umm Durman
El Khartum Bahri
Dahlak Archipelago
Wuday'ah
El Khartum
(Khartoum)
Kassala
Keren
Massawa
Harad
Al Ghay
Khashm el Girba
Teseney
Akordat
Asmara
3760
Jabal an Nabī Shu'ayb
San'ā
Mar'ib
Shabwah
Say'ūn
Hadhramaut
Qishn
Wad Medani
ERITREA
YEMEN
Sennar
Gedaref
Himora
Aksum
Adigrat
Al Hudaydah
Dhamār
Ash Shihr
Ras Dashen Terara
4620
Ed
Lawdar
Ḥabbān
Al Mukallā
Kosti
Mek'ele
Ta'izz
2514
Jabal Thamar
ETHIOPIA
Al Mukhā
Assab
Bāb al Mandab
At Turbah
'Adan
(Aden)
Ras Bir
Abd al
Tendaho
DJIBOUTI
Gulf of Aden
Caluula
Raas Cas
Lake Abbe
Dikhil
Djibouti
SOMALIA
Bereeda
Sāylac
Maydh
122
123
128
129

100 101

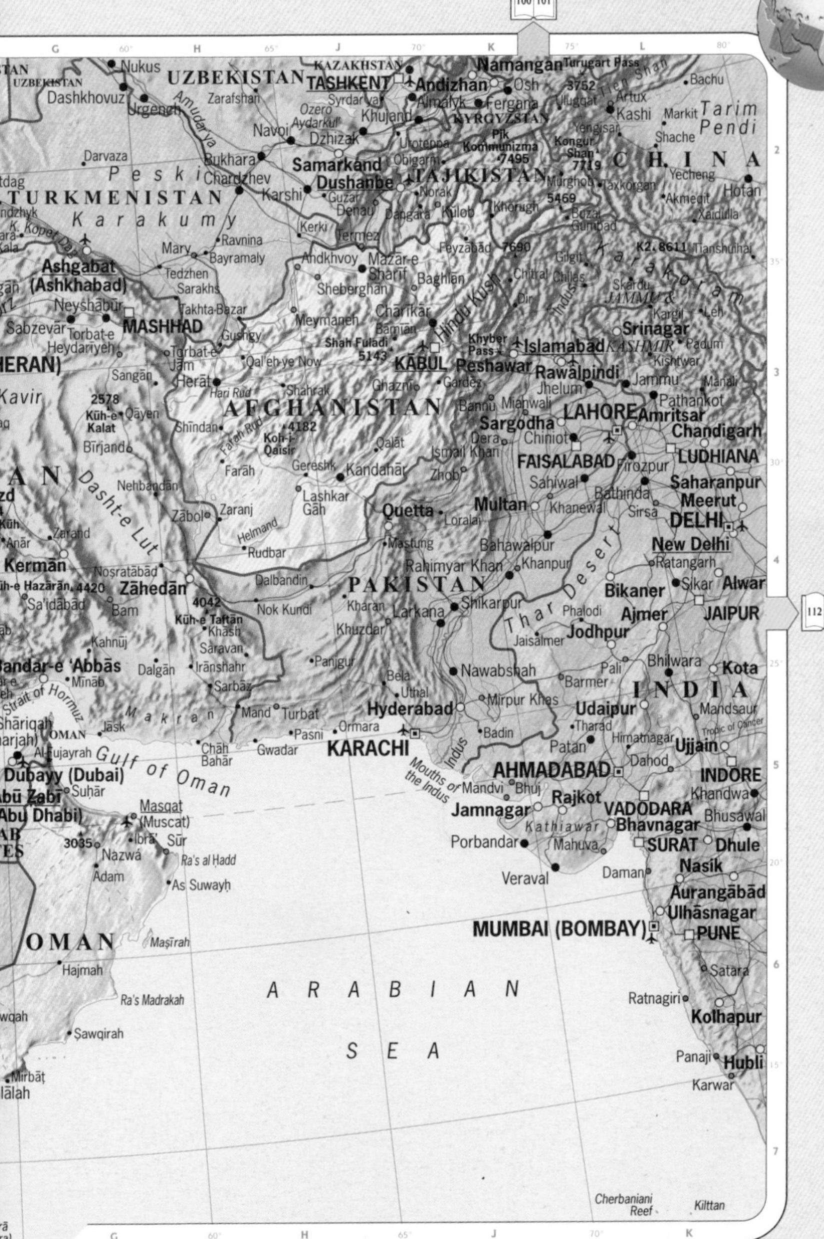

112 113

1 : 9 300 000
0
200
400
600 km
0
100
200
300 miles
ROMANIA
BUCUREŞTI (BUCHAREST)
Constanţa
BULGARIA
Varna
Burgas
Ruse
Dobrič
Šumen
Sliven
Stara Zagora
Jambol
Simferopol'
UKRAINE
Sevastopol'
Yalta
Feodosiya
Kerch
B L A C K S E A
Edirne
İSTANBUL
İstanbul Boğazı (Bosporus)
Marmara Denizi
Zonguldak
Kastamonu
Sinop
Samsun
İzmit
Bursa
Eskişehir
ANKARA
Kırıkkale
Çorum
Amasya
Tokat
Yozgat
Balıkesir
Çanakkale
Kütahya
İZMIR
Manisa
Uşak
Afyon
A N A T O L I A
T U R K E Y
Tuz Gölü
Kayseri
Aksaray
Konya
Aydın
Denizli
Isparta
Antalya
Antalya Körfezi
Alanya
Toros Dağları
İçel (Mersin)
Tarsus
ADANA
Gaziantep
İskenderun
Antakya
GREECE
Rodos
Karpathos
Lefkosia (Nicosia)
Lemesos (Limassol)
Larnaka
CYPRUS
Al Lādhiqīyah
Hamāh
Trâblous (Tripoli)
BAYROUTH (BEIRUT)
LEBANON
DIMASHQ (DAMASCUS)
M E D I T E R R A N E A N S E A
© Helicon Publishing Ltd

94 95

118 119

96 97
H
40°
J
42°
K
44°
L
46°
M
48°
N
KALMYKIYA
Krasnodar
Ust'-Labinsk
Armavir
Stavropol'
Budennovsk
Krymsk
Belorechensk
Novorossiysk
Nevinnomyssk
Zelenokumsk
Kizlyarskiy Zaliv
Yuzhno-Sukhokumsk
Gelendzhik
Maykop
ADYGEYA
R U S S I A
Os. Chechen'
Tuapse
Cherkessk
Pyatigorsk
Kizlyar
Agrakhanskiy Poluostrov
Psebay
KARACHAYEVO-CHERKESIYA
Mozdok
Kargalinskaya
KABARDINO-BALKARIYA
CHECHNYA
DAGESTAN
Sochi
Teberda
5642 Elbrus
Nal'chik
Nazran
INGUSHETIYA
Gudermes
Makhachkala
Gagra
Vladikavkaz
Groznyy
Kaspiysk
SEVERNAYA OSETIYA
C A S P I A N
Sokhumi
Buynaksk
Oni
5047 Kazbek
4494
Levashi
Och'amch'ire
Derbent
Zugdidi
K'ut'aisi
Ts'khinvali
S E A
P'ot'i
G E O R G I A
T'elavi
Samtredia
Khashuri
Gori
T'BILISI
Xaçmaz
Bat'umi
Zaqatala
Akhty
Rust'avi
4466 Gora Bazardyuzi
Quba
Arkhalts'ikhe
Şäki
Siyäzän
Bolnisi
Mingäçevir Su Anbarı
Qazax
Pazar
Artvin
Sumqayıt
Şämkir
Mingäçevir
Ardahan
Vanadzor
Yevlax
BAKI (BAKU)
Trabzon
Rize
Gäncä
A Z E R B A I J A N
Giresun
3937
Kars
Gyumri
Hrazdan
Sevana Lich
Kürdämir
Qazimämmäd
Anadolu Dağları
Oltu
ARMENIA
İmişli
Äli Bayramlı
Gümüşhane
Ejmiadzin
YEREVAN
Saatli
Suşehri
Pasinler
Horasan
Ararat
Xankändi
Salyan
Kür
Mt. Ararat 5165
Ağri
Araz
Erzincan
Aşkale
Erzurum
Şahbuz
Goris
Neftçala
AZER.
Naxçıvan
Masallı
Patnos
Ercis
Mākū
Khodā Āfarīn
Länkäran
Divriği
Tunceli
Murat
Keban Barajı
Bingöl
4434 Süphan Daği
Jolfā
Ahar
Astara
Van Gölü
Qoţūr
Marand
4810
Ardabīl
Elazığ
Muş
Van
Khvoy
TABRĪZ
Fırat (Euphrates)
Tatvan
Salmās
Sarāb
Tālesh
Malatya
Ergani
Silvan
Gevaş
Başkale
Daryācheh-ye Orūmīyeh
3710 Kuh-e Sahand
Bandar-e Anzalī
Lāhījān
Siverek
Siirt
Mīāneh
Rasht
Adıyaman
Diyarbakır
Batman
Orūmīyeh
Marāgheh
Qezel Owzan
Şırnak
Hakkâri
Miandowāb
Kızıltepe
Mardin
Kirk Bulāg D. 3107
Zanjān
Zākhō
Āmādīyah
Şanlıurfa
Al Qāmishlī
Mahābād
Dahūk
I R A N
Akçakale
Al Mawşil
Rānya
Saqqez
Manbij
Al Hasakah
Tall 'Afar
Arbīl
Bāneh
Dīvāndarreh
Bījār
Buhayrat al Asad
Sinjār
Ar Raqqah
Maskanah
As Sulaymānīyah
Marīvān
Kirkūk
Sanandaj
Qorveh
Pāveh
Dayr az Zawr
R I A
Baiji
Kifrī
MESOPOTAMIA
I R A Q
Kermānshāh
114 115
Tikrīt
Harsīn
Rāwah
Buhayrat ath Tharthār
Tigris
Āl Bū Kamāl
'Anah
Jalūlā
Gīlān Gharb
Tadmur
Īlām
Kūhdasht
Ba'qūbah
Khān al Baghdādī
Euphrates
BAGHDĀD
Mehrān
Ar Ramādī
Bādiyat ash Shām (Syrian Desert)
Dehlonān
Bar al Milh
Ar Rutba
122 123

Israel

1 : 4 600 000

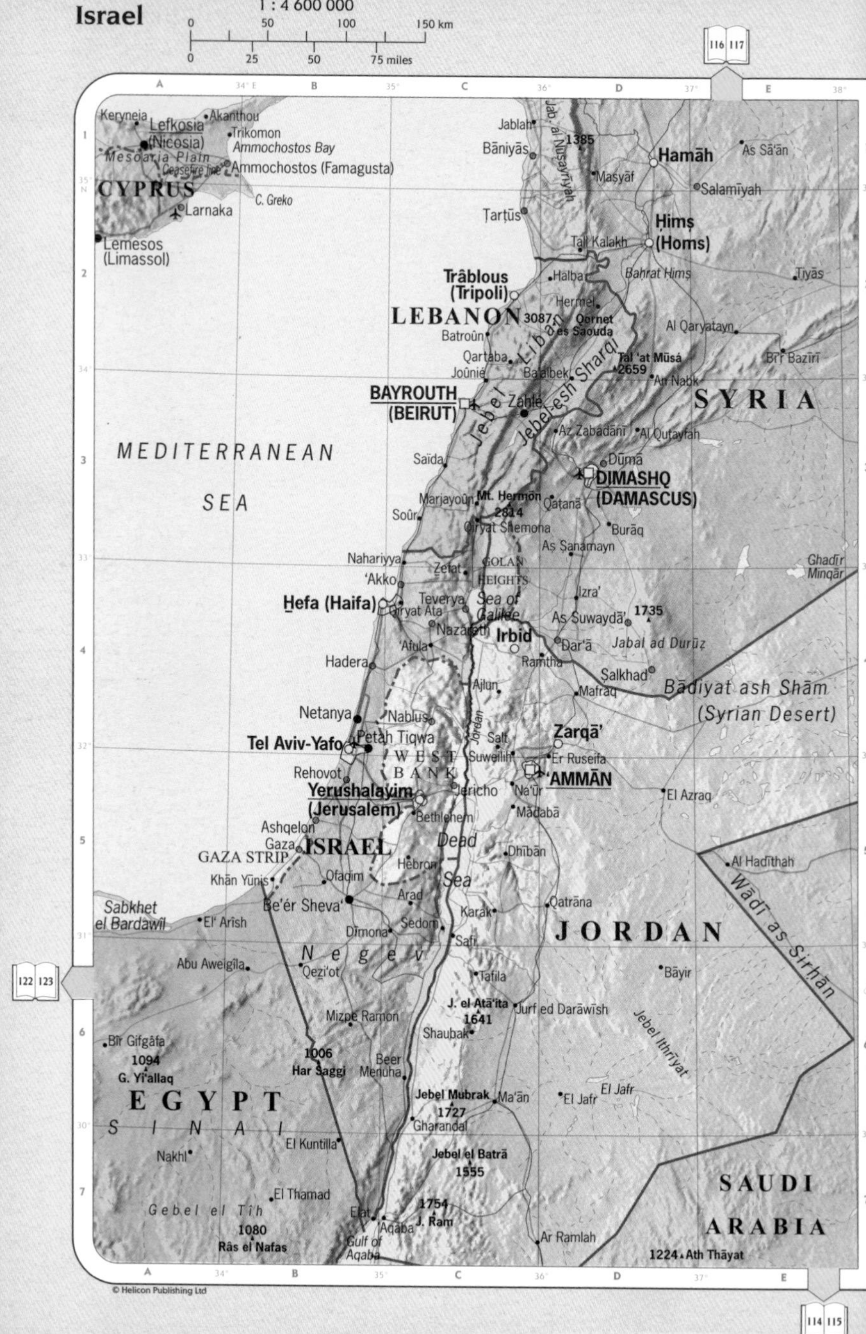

1 : 9 300 000

0 100 200 300 km

0 50 100 150 miles

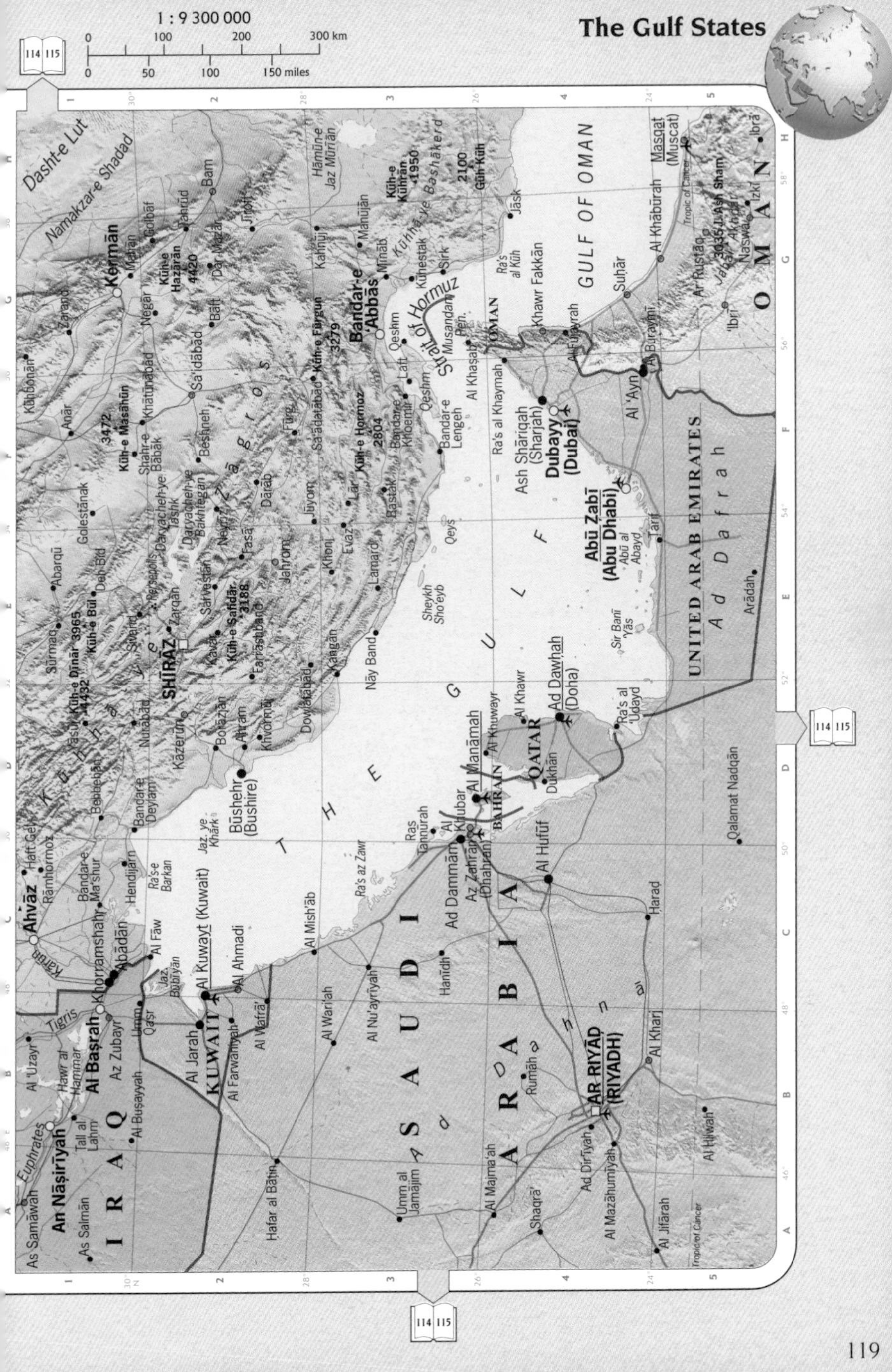

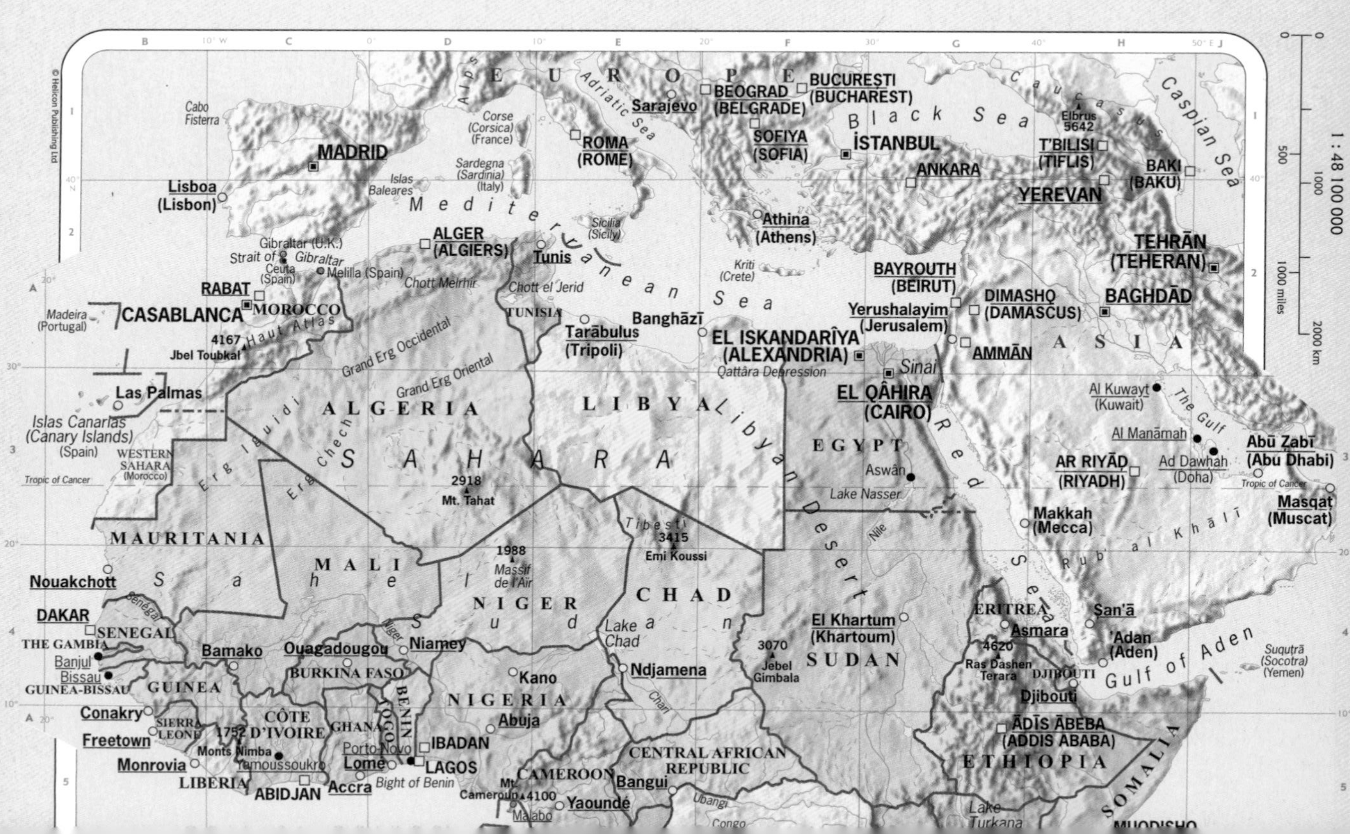

1 : 48 100 000
0
1000
2000 km
500
1000 miles
© Helicon Publishing Ltd
E U R O P E
Alps
Cabo Fisterra
MADRID
Lisboa (Lisbon)
Islas Baleares
Corse (Corsica) (France)
Sardegna (Sardinia) (Italy)
ROMA (ROME)
Adriatic Sea
Sarajevo
BEOGRAD (BELGRADE)
SOFIYA (SOFIA)
BUCUREȘTI (BUCHAREST)
Black Sea
İSTANBUL
ANKARA
Caucasus
Elbrus 5642
T'BILISI (TIFLIS)
BAKI (BAKU)
YEREVAN
Caspian Sea
TEHRĀN (TEHERAN)
BAGHDĀD
DIMASHQ (DAMASCUS)
AMMĀN
BAYROUTH (BEIRUT)
Yerushalayim (Jerusalem)
A S I A
Mediterranean Sea
Sicilia (Sicily)
Athina (Athens)
Kriti (Crete)
Gibraltar (U.K.)
Strait of Gibraltar
Ceuta (Spain)
Melilla (Spain)
ALGER (ALGIERS)
Tunis
TUNISIA
Chott Melrhir
Chott el Jerid
RABAT
CASABLANCA
MOROCCO
Haut Atlas
4167 Jbel Toubkal
Madeira (Portugal)
Las Palmas
Islas Canarias (Canary Islands) (Spain)
WESTERN SAHARA (Morocco)
Tropic of Cancer
Grand Erg Occidental
Grand Erg Oriental
ALGERIA
Erg Iguidi
Erg Chech
SAHARA
2918 Mt. Tahat
Tarābulus (Tripoli)
Banghāzī
LIBYA
Libyan Desert
EL ISKANDARÎYA (ALEXANDRIA)
Qattâra Depression
Sinai
EL QÂHIRA (CAIRO)
EGYPT
Aswân
Lake Nasser
Nile
Red Sea
Al Kuwayt (Kuwait)
The Gulf
Al Manāmah
Ad Dawhah (Doha)
Abū Zabī (Abu Dhabi)
AR RIYĀD (RIYADH)
Masqat (Muscat)
Makkah (Mecca)
Rub al Khālī
MAURITANIA
Nouakchott
DAKAR
SENEGAL
Sénégal
THE GAMBIA
Banjul
Bissau
GUINEA-BISSAU
GUINEA
Conakry
SIERRA LEONE
Freetown
Monrovia
LIBERIA
1752 Monts Nimba
CÔTE D'IVOIRE
Yamoussoukro
ABIDJAN
Bamako
MALI
Sahel
Ouagadougou
BURKINA FASO
GHANA
Accra
TOGO
Lomé
BENIN
Porto-Novo
Bight of Benin
Niger
Niamey
NIGER
1988 Massif de l'Aïr
Tibesti
3415 Emi Koussi
CHAD
Lake Chad
Ndjamena
Chari
Kano
NIGERIA
Abuja
IBADAN
LAGOS
Mt. Cameroun 4100
Malabo
CAMEROON
Yaoundé
Bangui
CENTRAL AFRICAN REPUBLIC
Ubangi
Congo
El Khartum (Khartoum)
SUDAN
3070 Jebel Gimbala
ERITREA
Asmara
4620 Ras Dashen Terara
Ṣan'ā
'Adan (Aden)
Gulf of Aden
Suquṭrā (Socotra) (Yemen)
DJIBOUTI
Djibouti
ĀDĪS ĀBEBA (ADDIS ABABA)
ETHIOPIA
Lake Turkana
SOMALIA
MUQDISHO

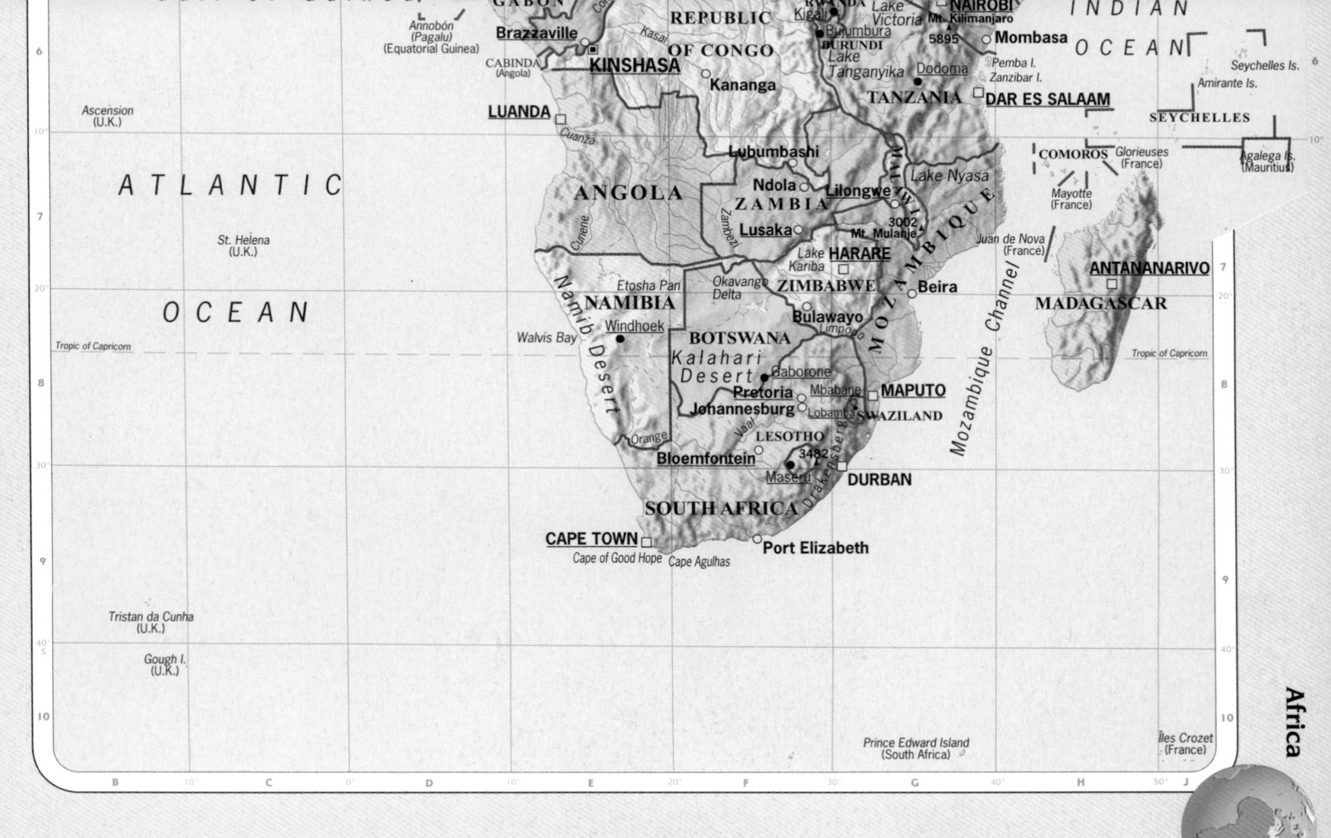
GABON
Annobón
(Pagalu)
(Equatorial Guinea)
Brazzaville
CABINDA
(Angola)
KINSHASA
Kasai
DEMOCRATIC REPUBLIC OF CONGO
Kananga
RWANDA
Kigali
Bujumbura
BURUNDI
Lake Victoria
Lake Tanganyika
NAIROBI
Mt. Kilimanjaro
5895
Mombasa
Dodoma
Pemba I.
Zanzibar I.
TANZANIA
DAR ES SALAAM
INDIAN OCEAN
Seychelles Is.
Amirante Is.
SEYCHELLES
Agalega Is.
(Mauritius)
COMOROS
Glorieuses
(France)
Mayotte
(France)
Ascension
(U.K.)
LUANDA
Cuanza
Lubumbashi
ATLANTIC
ANGOLA
Ndola
ZAMBIA
Lilongwe
MALAWI
Lake Nyasa
MOZAMBIQUE
3002
Mt. Mulanje
Juan de Nova
(France)
Lusaka
Zambezi
Cunene
St. Helena
(U.K.)
Lake Kariba
HARARE
ANTANANARIVO
Etosha Pan
Okavango Delta
ZIMBABWE
Beira
MADAGASCAR
OCEAN
NAMIBIA
Namib Desert
Windhoek
Walvis Bay
Bulawayo
Limpopo
BOTSWANA
Kalahari Desert
Mozambique Channel
Tropic of Capricorn
Gaborone
Pretoria
Mbabane
MAPUTO
Johannesburg
Lobamba
SWAZILAND
Vaal
LESOTHO
Orange
3482
Bloemfontein
Maseru
Drakensberg
DURBAN
SOUTH AFRICA
CAPE TOWN
Cape of Good Hope
Cape Agulhas
Port Elizabeth
Tristan da Cunha
(U.K.)
Gough I.
(U.K.)
Prince Edward Island
(South Africa)
Îles Crozet
(France)

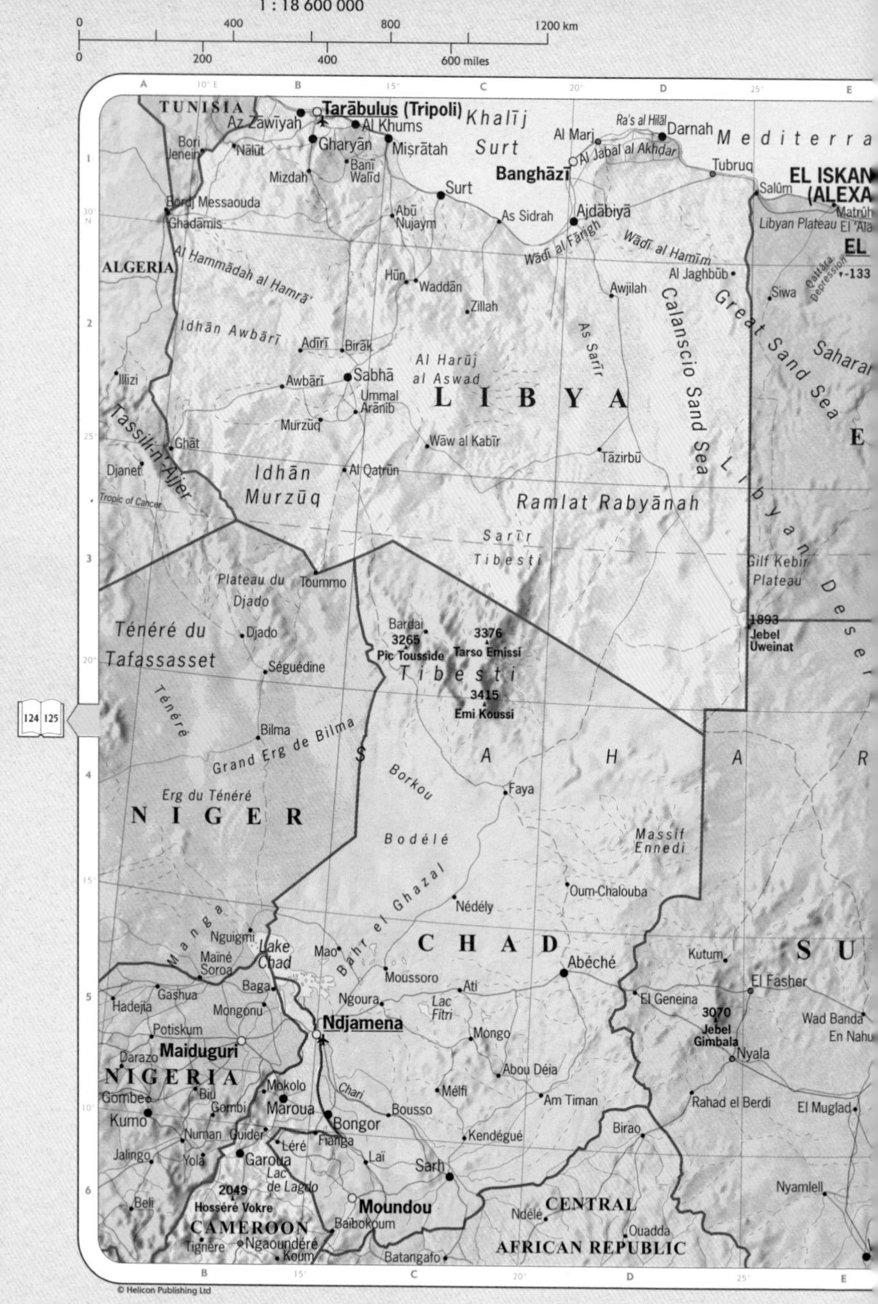
1 : 18 600 000
0
400
800
1200 km
200
600 miles
TUNISIA
Tarābulus (Tripoli)
Az Zawīyah
Al Khums
Gharyān
Mişrātah
Khalīj Surt
Bani Walid
Mizdah
Nālūt
Bordj Messaouda
Ghadāmis
ALGERIA
Surt
Banghāzī
Al Marj
Ra's al Hilāl
Darnah
Al Jabal al Akhdar
Tubruq
Mediterra
EL ISKAN (ALEXA
Salûm
Matrûh
Libyan Plateau
Ajdābiyā
As Sidrah
Abū Nujaym
Wādī al Fārigh
Wādī al Hamīm
Al Hammādah al Hamrā'
Hūn
Waddān
Zillah
Awjilah
Al Jaghbūb
Siwa
Qattara Depression
Idhān Awbārī
Adīrī
Birāk
Sabhā
Awbārī
Al Harūj al Aswad
LIBYA
As Sarīr
Calanscio Sand Sea
Great Sand Sea
Saharan
Illizi
Tassili-n'-Ajjer
Ummal Arānib
Murzūq
Ghāt
Djanet
Wāw al Kabīr
Tāzirbū
Idhān Murzūq
Al Qatrūn
Tropic of Cancer
Ramlat Rabyānah
Libyan Desert
Sarīr Tibesti
Gilf Kebir Plateau
Plateau du Djado
Toummo
1893 Jebel Uweinat
Ténéré du Tafassasset
Djado
Bardai
3265 Pic Tousside
3376 Tarso Emissi
Séguédine
Tibesti
3415 Emi Koussi
Ténéré
Bilma
Grand Erg de Bilma
SAHARA
Borkou
Faya
Erg du Ténéré
NIGER
Bodélé
Massif Ennedi
Bahr el Ghazal
Oum-Chalouba
Nédély
Manga
Nguigmi
Lake Chad
Maïné Soroa
Mao
CHAD
Abéché
Kutum
SU
El Fasher
Gashua
Baga
Moussoro
Ati
El Geneina
Hadejia
Mongonu
Ngoura
Lac Fitri
3070 Jebel Gimbala
Wad Banda
En Nahu
Potiskum
Ndjamena
Maiduguri
Mongo
Nyala
Darazo
NIGERIA
Abou Déia
Biu
Mokolo
Mélfi
Gombe
Gembi
Maroua
Chari
Am Timan
Rahad el Berdi
El Muglad
Kumo
Bongor
Bousso
Numan
Guider
Birao
Léré
Fianga
Kendégué
Jalingo
Yola
Garoua
Laï
Sarh
Lac de Lagdo
2049 Hosséré Vokre
Nyamlell
Beli
Moundou
CENTRAL
Ndélé
CAMEROON
Baibokoum
Ouadda
Tignère
Ngaoundéré
Koum
Batangafo
AFRICAN REPUBLIC
124 125
© Helicon Publishing Ltd

116 117  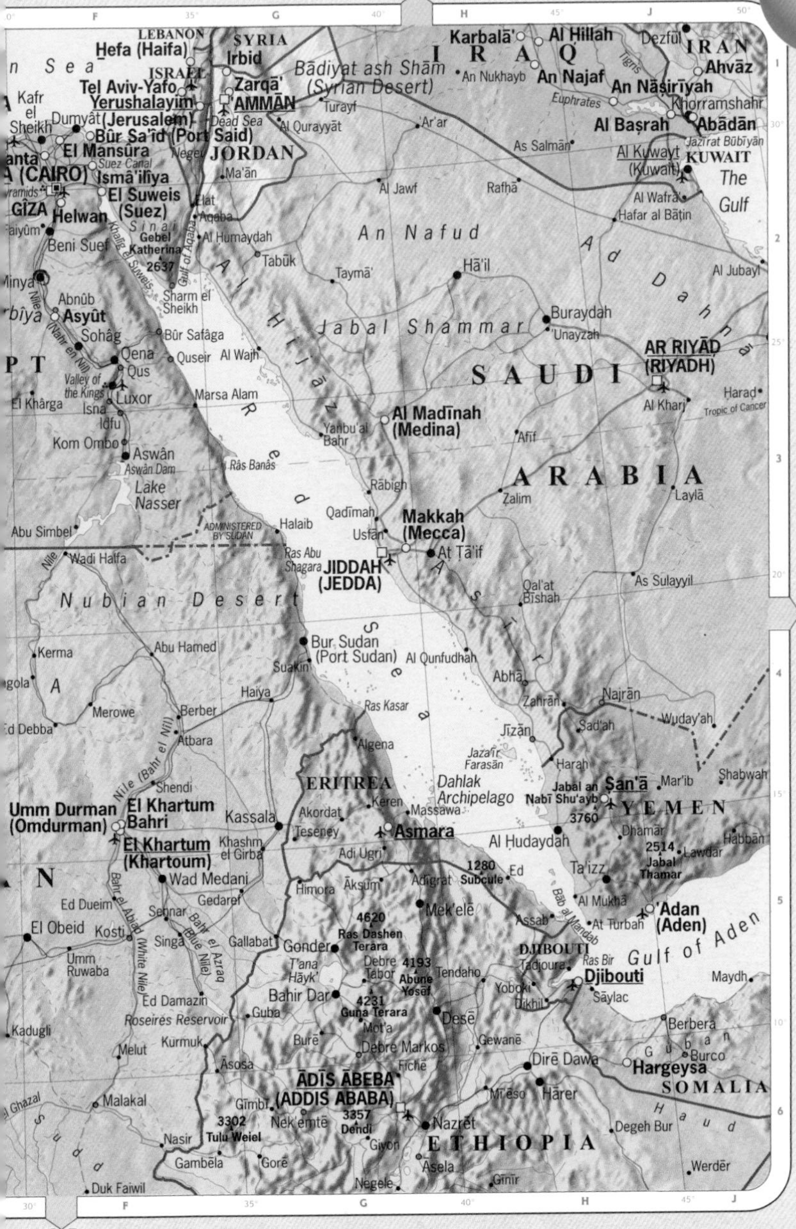
114 115
128 129

1 : 18 600 000

0 400 800 1200 km

0 200 400 600 miles

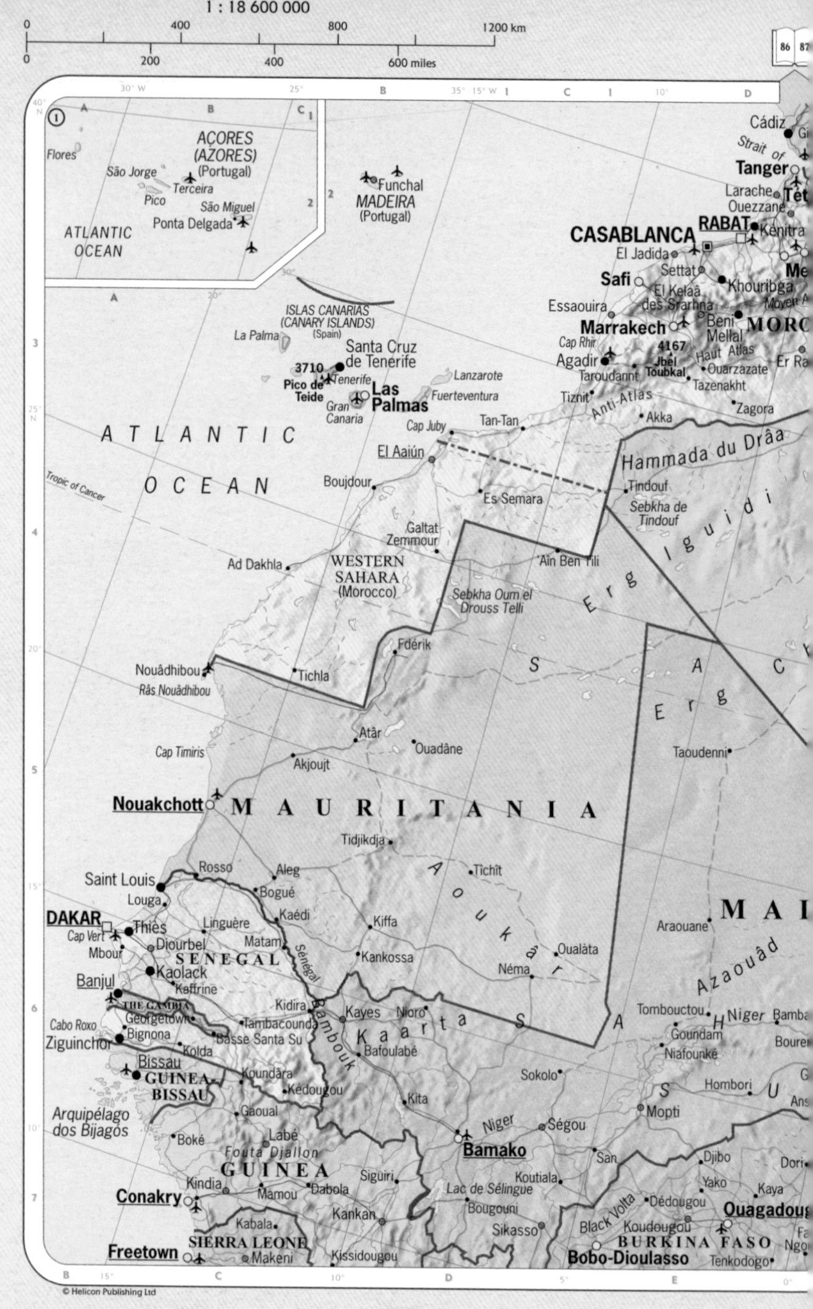

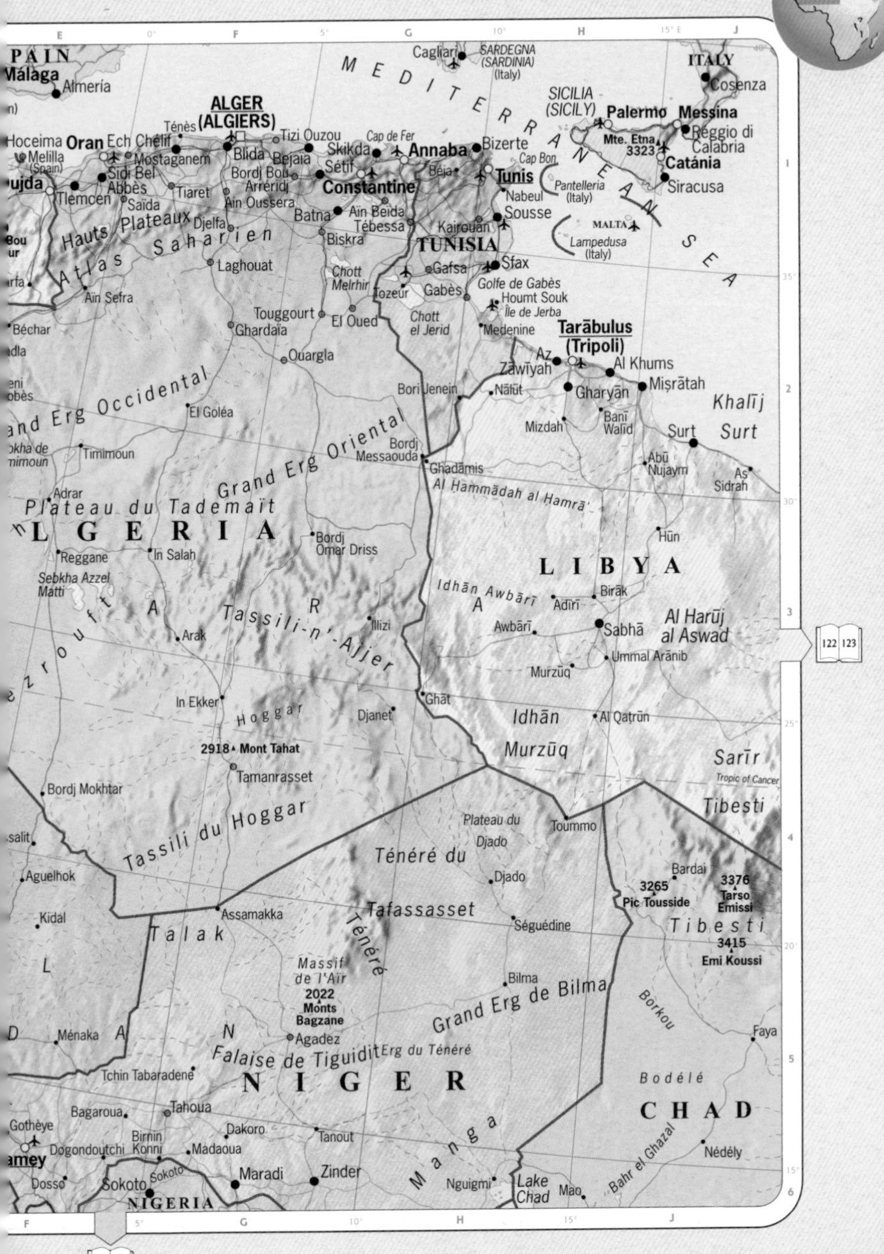

122 123

126 127

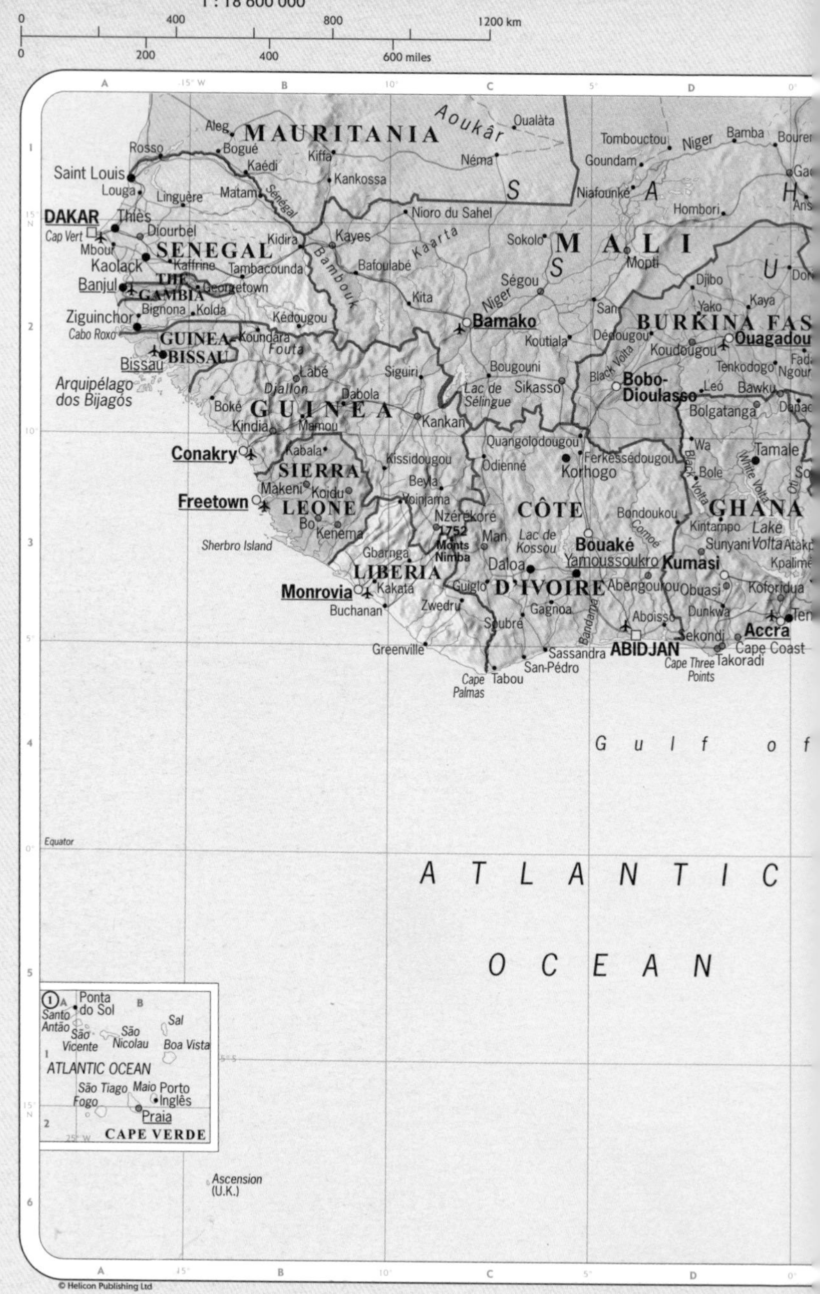

1 : 18 600 000
0
400
800
1200 km
0
200
400
600 miles
MAURITANIA
Aoukâr
Oualâta
Aleg
Rosso
Bogué
Kiffa
Kaédi
Néma
Kankossa
Saint Louis
Louga
Linguère
Matam
Sénégal
DAKAR
Thiès
Cap Vert
Diourbel
Mbour
SENEGAL
Kaolack
Kaffrine
Kidira
Tambacounda
Kayes
Bafoulabé
Bambouk
Kaarta
Nioro du Sahel
Banjul
THE GAMBIA
Georgetown
Bignona
Kolda
Ziguinchor
Cabo Roxo
Kédougou
Kita
GUINEA-BISSAU
Bissau
Koundara
Fouta Djallon
Labé
Arquipélago dos Bijagós
Boké
GUINEA
Dabola
Kindia
Mamou
Siguiri
Kankan
Conakry
Kabala
SIERRA LEONE
Makeni
Koidu
Freetown
Bo
Kenema
Sherbro Island
Kissidougou
Beyla
Voinjama
Nzérékoré
1752
Monts Nimba
Gbarnga
LIBERIA
Monrovia
Kakata
Buchanan
Zwedru
Greenville
Guiglo
Man
Cape Palmas
Tabou
Tombouctou
Niger
Bamba
Goundam
Niafounké
Hombori
S A H
Sokolo
M A L I
Mopti
Ségou
Niger
Bamako
San
Koutiala
Bougouni
Sikasso
Lac de Sélingue
Djibo
Yako
Kaya
BURKINA FAS
Ouagadou
Dédougou
Koudougou
Tenkodogo
Black Volta
Bobo-Dioulasso
Léo
Bawku
Bolgatanga
Quangolodougou
Ferkessédougou
Odienné
Korhogo
Wa
Tamale
Bole
White Volta
Black Volta
CÔTE D'IVOIRE
Lac de Kossou
Bouaké
Yamoussoukro
Bondoukou
Comoé
Daloa
Gagnoa
Soubré
Bandama
Abengourou
Aboisso
Sassandra
San-Pédro
ABIDJAN
GHANA
Kintampo
Lake Volta
Sunyani
Kumasi
Obuasi
Koforidua
Dunkwa
Sekondi
Accra
Cape Coast
Takoradi
Cape Three Points
Gulf of
ATLANTIC OCEAN
Equator
Ponta do Sol
Santo Antão
São Vicente
São Nicolau
Sal
Boa Vista
ATLANTIC OCEAN
São Tiago
Maio
Porto Inglês
Fogo
Praia
CAPE VERDE
Ascension (U.K.)
© Helicon Publishing Ltd

124 125

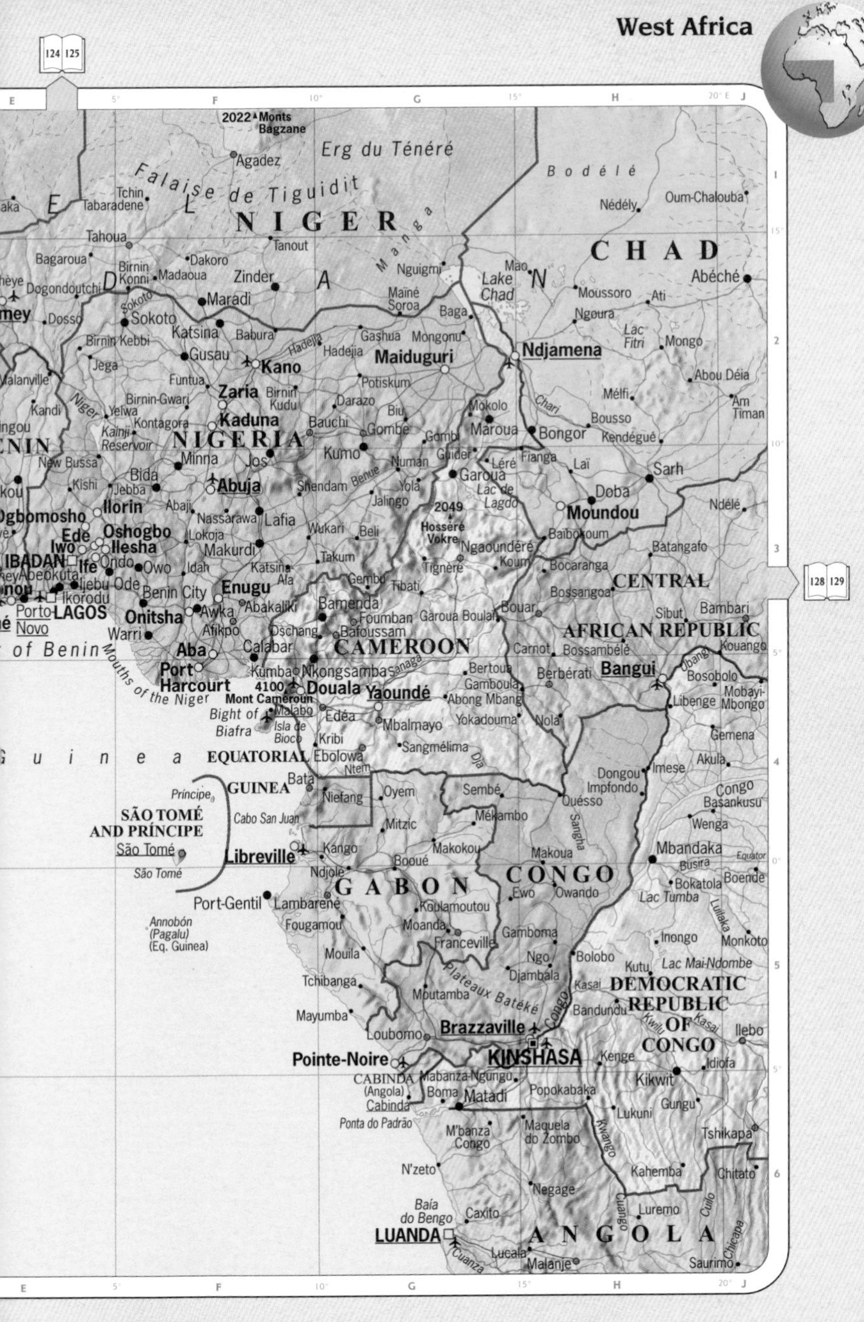

128 129

Central Africa

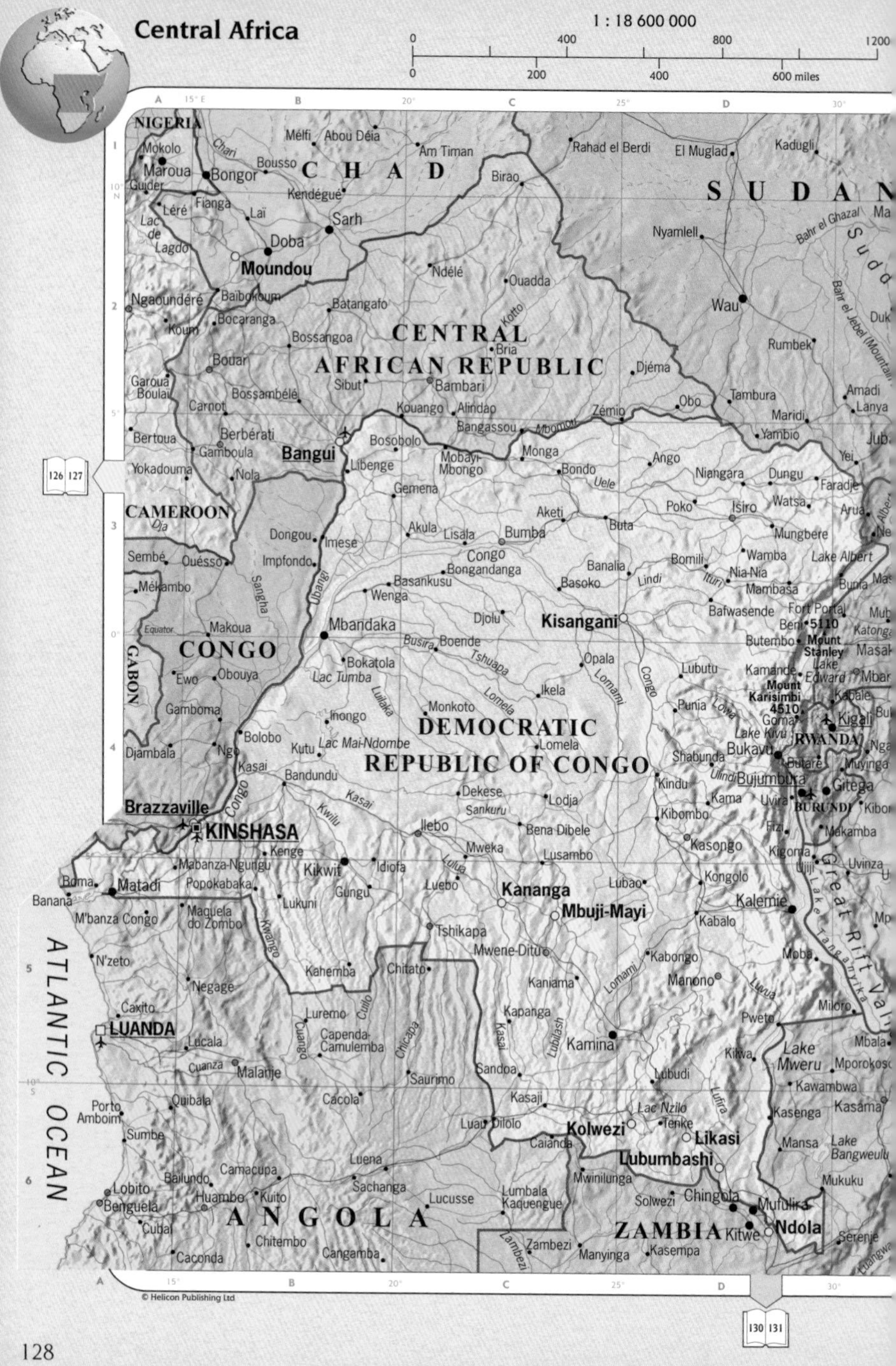

126 127

130 131

122 123

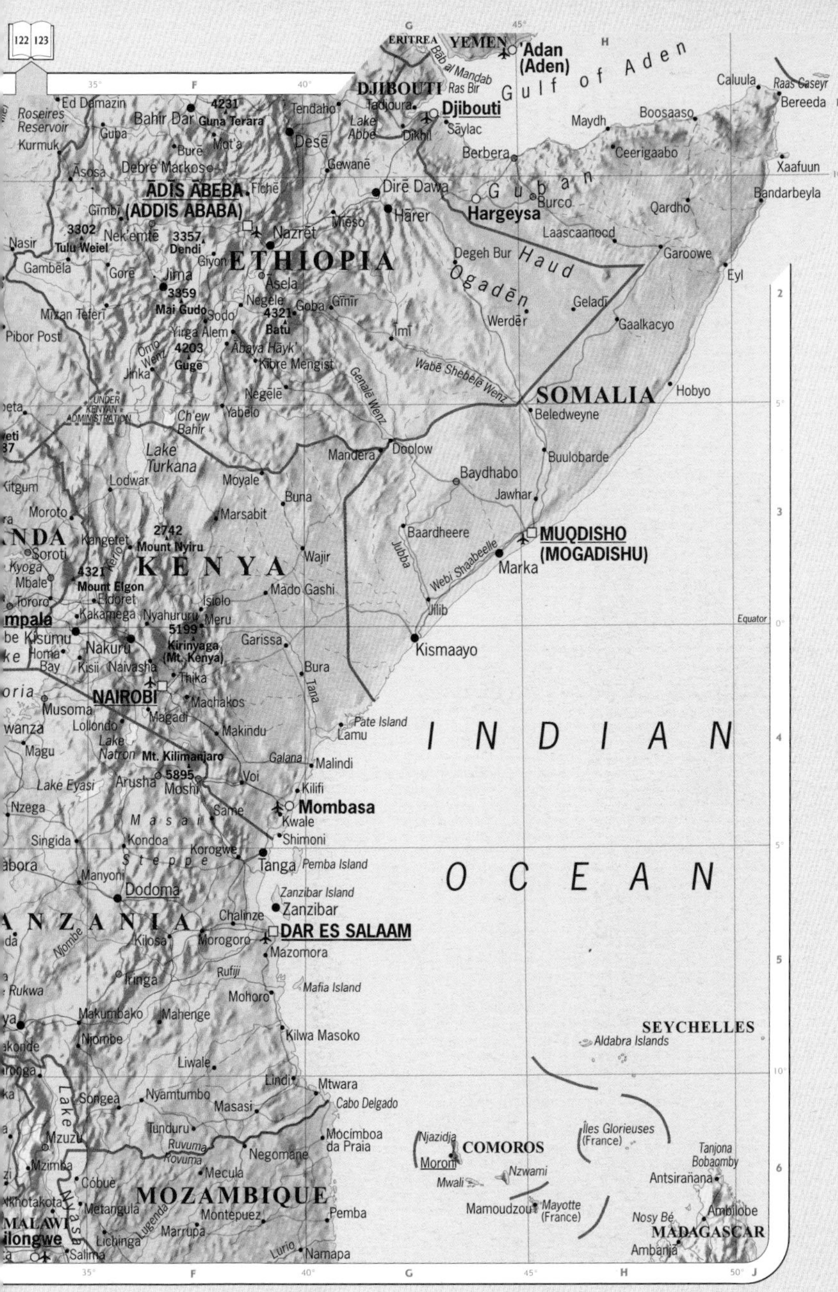
ETHIOPIA
SOMALIA
KENYA
DJIBOUTI
YEMEN
ERITREA
MOZAMBIQUE
COMOROS
SEYCHELLES
MADAGASCAR
MALAWI
INDIAN
OCEAN
Gulf of Aden
ĀDĪS ĀBEBA
(ADDIS ABABA)
MUQDISHO
(MOGADISHU)
NAIROBI
DAR ES SALAAM
Djibouti
'Adan
(Aden)
Hargeysa
Mombasa
Zanzibar
Dodoma
Kismaayo
Marka
Berbera
Boosaaso
Bereeda
Caluula
Raas Caseyr
Xaafuun
Bandarbeyla
Qardho
Garoowe
Eyl
Gaalkacyo
Hobyo
Beledweyne
Buulobarde
Jawhar
Baydhabo
Baardheere
Jilib
Doolow
Mandera
Dirē Dawa
Hārer
Nazrēt
Desē
Bahir Dar
Jīma
Gambēla
Lake Turkana
Moyale
Marsabit
Wajir
Garissa
Lamu
Malindi
Kilifi
Tanga
Mt. Kilimanjaro
5895
Moshi
Arusha
Nakuru
Kisumu
Kampala
Eldoret
Mount Elgon
Kirinyaga
(Mt. Kenya)
5199
Pemba Island
Zanzibar Island
Mafia Island
Kilwa Masoko
Lindi
Mtwara
Cabo Delgado
Mocímboa
da Praia
Pemba
Aldabra Islands
Îles Glorieuses
(France)
Njazidja
Moroni
Nzwani
Mwali
Mamoudzou
Mayotte
(France)
Antsirañana
Nosy Bé
Ambanja
Ambilobe
Equator
Laascaanood
Burco
Guban
Haud
Ogadēn
Wabē Shebelē Wenz
Webi Shaabeelle
Jubba
Tana
Pate Island
Lake Natron
Lake Eyasi
Masai Steppe
Morogoro
Iringa
Songea
Lake Nyasa
Mzuzu
Lilongwe

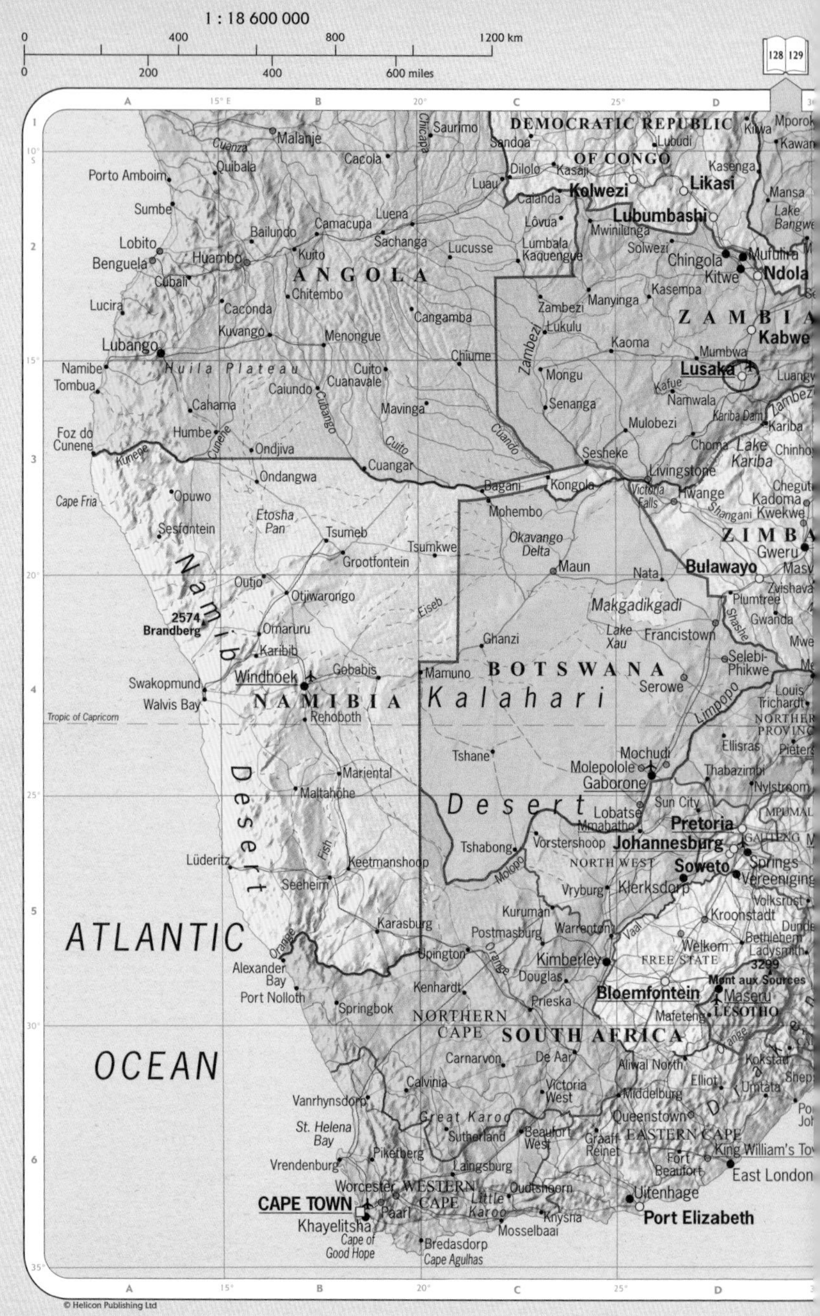

1 : 18 600 000
0
400
800
1200 km
0
200
400
600 miles
128 129
A
15° E
B
20°
C
25°
D
10°
15°
20°
25°
30°
35°
1
2
3
4
5
6
DEMOCRATIC REPUBLIC
OF CONGO
ANGOLA
ZAMBIA
ZIMBA
BOTSWANA
NAMIBIA
SOUTH AFRICA
LESOTHO
ATLANTIC
OCEAN
Namib Desert
Kalahari Desert
Huila Plateau
Etosha Pan
Okavango Delta
Makgadikgadi
Lake Xau
Lake Kariba
Lake Bangweulu
Great Karoo
Little Karoo
Tropic of Capricorn
Cape Fria
Cape of Good Hope
Cape Agulhas
St. Helena Bay
Cuanza
Chicapa
Kasaji
Zambezi
Kunene
Cunene
Cubango
Cuito
Cuando
Kafue
Shangani
Shashe
Limpopo
Eiseb
Fish
Molopo
Orange
Vaal
Malanje
Saurimo
Sandoa
Lubudi
Kilwa
Mporokoso
Kawambwa
Porto Amboim
Quibala
Cacola
Dilolo
Kasenga
Luau
Calanda
Kolwezi
Likasi
Mansa
Sumbe
Luena
Lubumbashi
Lobito
Bailundo
Camacupa
Lôvua
Mwinilunga
Benguela
Huambo
Kuito
Sachanga
Lucusse
Lumbala Kaquengue
Solwezi
Chingola
Mufulira
Kitwe
Ndola
Cubal
Chitembo
Kasempa
Lucira
Caconda
Zambezi
Manyinga
Cangamba
Lukulu
Kabwe
Kuvango
Menongue
Kaoma
Lubango
Chiume
Mumbwa
Namibe
Cuito Cuanavale
Mongu
Lusaka
Tombua
Caiundo
Cahama
Mavinga
Senanga
Namwala
Kariba Dam
Kariba
Foz do Cunene
Humbe
Mulobezi
Ondjiva
Sesheke
Choma
Chinhoyi
Cuangar
Livingstone
Ondangwa
Bagani
Kongola
Victoria Falls
Hwange
Chegutu
Kadoma
Kwekwe
Opuwo
Mohembo
Sesfontein
Tsumeb
Tsumkwe
Gweru
Grootfontein
Maun
Nata
Bulawayo
Masvingo
Outjo
Otjiwarongo
Zvishavane
Plumtree
Gwanda
2574
Brandberg
Omaruru
Ghanzi
Francistown
Karibib
Selebi-Phikwe
Windhoek
Gobabis
Mamuno
Swakopmund
Serowe
Louis Trichardt
Walvis Bay
Rehoboth
NORTHERN PROVINCE
Tshane
Mochudi
Ellisras
Molepolole
Gaborone
Thabazimbi
Mariental
Maltahöhe
Nylstroom
Lobatse
Sun City
Mmabatho
Pretoria
MPUMALANGA
GAUTENG
Tshabong
Vorstershoop
Johannesburg
NORTH WEST
Springs
Lüderitz
Keetmanshoop
Soweto
Vereeniging
Seeheim
Vryburg
Klerksdorp
Volksrust
Kuruman
Kroonstadt
Karasburg
Warrenton
Postmasburg
Welkom
Bethlehem
Upington
Kimberley
FREE STATE
Ladysmith
Alexander Bay
Douglas
3299
Mont aux Sources
Kenhardt
Bloemfontein
Maseru
Port Nolloth
Springbok
Prieska
Mafeteng
NORTHERN CAPE
Carnarvon
De Aar
Aliwal North
Kokstad
Elliot
Umtata
Calvinia
Victoria West
Middelburg
Vanrhynsdorp
Queenstown
Sutherland
Beaufort West
Graaff-Reinet
EASTERN CAPE
King William's Town
Piketberg
Fort Beaufort
Vrendenburg
Laingsburg
East London
Worcester
WESTERN CAPE
Oudtshoorn
Uitenhage
CAPE TOWN
Paarl
Knysna
Port Elizabeth
Khayelitsha
Mosselbaai
Bredasdorp

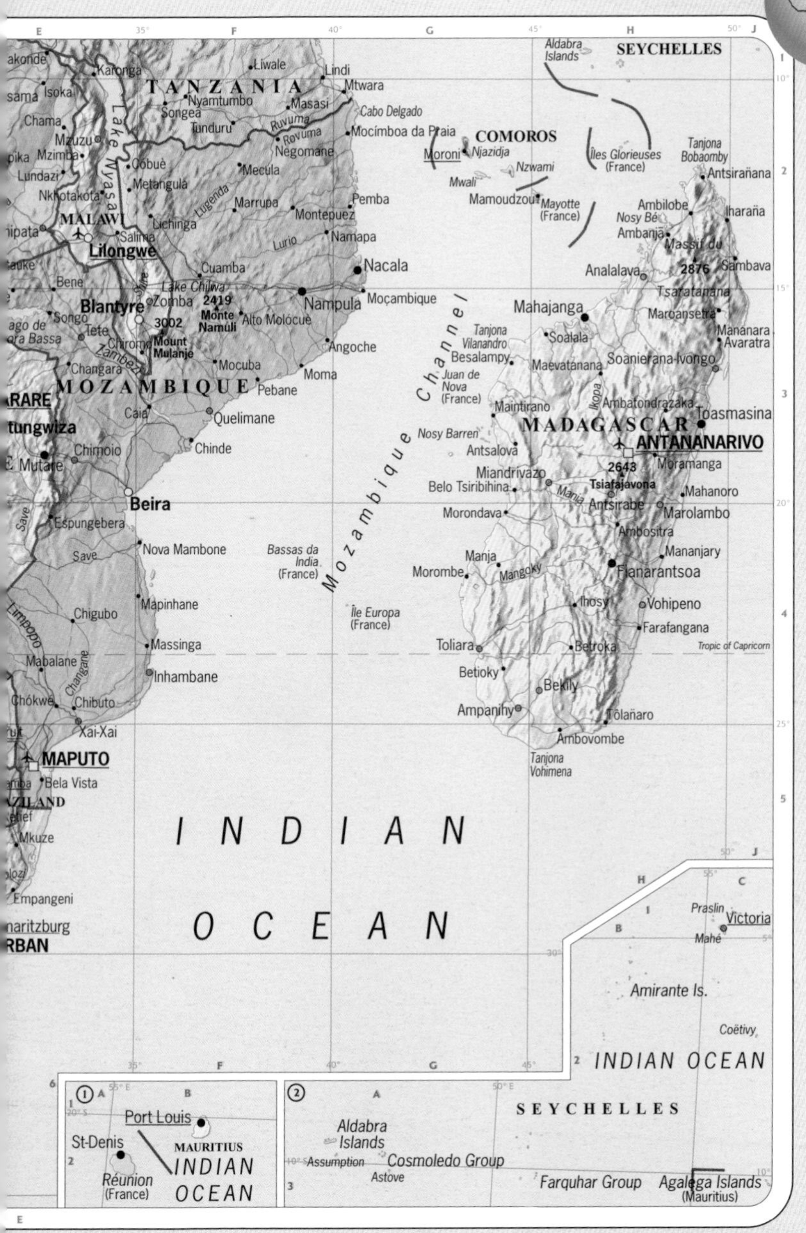

SEYCHELLES
Aldabra Islands
TANZANIA
Liwale
Lindi
Mtwara
Karonga
Isoka
Nyamtumbo
Songea
Masasi
Tunduru
Ruvuma
Cabo Delgado
Mocímboa da Praia
Negomane
Chama
Mzuzu
Mzimba
Lundazi
Nkhotakota
Lake Nyasa
Cóbuè
Metangula
Mecula
COMOROS
Moroni
Njazidja
Nzwani
Mwali
Mamoudzou
Mayotte (France)
Îles Glorieuses (France)
Tanjona Bobaomby
Antsirañana
Ambilobe
Nosy Bé
Ambanja
Iharaña
Massif du
2876
Sambava
Analalava
Tsaratanana
MALAWI
Lilongwe
Salima
Lichinga
Lugenda
Marrupa
Montepuez
Pemba
Namapa
Lurio
Nacala
Cuamba
Lake Chilwa
Zomba
2419
Monte Namúli
Alto Molócuè
Nampula
Moçambique
Blantyre
3002
Mount Mulanje
Bene
Songo
Tete
Chiromo
Zambezi
Changara
Mocuba
Angoche
Moma
Pebane
MOZAMBIQUE
Mozambique Channel
Tanjona Vilanandro
Besalampy
Juan de Nova (France)
Mahajanga
Soalala
Maevatanana
Maroansetra
Mananara
Avaratra
Soanierana-Ivongo
Ikopa
Ambatondrazaka
Toamasina
Maintirano
MADAGASCAR
ANTANANARIVO
Moramanga
2643
Tsiafajavona
Antsirabe
Mania
Mahanoro
Marolambo
Ambositra
Mananjary
Fianarantsoa
Vohipeno
Farafangana
Ihosy
Betroka
Tropic of Capricorn
Nosy Barren
Antsalova
Miandrivazo
Belo Tsiribihina
Morondava
Manja
Mangoky
Morombe
Toliara
Betioky
Bekily
Ampanihy
Tôlañaro
Ambovombe
Tanjona Vohimena
Île Europa (France)
Bassas da India (France)
Caia
Quelimane
Chinde
Chimoio
Mutare
Beira
Save
Espungebera
Nova Mambone
Limpopo
Chigubo
Mapinhane
Massinga
Inhambane
Mabalane
Changane
Chókwè
Chibuto
Xai-Xai
MAPUTO
Bela Vista
Mkuze
Empangeni
INDIAN OCEAN
Praslin
Victoria
Mahé
Amirante Is.
Coëtivy
INDIAN OCEAN
Port Louis
St-Denis
MAURITIUS
Réunion (France)
INDIAN OCEAN
SEYCHELLES
Aldabra Islands
Assumption
Cosmoledo Group
Astove
Farquhar Group
Agalega Islands (Mauritius)

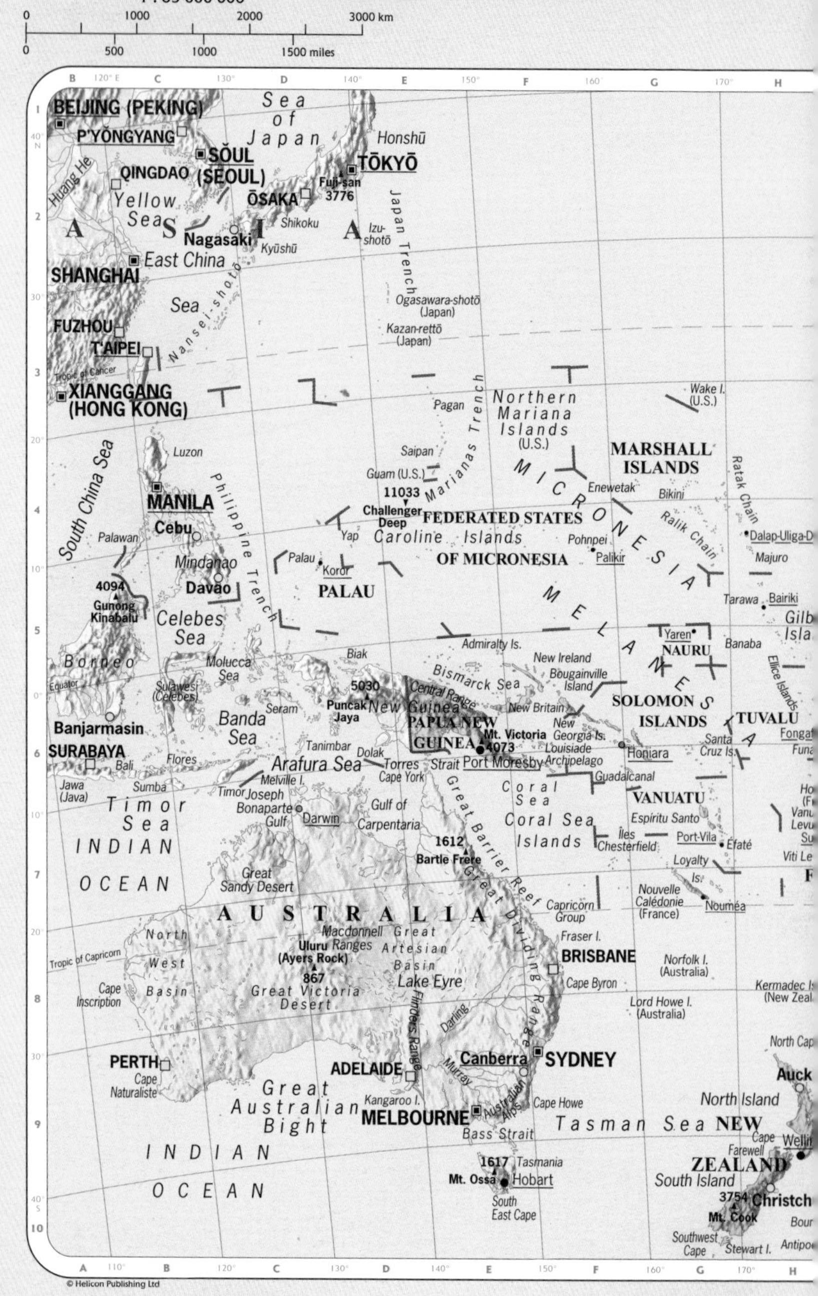
1 : 65 000 000
0 1000 2000 3000 km
0 500 1000 1500 miles
BEIJING (PEKING)
P'YŎNGYANG
SŎUL (SEOUL)
QINGDAO
Huang He
Yellow Sea
Sea of Japan
Honshū
TŌKYŌ
Fuji-san 3776
ŌSAKA
Shikoku
Nagasaki
Kyūshū
Izu-shotō
Japan Trench
A S I A
East China Sea
SHANGHAI
Nansei-shotō
Ogasawara-shotō (Japan)
Kazan-rettō (Japan)
FUZHOU
T'AIPEI
Tropic of Cancer
XIANGGANG (HONG KONG)
Pagan
Northern Mariana Islands (U.S.)
Marianas Trench
Saipan
Guam (U.S.)
11033 Challenger Deep
Wake I. (U.S.)
MARSHALL ISLANDS
Enewetak
Bikini
Ralik Chain
Ratak Chain
Dalap-Uliga-D
Majuro
MICRONESIA
FEDERATED STATES OF MICRONESIA
Caroline Islands
Pohnpei
Palikir
Yap
Palau
Koror
PALAU
South China Sea
Luzon
MANILA
Philippine Trench
Palawan
Cebu
Mindanao
Davao
4094 Gunong Kinabalu
Celebes Sea
Borneo
Equator
Molucca Sea
Sulawesi (Celebes)
Biak
5030 Puncak Jaya
New Guinea
Central Range
PAPUA NEW GUINEA
Mt. Victoria 4073
Port Moresby
Admiralty Is.
Bismarck Sea
New Ireland
Bougainville Island
New Britain
New Georgia Is.
Louisiade Archipelago
Honiara
SOLOMON ISLANDS
Guadalcanal
MELANESIA
Tarawa
Bairiki
Yaren
NAURU
Banaba
Ellice Islands
TUVALU
Santa Cruz Is.
Banjarmasin
SURABAYA
Seram
Banda Sea
Tanimbar
Dolak
Torres Strait
Bali
Flores
Arafura Sea
Cape York
Jawa (Java)
Sumba
Melville I.
Timor
Joseph Bonaparte Gulf
Darwin
Gulf of Carpentaria
Timor Sea
INDIAN OCEAN
Coral Sea
Coral Sea Islands
VANUATU
Espíritu Santo
Îles Chesterfield
Port-Vila
Éfaté
Loyalty Is.
1612 Bartle Frere
Great Barrier Reef
Great Sandy Desert
AUSTRALIA
Great Dividing Range
Capricorn Group
Nouvelle Calédonie (France)
Nouméa
North West Basin
Macdonnell Ranges
Great Artesian Basin
Uluru (Ayers Rock) 867
Fraser I.
BRISBANE
Tropic of Capricorn
Norfolk I. (Australia)
Cape Inscription
Great Victoria Desert
Lake Eyre
Cape Byron
Lord Howe I. (Australia)
Kermadec Is. (New Zeal
Darling
Flinders Ranges
North Cap
PERTH
Cape Naturaliste
ADELAIDE
Murray
Canberra
SYDNEY
Great Australian Bight
Kangaroo I.
MELBOURNE
Australian Alps
Cape Howe
Bass Strait
Tasman Sea
North Island
NEW ZEALAND
Cape Farewell
1617 Tasmania
Mt. Ossa
Hobart
South East Cape
South Island
3754 Mt. Cook
Southwest Cape
Stewart I.
Antipo
© Helicon Publishing Ltd

NORTH AMERICA
LOS ANGELES
SAN DIEGO
Guadalupe (Mexico)
Tropic of Cancer
Is. Revillagigedo (Mexico)
PACIFIC
OCEAN
HAWAII (U.S.)
Hawaiian Islands
Necker I.
Oahu
Honolulu
Hawaii
N.W. Christmas Island Ridge
Johnston I. (U.S.)
Palmyra I. (U.S.)
Line Islands
Kiritimati
Howland (U.S.)
Baker (U.S.)
Jarvis (U.S.)
Phoenix Islands
KIRIBATI
Starbuck I.
POLYNESIA
Equator
Tokelau (New Zealand)
Tongareva
Danger Is.
Caroline I.
Marquesas Islands
Vostok I.
Flint I.
SAMOA
American Samoa
Apia
Upolu
Cook Islands (New Zealand)
Îles Palliser
Archipel des Tuamotu
Îles de Désappointement
TONGA
Niue (New Zealand)
Palmerston I.
Arch. de la Société
Tahiti
Rarotonga
French Polynesia
Tonga Trench
Tubuai
Mururoa
Gambier Is.
Tubuai Islands
Rapa
Oeno
Henderson I.
Ducie I.
Pitcairn Is. (U.K.)
Tropic of Capricorn
Easter I. (Chile)
Kermadec Trench
South West Pacific Basin
Chatham Is. (New Zealand)

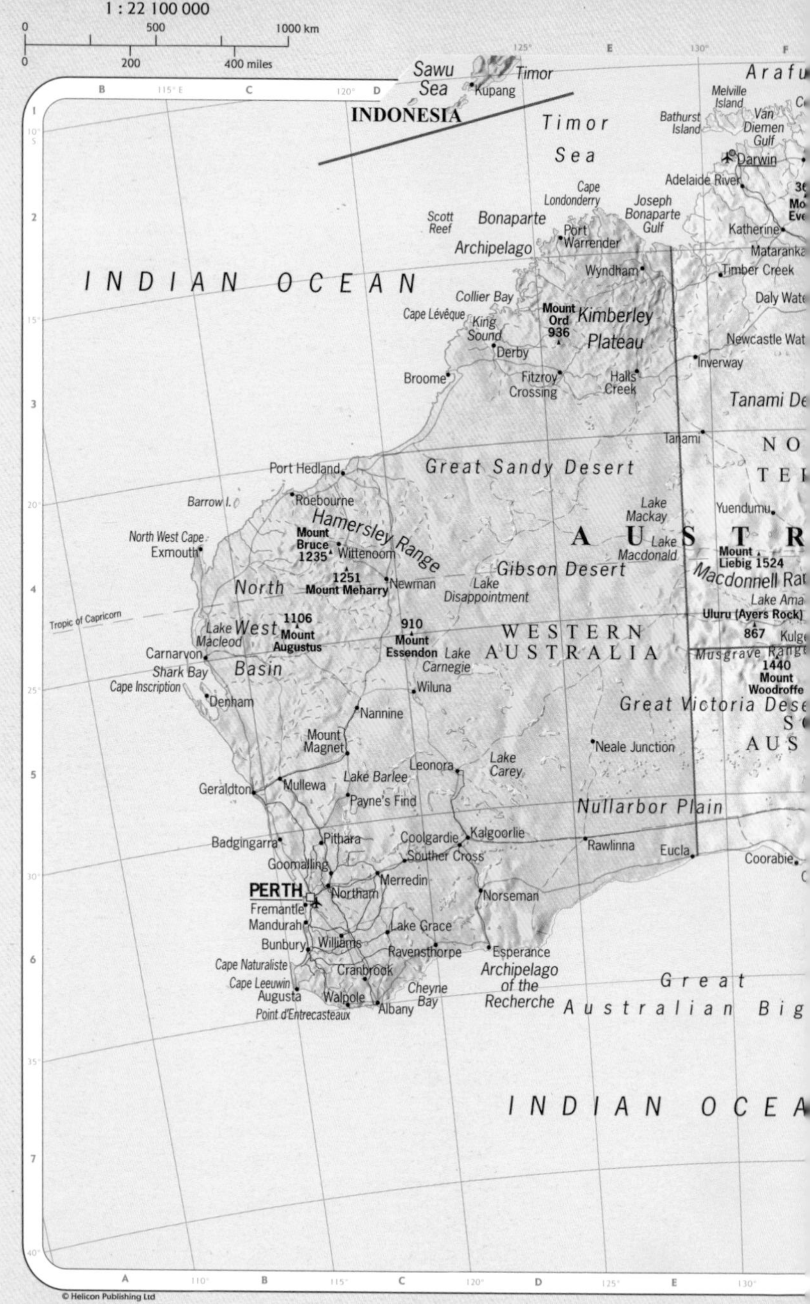
1 : 22 100 000
0 500 1000 km
0 200 400 miles
Sawu Sea
Timor
Kupang
INDONESIA
Timor Sea
Arafu
Melville Island
Bathurst Island
Van Diemen Gulf
Darwin
Adelaide River
Cape Londonderry
Joseph Bonaparte Gulf
Scott Reef
Bonaparte Archipelago
Port Warrender
Katherine
Mataranka
Wyndham
Timber Creek
INDIAN OCEAN
Collier Bay
Daly Wate
Cape Lévêque
King Sound
Mount Ord 936
Kimberley Plateau
Newcastle Wat
Derby
Inverway
Broome
Fitzroy Crossing
Halls Creek
Tanami De
Tanami
Port Hedland
Great Sandy Desert
Barrow I.
Roebourne
Lake Mackay
Yuendumu
Hamersley Range
North West Cape
Exmouth
Mount Bruce 1235
Wittenoom
A U S T R
Lake Macdonald
Mount Liebig 1524
1251 Mount Meharry
Newman
Gibson Desert
Lake Disappointment
Macdonnell Ra
Lake Ama
North West Basin
Tropic of Capricorn
1106 Mount Augustus
Uluru (Ayers Rock) 867
Lake Macleod
910 Mount Essendon
WESTERN AUSTRALIA
Kulg
Carnarvon
Lake Carnegie
Musgrave Range
1440 Mount Woodroffe
Shark Bay
Cape Inscription
Wiluna
Denham
Great Victoria Dese
Nannine
Mount Magnet
Neale Junction
Leonora
Lake Carey
Geraldton
Mullewa
Lake Barlee
Payne's Find
Nullarbor Plain
Badgingarra
Pithara
Coolgardie
Kalgoorlie
Goomalling
Southern Cross
Rawlinna
Eucla
Coorabie
Merredin
PERTH
Northam
Norseman
Fremantle
Mandurah
Lake Grace
Bunbury
Williams
Ravensthorpe
Esperance
Cape Naturaliste
Cranbrook
Archipelago of the Recherche
Cape Leeuwin
Augusta
Walpole
Cheyne Bay
Albany
Point d'Entrecasteaux
Great Australian Big
INDIAN OCEA
© Helicon Publishing Ltd

110 111
Port Moresby
PAPUA NEW GUINEA
Moa (Banks Island)
Torres Strait
Cape York
Bamaga
Cape York Peninsula
Weipa
Aurukun
Cape Wessel
Wessel Islands
Cape Arnhem
Nhulunbuy
Groote Eylandt
Numbulwar
Gulf of Carpentaria
Wellesley Islands
Louisiade Archipelago
CORAL SEA ISLANDS
CORAL SEA
TERRITORY
(Australia)
Cape Melville
Cape Flattery
Laura
Cooktown
Dunbar
GREAT BARRIER REEF
Cairns
Mareeba
1612 Mount Bartle Frere
Innisfail
Mount Garnet
Flinders Reefs
Willis Group
Diamond Islets
Tregosse Islets
Karumba
Normanton
Barkly Tableland
Lorraine
Greenvale
Ingham
Townsville
Ayr
Bowen
The Whitsundays
Repulse Bay
Mackay
Sarina
Clairview
PACIFIC
OCEAN
Swain Reefs
Camooweal
Mount Isa
Richmond
Charters Towers
QUEENSLAND
GREAT DIVIDING RANGE
Tobermorey
Winton
Boulia
Great Artesian Basin
Clermont
Emerald
Rockhampton
Curtis I.
Gladstone
Tropic of Capricorn
Barcaldine
Springsure
Banana
Bundaberg
Sandy Cape
Hervey Bay
Fraser I.
Maryborough
Simpson Desert
Birdsville
Windorah
Augathella
Charleville
Gayndah
Gympie
Kingaroy
Roma
Miles
Muckadilla
Quilpie
Lake Eyre Basin
Sturt Stony Desert
Oodnadatta
Lake Eyre North
Lake Eyre South
Saint George
Dalby
BRISBANE
Beenleigh
Gold Coast
Toowoomba
Grey Range
Cunnamulla
Hungerford
Dirranbandi
Goondiwindi
Tibbooburra
Marree
Moree
Casino
Cape Byron
Ballina
Brewarrina
Bourke
Glenn Innes
Walgett
Narrabi
Round Mountain
1608
Grafton
Armidale
Coffs Harbour
Lake Torrens
Lake Frome
Flinders Ranges
Lake Gairdner
Pimba
Broken Hill
Wilcannia
Darling
Nyngan
Gunnedah
Tamworth
Hawker
Port Augusta
NEW SOUTH WALES
Gilgandra
Port Macquarie
Whyalla
Kyancutta
Orroroo
Murray River
Dubbo
Taree
Lord Howe I.
Cowell
Port Pirie
Ivanhoe
Condobolin
Orange
Cessnock
Newcastle
Eyre Pen.
Morgan
Wentworth
Goolgowi
Marsden
Bathurst
Lithgow
Spencer Gulf
Gawler
Renmark
Murray Basin
Balranald
Hay
Cowra
SYDNEY
ADELAIDE
Ouyen
Swan Hill
Narrandera
Cootamundra
Wollongong
Murray Bridge
Deniliquin
Wagga Wagga
Nowra
Kingscote
Victor Harbor
Canberra
Kangaroo I.
A.C.T.
Batemans Bay
Border Town
VICTORIA
Albury
Shepparton
2230
Cooma
Lacepede Bay
Horsham
Seymour
Mount Kosciuszko
Robe
Ballarat
Eden
Mount Gambier
MELBOURNE
Cape Howe
Portland
Geelong
Morwell
Bairnsdale
Cape Nelson
Warrnambool
Sale
Port Albert
Walkerville
Wilson's Promontory
136 137
King Island
Bass Strait
Flinders I.
Furneaux Group
Whitemark
Cape Grim
TASMAN SEA
Burnie
George Town
TASMANIA
Devonport
1617
Launceston
Queenstown
Mount Ossa
Swansea
A.C.T. = Australian Capital Territory
Hobart
Port Arthur
Dover
South East Cape

1 : 7 400 000
0
100
200
400 km
0
200 miles
P A C I F I C
O C E A N
T A S M A N
S E A
NORTH ISLAND
NEW ZEALAND
Three Kings Island
Cape Reinga
North Cape
Te Hapua
Great Exhibition Bay
Mangonui
Bay of Islands
Kaitaia
Tauroa Point
Kaikohe
Kawakawa
Omapere
Pakotai
Whangarei
Dargaville
Paparoa
Little Barrier Island
Great Barrier Island
Port Fitzroy
Ruawai
Wellsford
Kaipara Harbour
Hauraki Gulf
Cape Colville
Mercury Islands
Helensville
Waiheke I.
Coromandel
Takapuna
Auckland
Manukau
Coromandel Peninsula
Manukau Harbour
Firth of Thames
Papakura
Mayor Island
Waiuku
Waitakaruru
Paeroa
Waihi
White Island
Huntly
Mount Maunganui
Bay of Plenty
Hamilton
Tauranga
Raglan
Cambridge
Te Araroa
East Cape
Te Awamutu
Putaruru
Whakatane
1754
Ruatoria
Kawhia
Rotorua
Lake Rotorua
Opotiki
Hikurangi
Otorohanga
Tokoroa
North Taranaki
Te Kuiti
Waikato
Atiamuri
Matawai
Raukumara Range
Tolaga Bay
Murupara
Mokau
Bight
Taupo
Gisborne
Ohura
Taumarunui
Waikaremoana
Lake Taupo
Waitara
New Plymouth
Wanganui
Turangi
Wairoa
Nuhaka
Okato
Mt. Egmont
1727
Te Haroto
Cape Egmont
National Park
2797
Makorako
Hawke Bay
Mahia Peninsula
2518
Ruapehu
Bay View
Opunake
Raetihi
Waiouru
Napier
South Taranaki Bight
Hawera
Taihape
Hastings
Havelock North
Wanganui
Mangaweka
Marton
1733
Waipukurau
Feilding
Ruahine Range
Pourerere
Palmerston North
Dannevirke
Woodville
Cape Farewell
Pahiatua
Weber
Paturau River
Golden Bay
D'Urville Island
Cook
Levin
Cape Turnagain
Otaki
© Helicon Publishing Ltd
134
135

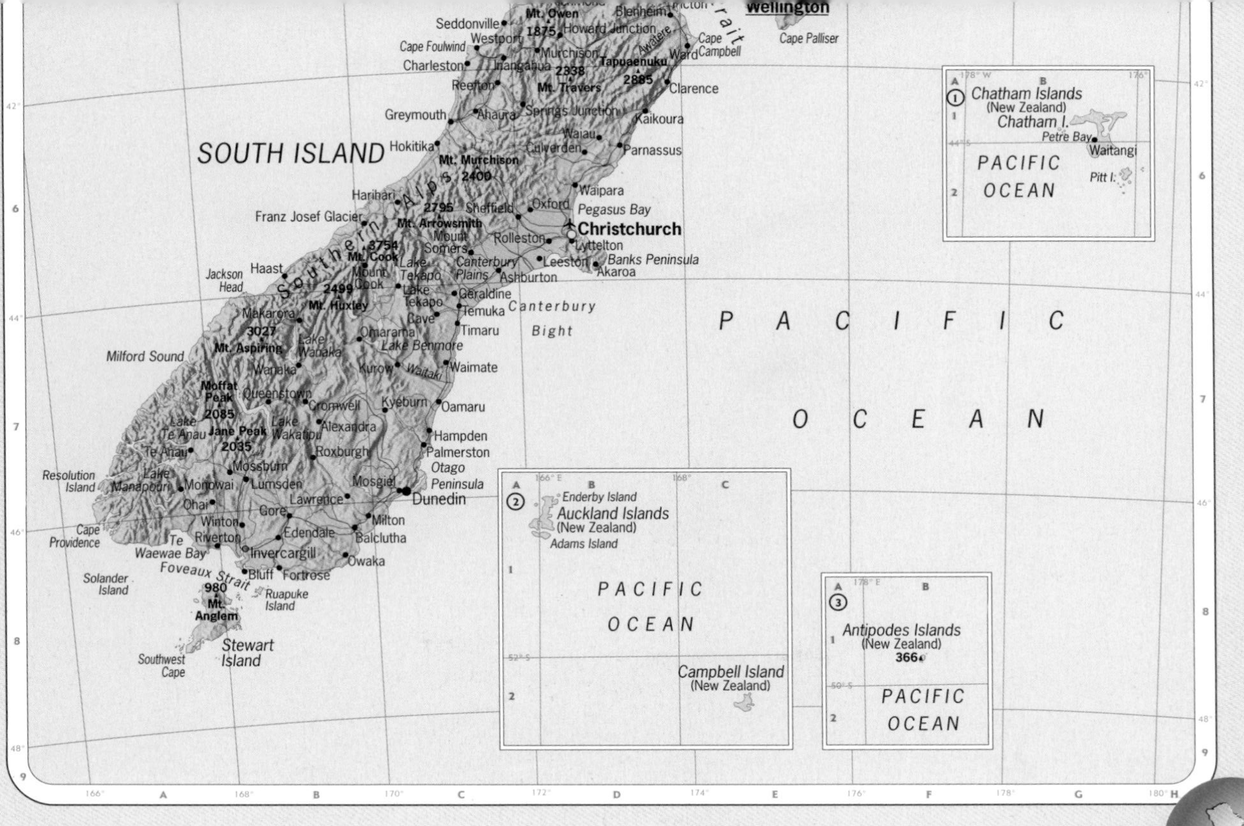
SOUTH ISLAND
PACIFIC OCEAN
Wellington
Cape Palliser
Strait
Cape Campbell
Ward
Awatere
Blenheim
Howard Junction
Mt. Owen 1875
Seddonville
Westport
Cape Foulwind
Charleston
Inangahua
Murchison
2338
Mt. Travers
Tapuaenuku 2885
Clarence
Reefton
Ahaura
Springs Junction
Greymouth
Kaikoura
Waiau
Culverden
Parnassus
Hokitika
Mt. Murchison 2400
Southern Alps
Harihari
2795
Mt. Arrowsmith
Sheffield
Oxford
Waipara
Pegasus Bay
Christchurch
Lyttelton
Rolleston
Franz Josef Glacier
Mount Somers
3754
Mt. Cook
Canterbury Plains
Leeston
Banks Peninsula
Akaroa
Ashburton
Haast
Jackson Head
Mount Cook
Lake Tekapo
Tekapo
2499
Mt. Huxley
Geraldine
Temuka
Cave
Timaru
Canterbury Bight
Makarora
3027
Mt. Aspiring
Lake Wanaka
Omarama
Lake Benmore
Milford Sound
Wanaka
Kurow
Waitaki
Waimate
Moffat Peak 2085
Queenstown
Cromwell
Kyeburn
Oamaru
Lake Te Anau
Lake Wakatipu
Alexandra
Jane Peak 2035
Te Anau
Roxburgh
Hampden
Palmerston
Otago Peninsula
Resolution Island
Lake Manapouri
Mossburn
Monowai
Lumsden
Mosgiel
Dunedin
Ohai
Lawrence
Gore
Winton
Milton
Cape Providence
Te Waewae Bay
Riverton
Edendale
Balclutha
Invercargill
Owaka
Foveaux Strait
Bluff
Fortrose
Solander Island
980
Mt. Anglem
Ruapuke Island
Stewart Island
Southwest Cape
① Chatham Islands (New Zealand)
Chatham I.
Petre Bay
Waitangi
Pitt I.
PACIFIC OCEAN
② Enderby Island
Auckland Islands (New Zealand)
Adams Island
PACIFIC OCEAN
Campbell Island (New Zealand)
③ Antipodes Islands (New Zealand)
366
PACIFIC OCEAN

1 : 55 700 000
0
1000
2000
3000 km
500
1500 miles
ASIA
RUSSIA
East Siberian Sea
ARCTIC OCEAN
North Pole
Wandel Sea
Svalbard (Spitzbergen) (Norway)
Greenland Sea
NORWAY
Shetland Is. (U.K.)
Faeroes (Denmark)
Jan Mayen (Norway)
Arctic Circle
Bering Sea
O. Vrangelya
International Date Line
St. Lawrence I.
Bering Strait
Point Hope
Point Barrow
St. Matthew I.
Norton Sound
Nunivak I.
Yukon
ALASKA (U.S.)
Brooks Range
Aleutian Islands
Aleutian Trench
Mt. McKinley 6194
Fairbanks
Anchorage
Kodiak I.
Gulf of Alaska
Mt. Logan 6059
Whitehorse
Juneau
Alexander Archipelago
Queen Charlotte Islands
Prince Rupert
Coast Mountains
Mt. Roosevelt 2972
Mackenzie Mts.
Mackenzie
Inuvik
Mt. Waddington 4042
Vancouver I.
Vancouver
Seattle
Portland
Cascade Range
Columbia
Fraser
ROCKY M
Edmonton
Calgary
Saskatchewan
Regina
Lake Winnipegosis
Winnipeg
Lake Winnipeg
Thunder Bay
Lake Nipigon
Sudbury
MONTRÉAL
Ottawa
Québec
Beaufort Sea
Prince Patrick Island
Banks Island
Melville Island
Parry Islands
Queen Elizabeth Islands
Ellesmere Island
Nares Strait
Viscount Melville Sound
Amundsen Gulf
Victoria Island
Great Bear Lake
Great Slave Lake
Yellowknife
Bathurst Inlet
Baker Lake
Boothia Pen.
Gulf of Boothia
Melville Pen.
Arctic Bay
Baffin Bay
Baffin Island
Foxe Basin
Southampton Island
Coats I.
Mansel I.
Hudson Bay
Cape Churchill
Churchill
Reindeer Lake
Nelson
Lake Athabasca
Peace
CANADA
Belcher Islands
James Bay
Fort George
Iqaluit
Hudson Strait
Péninsule d'Ungava
Ungava Bay
Schefferville
Smallwood Reservoir
Cape Dyer
Davis Strait
GREENLAND (Denmark)
Nuuk (Godthåb)
Cape Farewell
Denmark Strait
ICELAND
Reykjavík
ATLANTIC OCEAN
Labrador Sea
Cape Harrison
Newfoundland
St. John's
Cape Race
Île d'Anticosti
Gulf of St. Lawrence
St-Pierre-et-Miquelon (France)
St. Lawrence
Cape Breton I.
Nova Scotia
Halifax
Cape Sable

UNITED STATES
MEXICO
THE BAHAMAS
CUBA
JAMAICA
HAITI
DOMINICAN REPUBLIC
BELIZE
GUATEMALA
HONDURAS
EL SALVADOR
NICARAGUA
COSTA RICA
PANAMA
SOUTH AMERICA
PACIFIC OCEAN
OCEAN
Gulf of Mexico
Caribbean Sea
Greater Antilles
Lesser Antilles
Bahía de Campeche
Golfo de California
Baja California
Yucatan Channel
Yucatán
Straits of Florida
Florida Keys
Puerto Rico Trench
Sierra Madre Occidental
Sierra Madre del Sur
Great Basin
Great Salt Lake Desert
Great Salt Lake
Mojave Desert
Death Valley
Grand Canyon
Great Plains
Edwards Plateau
Appalachian Mts.
Rio Grande
Colorado
Arkansas
Missouri
Mississippi
Red
Ohio
Tennessee
Orinoco
Amazonas
Cordillera Occidental
Cordillera Central
Cordillera Oriental
Lake Erie
Tropic of Cancer
Equator
Sacramento
San Francisco
Fresno
LOS ANGELES
SAN DIEGO
Mexicali
Las Vegas
Salt Lake City
4123
4011
Denver
Albuquerque
PHOENIX
Tucson
El Paso
Ciudad Juárez
Hermosillo
Oklahoma City
Kansas City
DALLAS
Fort Worth
Austin
HOUSTON
Corpus Christi
Matamoros
MONTERREY
St. Louis
Indianapolis
Columbus
CHICAGO
DETROIT
Cleveland
Cincinnati
Nashville
Memphis
Atlanta
Charlotte
New Orleans
Mobile
Jacksonville
Tampa
Miami
Cape Canaveral
Cape Hatteras
Virginia Beach
Washington D.C.
PHILADELPHIA
NEW YORK
Bermuda (U.K.)
GUADALAJARA
León
CIUDAD DE MÉXICO
5610
Vol. Citlaltépetl
Veracruz
Acapulco
Mérida
Belmopan
GUATEMALA
San Salvador
Tegucigalpa
Managua
Lago de Nicaragua
San José
Canal de Panamá (Panama Canal)
Panamá
Punta Mariato
Cabo Gracias á Dios
Swan Is. (Honduras)
Cayman Is. (U.K.)
LA HABANA (HAVANA)
Santiago de Cuba
Nassau
Turks and Caicos Is. (U.K.)
PORT-AU-PRINCE
Kingston
SANTO DOMINGO
Puerto Rico (U.S.)
Virgin Is. (U.S.)
Virgin Is. (U.K.)
Netherlands Antilles
CARACAS
Punta Gallinas
Cristóbal Colón
5775
BARRANQUILLA
MEDELLÍN
BOGOTÁ
CALI
QUITO
6310
GUAYAQUIL
Iquitos
Chiclayo
Isla de Malpelo (Colombia)
I. de Coco (Costa Rica)
Islas Galápagos (Galapagos Is.) (Ecuador)
Clipperton Island (France)
Islas Revillagigedo (Mexico)
Cabo San Lucas
Guadalupe (Mexico)

1 : 22 100 000

0 400 800 1200 km

0 200 400 600 miles

150 151

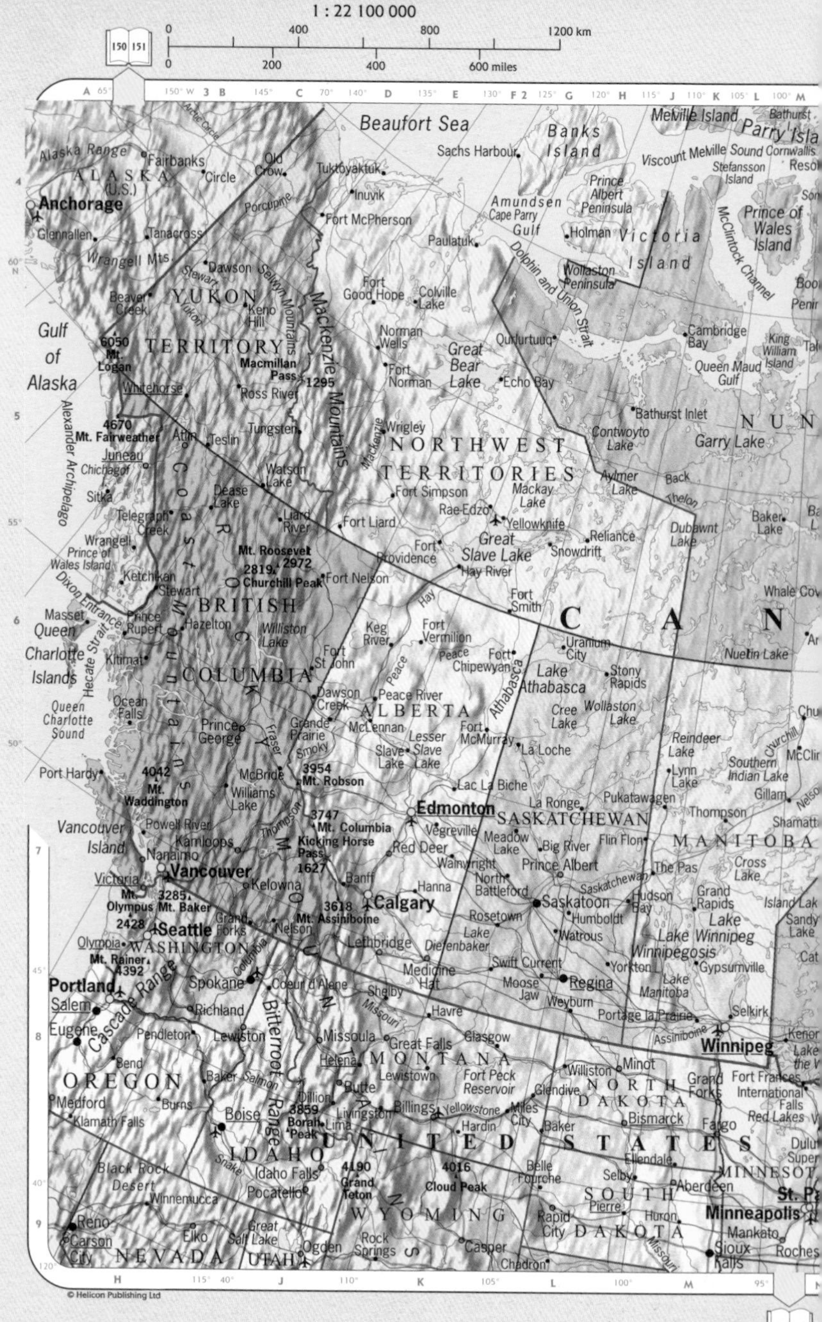

142 143

Baffin Bay
Upernavik
Uummannaq
GREENLAND (Denmark)
Ammassalik (Angmagssalik)
Qeqertsuaq (Disko)
Ilulissat (Jakobshavn)
Kangaatsiaq
Kong Frederick VI Kyst
Davis Strait
Maniitsoq (Sukkertoppen)
Nuuk (Godthåb)
Qeqertarsuatsiaat (Fiskenæsset)
Paamiut (Frederikshåb)
Nanortalik
Ivittuut
Nunap Isua (Kap Farvel)
Arctic Circle
Devon Island
Lancaster Sound
Arctic Bay
Bylot Island
Pond Inlet
Borden Peninsula
Baffin Island
Clyde River
Home Bay
Cape Dyer
Igloolik
Hall Beach
Melville Peninsula
Prince Charles Island
Nettilling Lake
Cumberland Peninsula
Pangnirtung
Cumberland Sound
Foxe Basin
Bowman Bay
Amadjuak Lake
Foxe Peninsula
Foxe Channel
Iqaluit
Frobisher Bay
Cape Dorset
Lake Harbour
Resolution Island
Southampton Island
Roes Welcome Sound
Nottingham I.
Hudson Strait
LABRADOR SEA
ATLANTIC OCEAN
Fisher Strait
Coats Island
Mansel Island
Ivujivik
Quaqtaq
Akpatok Island
Port Burwell
Ungava Bay
Péninsule d'Ungava
Kangiqsualujjuaq
Hebron
Nutak
Nain
Hopedale
Kuujjuaq
NEWFOUNDLAND
Cape Harrison
Groswater Bay
Cartwright
HUDSON BAY
Inukjuak
Lac Minto
Lac à l'Eau Claire
Schefferville
Lake Melville
Labrador
Smallwood Reservoir
Churchill Falls
Battle Harbour
Cape Bauld
St. Anthony
White Bay
Belcher Islands
Réservoir Caniapiscau
Kuujjuarapik
Fort Severn
Winisk
Cape Henrietta Maria
Rés. de La Grande 2
QUÉBEC
Labrador City
Gander
St. John's
Deer Lake
Grand Falls
Newfoundland
James Bay
Fort George
Réservoir Opinaca
Eastmain
1021
Réservoir Manicouagan
Natashquan
Stephenville
Grand Bank
Cape Race
Channel-Port aux Basques
Big Trout Lake
Attawapiskat
Akimiski Island
Charlton I.
Sept-Îles
Île d'Anticosti
Port-Menier
Gulf of St. Lawrence
Cabot Strait
St-Pierre-et-Miquelon (France)
Albany
Fort Rupert
Chute des Passes
St. Lawrence
Péninsule de Gaspé
Moosonee
Chibougamau
Réservoir Pipmuacan
Rimouski
Sydney
ONTARIO
Lac St-Jean
Chicoutimi
Bathurst
PRINCE EDWARD ISLAND
Cape Breton Island
Nakina
Hearst
Edmundston
NEW BRUNSWICK
Charlottetown
Geraldton
Kapuskasing
Cochrane
Baie St. Paul
Presque Isle
Truro
NOVA SCOTIA
Sable I.
Nipigon
Timmins
Val-d'Or
La Tuque
Fredericton
Dartmouth
Halifax
Thunder Bay
Rouyn
Réservoir Cabonga
Trois Rivières
Québec
St. John
Bay of Fundy
Kirkland Lake
Wawa
MAINE
Lake Superior
North Bay
MONTRÉAL
Sherbrooke
White Mts.
Mt. Washington 1917
Yarmouth
Cape Sable
Sault Ste. Marie
Ottawa
Sudbury
Burlington
Augusta
Marquette
Smiths Falls
Ironwood
Parry Sound
Montpelier
NEW HAMPSHIRE
Portland
Massachusetts Bay
MICHIGAN
Lake Huron
Owen Sound
Kingston
WISCONSIN
Marinette
Barrie
Oshawa
Lake Ontario
VERMONT
Concord
Green Bay
Alpena
Toronto
Syracuse
Albany
Boston
Lake Michigan
Rochester
MASS.
Cape Cod
Appleton
Hamilton
NEW YORK
Springfield
Providence
Sheboygan
Grand Rapids
Saginaw
London
Buffalo
Hartford
CONN.
RHODE ISLAND
Milwaukee
Lake Erie
Erie
Bridgeport
NEW YORK
DETROIT
Windsor
PENNSYLVANIA
Newark

1 : 24 900 000

0 400 800 1200 km

0 200 400 600 miles

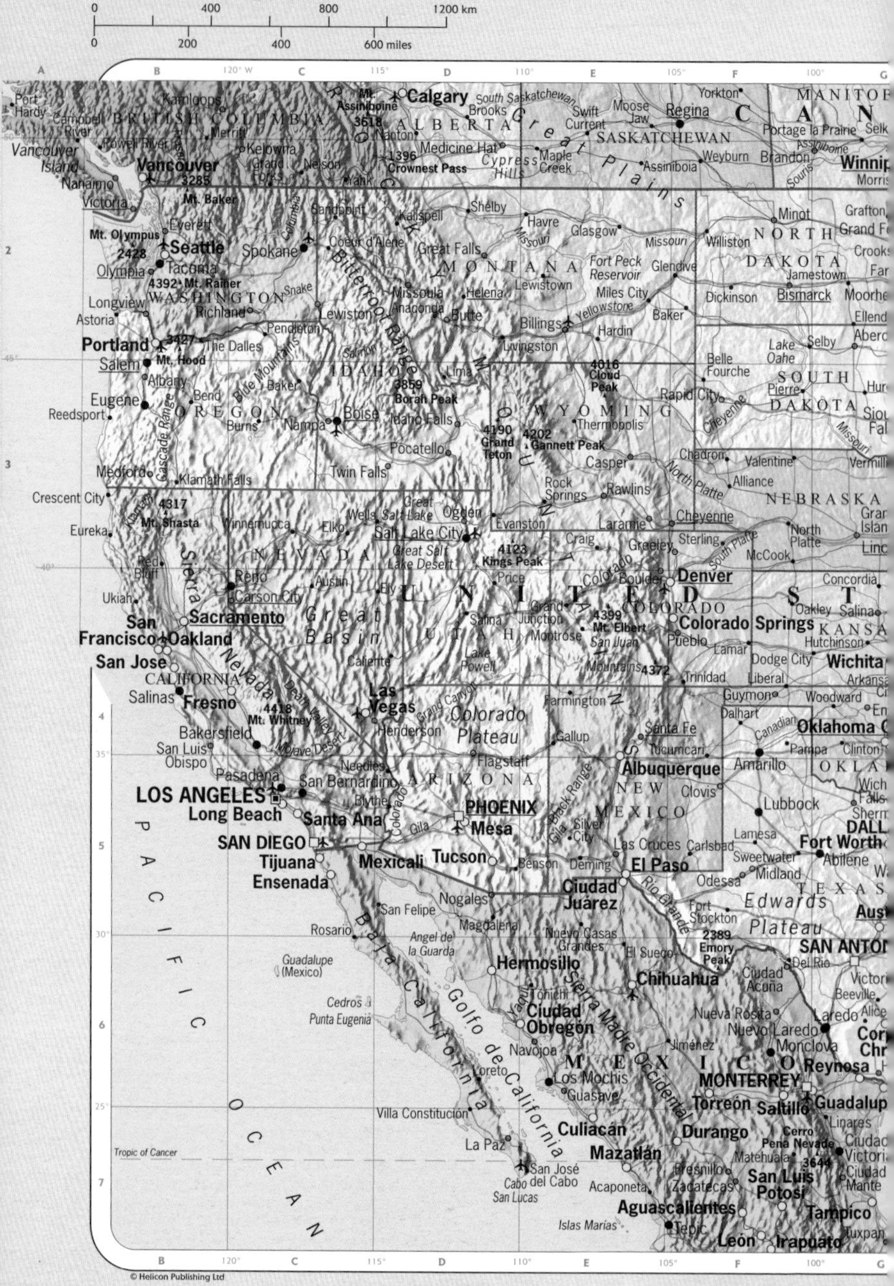

140 141

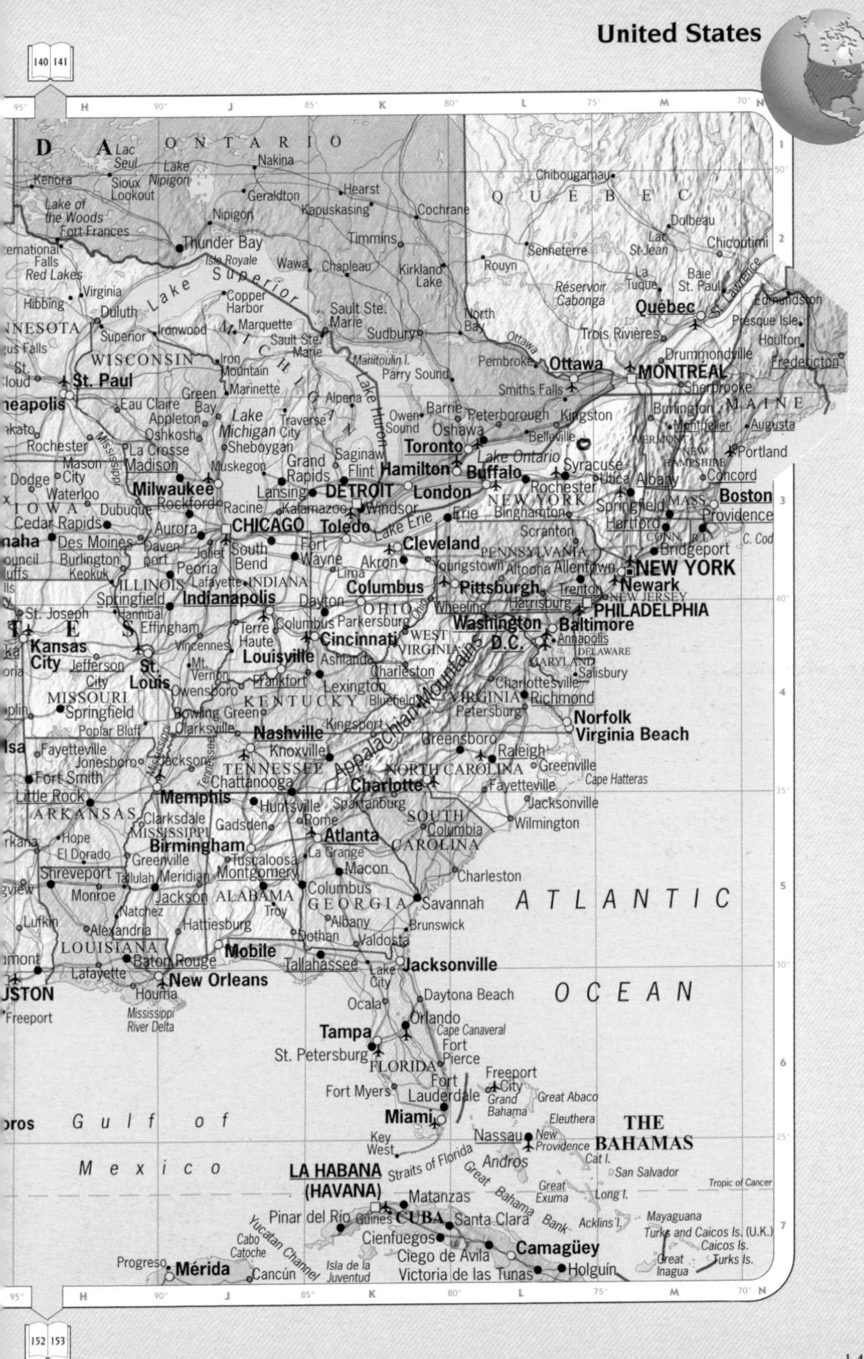

152 153

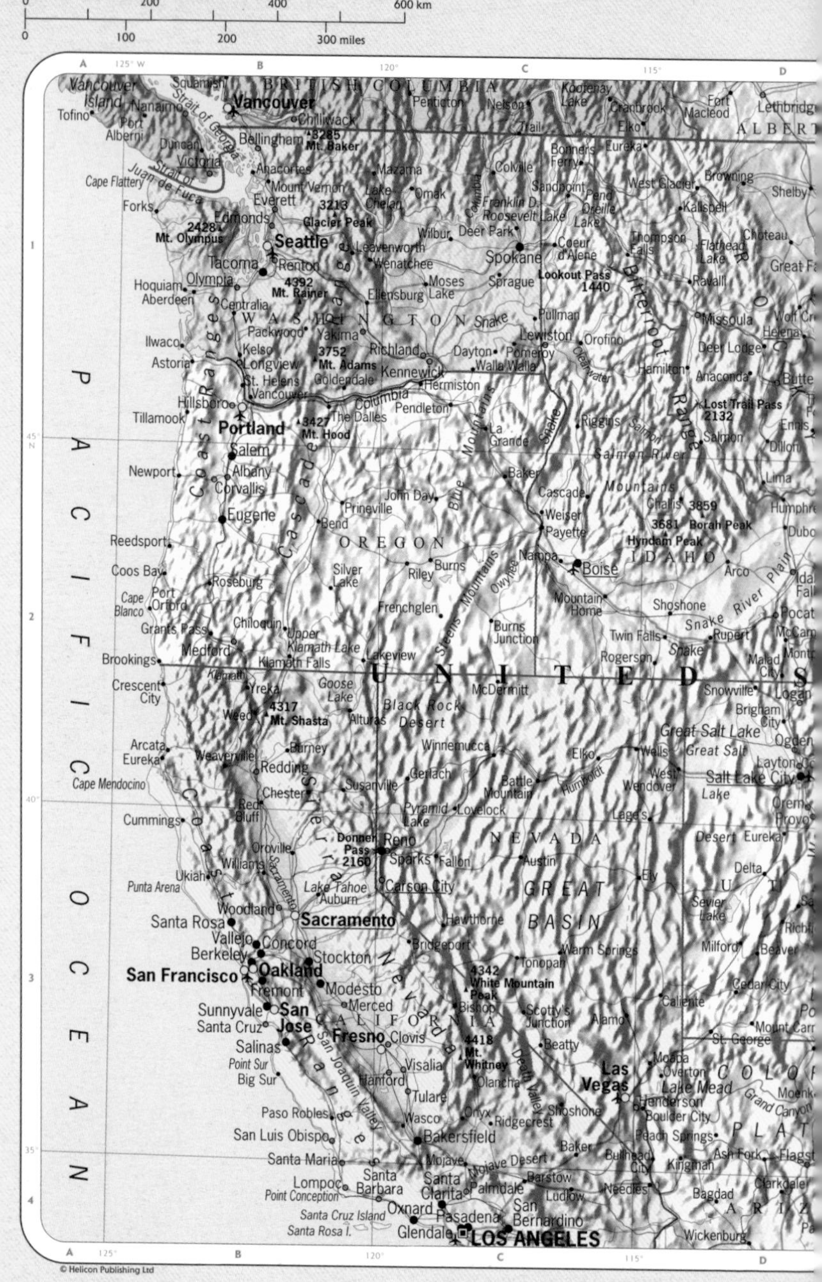

1 : 11 600 000
0
200
400
600 km
0
100
200
300 miles
A
125° W
B
120°
C
115°
D
1
2
3
4
45° N
40°
35°
BRITISH COLUMBIA
ALBERTA
WASHINGTON
OREGON
IDAHO
NEVADA
CALIFORNIA
UNITED S
PACIFIC OCEAN
Vancouver Island
Tofino
Nanaimo
Port Alberni
Squamish
Strait of Georgia
Vancouver
Chilliwack
Penticton
Nelson
Trail
Kootenay Lake
Cranbrook
Elko
Fort Macleod
Lethbridge
Duncan
Victoria
Strait of Juan de Fuca
Cape Flattery
Bellingham
3285 Mt. Baker
Anacortes
Mount Vernon
Everett
Mazama
Lake Chelan
Omak
Colville
Bonners Ferry
Eureka
West Glacier
Browning
Shelby
Forks
2428 Mt. Olympus
Edmonds
3213 Glacier Peak
Seattle
Leavenworth
Wenatchee
Tacoma
Renton
Wilbur
Deer Park
Franklin D. Roosevelt Lake
Sandpoint
Pend Oreille Lake
Kalispell
Spokane
Coeur d'Alene
Thompson Falls
Flathead Lake
Choteau
Great Falls
Hoquiam
Aberdeen
Olympia
Centralia
4392 Mt. Rainier
Ellensburg
Moses Lake
Sprague
Lookout Pass 1440
Bitterroot
Ravalli
Missoula
Wolf Creek
Helena
Packwood
Yakima
Snake
Pullman
Lewiston
Orofino
Ilwaco
Astoria
Kelso
Longview
3752 Mt. Adams
Richland
Kennewick
Dayton
Pomeroy
Walla Walla
Clearwater
Deer Lodge
Hamilton
Anaconda
Butte
St. Helens
Goldendale
Vancouver
Hermiston
Columbia
Pendleton
Hillsboro
Tillamook
Portland
3427 Mt. Hood
The Dalles
Blue Mountains
La Grande
Riggins
Salmon
Lost Trail Pass 2132
Salmon
Ennis
Dillon
Salem
Newport
Albany
Corvallis
Coast Ranges
Cascade Range
Baker
Salmon River Mountains
Cascade
Challis
3859 Borah Peak
3681 Hyndam Peak
Lima
Humphrey
Dubois
Eugene
Prineville
John Day
Bend
Weiser
Payette
Reedsport
Coos Bay
Nampa
Boise
Arco
Idaho Falls
Roseburg
Silver Lake
Riley
Burns
Owyhee
Steens Mountains
Cape Blanco
Port Orford
Frenchglen
Mountain Home
Shoshone
Snake River Plain
Pocatello
Grants Pass
Chiloquin
Upper Klamath Lake
Burns Junction
Twin Falls
Rupert
McCammon
Medford
Klamath Falls
Lakeview
Rogerson
Malad City
Brookings
Klamath
Crescent City
Yreka
Goose Lake
McDermitt
Snowville
Logan
4317 Mt. Shasta
Weed
Alturas
Black Rock Desert
Brigham City
Great Salt Lake
Ogden
Arcata
Eureka
Burney
Winnemucca
Elko
Wells
Great Salt Lake Desert
Weaverville
Redding
Gerlach
Battle Mountain
Humboldt
West Wendover
Layton
Salt Lake City
Cape Mendocino
Chester
Susanville
Lake
Red Bluff
Pyramid Lake
Lovelock
Lages
Orem
Provo
Cummings
Coast Ranges
Donner Pass 2160
Reno
Sparks
Fallon
Desert
Eureka
Oroville
Williams
Sacramento
Sierra Nevada
Austin
Delta
Ukiah
Punta Arena
Lake Tahoe
Auburn
Carson City
GREAT BASIN
Ely
Sevier Lake
Woodland
Sacramento
Hawthorne
Richfield
Santa Rosa
Vallejo
Concord
Berkeley
Stockton
Bridgeport
Warm Springs
Milford
Beaver
San Francisco
Oakland
Tonopah
Fremont
Modesto
4342 White Mountain Peak
Cedar City
Merced
Bishop
Scotty's Junction
Alamo
Caliente
Sunnyvale
San Jose
Santa Cruz
Salinas
Fresno
Clovis
4418 Mt. Whitney
Beatty
Mount Carmel
St. George
Point Sur
Big Sur
San Joaquin Valley
Visalia
Hanford
Tulare
Olancha
Death Valley
Las Vegas
Mesquite
Overton
Lake Mead
COLORADO PLATEAU
Henderson
Boulder City
Grand Canyon
Paso Robles
Wasco
Onyx
Ridgecrest
Shoshone
San Luis Obispo
Bakersfield
Peach Springs
Baker
Santa Maria
Mojave
Mojave Desert
Bullhead City
Kingman
Ash Fork
Flagstaff
Lompoc
Point Conception
Santa Barbara
Santa Clarita
Palmdale
Barstow
Ludlow
Needles
Bagdad
Clarkdale
ARIZONA
Oxnard
Pasadena
San Bernardino
Santa Cruz Island
Santa Rosa I.
Glendale
LOS ANGELES
Wickenburg

Northwest United States

140 141

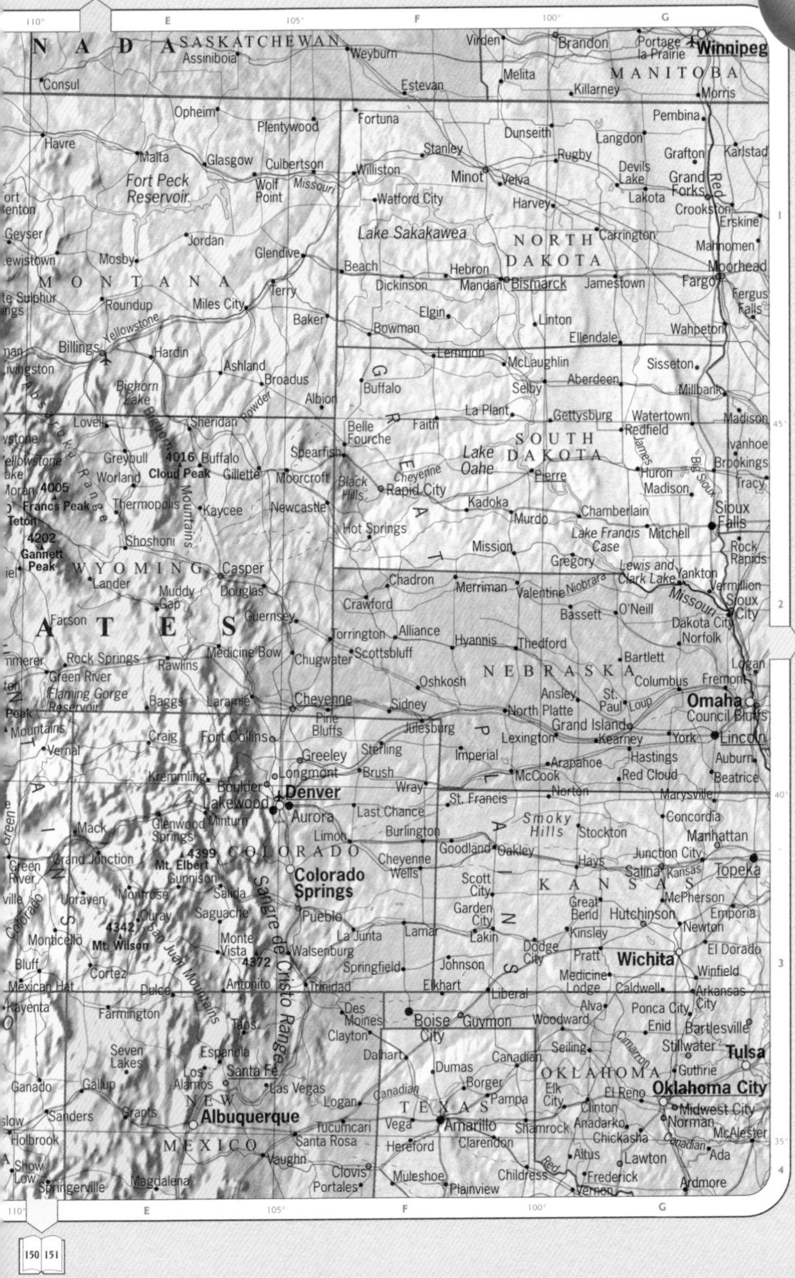

146 147

150 151

1 : 11 600 000
0
200
400
600 km
0
100
200
300 miles
140 141
144 145
A
B
C
D
1
2
3
4
95° W
90°
85°
45° N
40°
35°
95°
MANITOBA
Morris
Lake of the Woods
Rainy Lake
Fort Frances
International Falls
Atikokan
Karlstad
Red
Red Lakes
Crookston
Grand Forks
Erskine
Mahnomen
Bemidji
Virginia
Hibbing
Grand Rapids
Detroit Lakes
Fargo
Moorhead
MINNESOTA
Fergus Falls
Brainerd
Long Prairie
Wahpeton
Alexandria
Little Falls
Pine City
Willow River
Sauk Centre
St. Cloud
Sisseton
Millbank
Benson
Coon Rapids
Madison
Litchfield
St. Paul
Montevideo
Minneapolis
Watertown
Big Sioux
Ivanhoe
Brookings
Redwood Falls
Red Wing
Mankato
Tracy
Madison
Luverne
Worthington
Fairmont
Rochester
Austin
Albert Lea
Winona
Sioux Falls
Rock Rapids
Spencer
Vermillion
Cherokee
Sioux City
Dakota City
Fort Dodge
Mason City
Decorah
Cedar Falls
Waterloo
IOWA
Denison
Missouri
Ames
Marshalltown
Logan
Des Moines
Newton
Iowa City
Cedar Rapids
Davenport
Fremont
Atlantic
Omaha
Council Bluffs
Creston
Indianola
Oskaloosa
Ottumwa
Rock Island
Moline
Lincoln
Shenandoah
Osceola
Centerville
Mount Pleasant
Auburn
Tarkio
Beatrice
Falls City
Maryville
Lancaster
Keokuk
Oregon
Bethany
Marysville
Hiawatha
Atchison
St. Joseph
Manhattan
Kansas City
Carrollton
Topeka
Kansas City
Independence
Junction City
Olathe
KANSAS
Ottawa
Emporia
El Dorado
Iola
Nevada
Chanute
Fort Scott
Winfield
Pittsburg
Joplin
Bartlesville
Tulsa
Muskogee
OKLAHOMA
Poteau
McAlester
Ada
Antlers
Durant
Denison
Lake Superior
Lake Nipigon
Geraldton
Nipigon
Schreiber
Marathon
Thunder Bay
Isle Royale
Grand Marais
Grand Portage
Michipicoten I.
Copper Harbor
Keweenaw Pen.
Hancock
Houghton
Apostle Is.
Duluth
Superior
Ashland
Ironwood
Hearst
Kapuskasing
Foleyet
Wawa
Chapleau
ONT
CA
Marquette
Whitefish Point
Grand Marais
Sault Ste. Marie
Sault Ste. Marie
Blind R
Little Cur
Iron Mountain
Rapid River
Prentice
Barron
Rhinelander
Escanaba
Mackinaw City
Manito
Lake H
Gills Rock
Chippewa Falls
Eau Claire
Wausau
Marinette
Menominee
Gaylord
Alpena
WISCONSIN
Shawano
Traverse City
Grayling
Stevens Point
Green Bay
Wisconsin Rapids
Alma
Appleton
Cadillac
Tawas City
Tomah
Oshkosh
Manitowoc
Ludington
Port Austin
La Crosse
Fond du Lac
Sheboygan
Mount Pleasant
Big Rapids
Bay City
Portage
Baraboo
Lake Michigan
Midland
Saginaw
Prairie du Chien
Madison
Milwaukee
Muskegon
Grand Rapids
Flint
Port Huron
Janesville
Waukesha
Dubuque
Platteville
Beloit
Racine
Holland
Lansing
Freeport
Kalamazoo
Ann Arbor
Warren
Battle Creek
DETROIT
Elgin
Waukegan
Rockford
Rochelle
Evanston
CHICAGO
Elkhart
Toledo
Aurora
Gary
South Bend
Sylvania
Joliet
Plymouth
Peru
Galesburg
UNITED S
Illinois
Kankakee
Findlay
Watseka
Huntington
Fort Wayne
Mansfield
Peoria
Burlington
Bloomington
Lafayette
Logansport
St. Marys
Lima
Havana
Kokomo
Marion
OHIO
Rushville
ILLINOIS
Champaign
Crawfordsville
Portland
Urbana
Macon
Quincy
Decatur
Danville
INDIANA
Springfield
Columbus
Springfield
Indianapolis
Moberly
Hannibal
Tuscola
Rushville
Dayton
Lancaster
Bowling Green
Jacksonville
Marshall
Terre Haute
Greensburg
Hamilton
Chillicothe
Pana
Bloomington
Alton
Vandalia
Effingham
Columbus
Cincinnati
Columbia
Warrensburg
Missouri
Bloomfield
Covington
Ripley
Jefferson City
St. Louis
East St. Louis
Salem
Vincennes
Carrollton
Portsmouth
MISSOURI
Union
Bedford
Ashland
Mount Vernon
Grayville
New Albany
Frankfort
Festus
Evansville
Louisville
Huntington
Preston
Rolla
Carbondale
Lexington
Harrisburg
Owensboro
Springfield
Bixby
Marion
Danville
Richmond
Cape Girardeau
Ohio
Princeton
Willow Springs
Cairo
KENTUCKY
Aurora
Sikeston
Manchester
Poplar Bluff
Paducah
Bowling Green
Glasgow
West Plains
London
Harrison
Hardy
Fulton
Clarksville
Middlesboro
Lake Hudson
Fayetteville
Hoxie
Kennett
Hendersonville
Nashville
Oak Ridge
Kingsport
Dyersburg
Jonesboro
Mississippi
Dickson
Murfreesboro
Milan
Knoxville
ARKANSAS
Blytheville
Jackson
Crossville
Fort Smith
Russellville
TENNESSEE
Searcy
Columbia
Athens
Ouachita Mountains
Conway
Memphis
Brownsville
Savannah
Fayetteville
Cleveland
Murphy
North Little Rock
West Memphis
Germantown
Mena
Brinkley
Corinth
Florence
Huntsville
Chattanooga
Spartanburg
Little Rock
Senatobia
Glenwood
Hot Springs
Decatur
Dalton
Greenville
Helena
Tupelo
Fort Payne
Clarksdale
ALABAMA
Dahlonega
Pine Bluff
Arkansas
Arkadelphia
MISSISSIPPI
Winfield
Gadsden
Rome
Gainesville
GEORGIA
Greenville
© Helicon Publishing Ltd

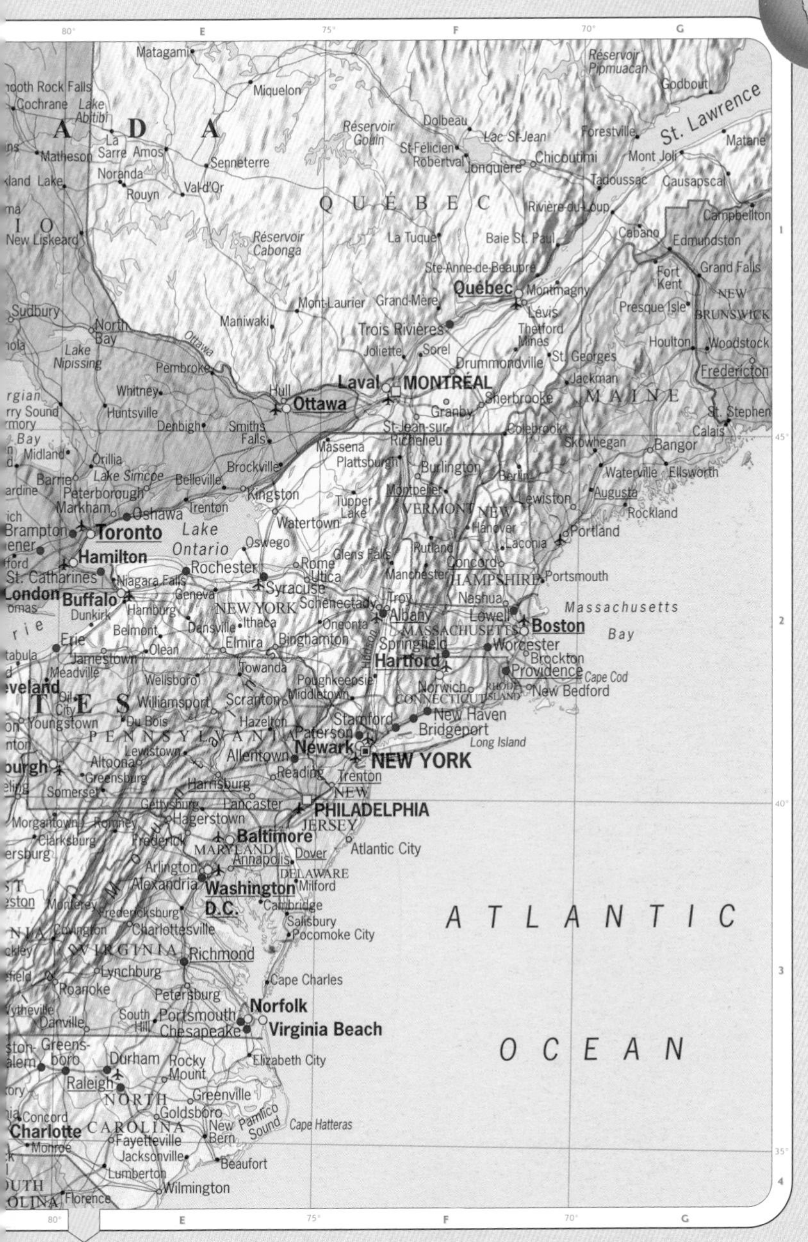
Matagami
Miquelon
Lake Abitibi
Cochrane
Matheson
La Sarre
Amos
Senneterre
Noranda
Rouyn
Val-d'Or
Réservoir Pipmuacan
Godbout
St. Lawrence
Matane
Mont Joli
Causapscal
Forestville
Dolbeau
Lac St-Jean
Réservoir Gouin
St-Félicien
Robertval
Jonquière
Chicoutimi
Tadoussac
Rivière-du-Loup
Campbellton
QUÉBEC
Réservoir Cabonga
La Tuque
Baie St. Paul
Cabano
Edmundston
New Liskeard
Ste-Anne-de-Beaupré
Fort Kent
Grand Falls
Québec
Montmagny
Lévis
NEW BRUNSWICK
Presque Isle
Mont-Laurier
Grand-Mère
Sudbury
North Bay
Lake Nipissing
Maniwaki
Trois Rivières
Thetford Mines
Houlton
Woodstock
Joliette
Sorel
Drummondville
St. Georges
Fredericton
Pembroke
Ottawa
Jackman
Whitney
Laval
MONTRÉAL
Sherbrooke
MAINE
Hull
Ottawa
Granby
Huntsville
St. Stephen
Calais
Denbigh
Smiths Falls
St-Jean-sur-Richelieu
Colebrook
Massena
Skowhegan
Bangor
Midland
Orillia
Plattsburgh
Burlington
Brockville
Berlin
Waterville
Ellsworth
Barrie
Lake Simcoe
Belleville
Peterborough
Kingston
Montpelier
Lewiston
Augusta
Rockland
Tupper Lake
Markham
Oshawa
Trenton
VERMONT
NEW
Brampton
Toronto
Watertown
Hanover
Portland
Lake Ontario
Oswego
Laconia
Hamilton
Rutland
Rochester
Rome
Glens Falls
Concord
St. Catharines
Niagara Falls
Utica
Manchester
HAMPSHIRE
Portsmouth
Syracuse
London
Buffalo
Geneva
Schenectady
Troy
Nashua
Massachusetts Bay
NEW YORK
Dunkirk
Hamburg
Albany
Lowell
Ithaca
Oneonta
MASSACHUSETTS
Boston
Belmont
Dansville
Erie
Elmira
Binghamton
Springfield
Worcester
Olean
Hudson
Hartford
Brockton
Jamestown
Towanda
Providence
Cape Cod
Meadville
Wellsboro
Poughkeepsie
New Bedford
Cleveland
Middletown
Norwich
RHODE ISLAND
Oil City
Williamsport
Scranton
CONNECTICUT
New Haven
Youngstown
Du Bois
Hazelton
Stamford
Bridgeport
PENNSYLVANIA
Paterson
Long Island
Lewistown
Newark
Altoona
Allentown
NEW YORK
Pittsburgh
Greensburg
Reading
Trenton
Somerset
Harrisburg
NEW
Gettysburg
Lancaster
PHILADELPHIA
Morgantown
Romney
Hagerstown
JERSEY
Clarksburg
Frederick
Baltimore
Atlantic City
MARYLAND
Dover
Annapolis
Arlington
DELAWARE
Alexandria
Washington D.C.
Milford
Monterey
Fredericksburg
Cambridge
ATLANTIC
Covington
Charlottesville
Salisbury
Pocomoke City
VIRGINIA
Richmond
Lynchburg
Cape Charles
Roanoke
Petersburg
Norfolk
Danville
South Hill
Portsmouth
Chesapeake
Virginia Beach
OCEAN
Greensboro
Durham
Rocky Mount
Elizabeth City
Raleigh
NORTH
Greenville
Goldsboro
Concord
Charlotte
CAROLINA
New Bern
Pamlico Sound
Cape Hatteras
Fayetteville
Monroe
Jacksonville
Beaufort
Lumberton
Wilmington
Florence
148 149

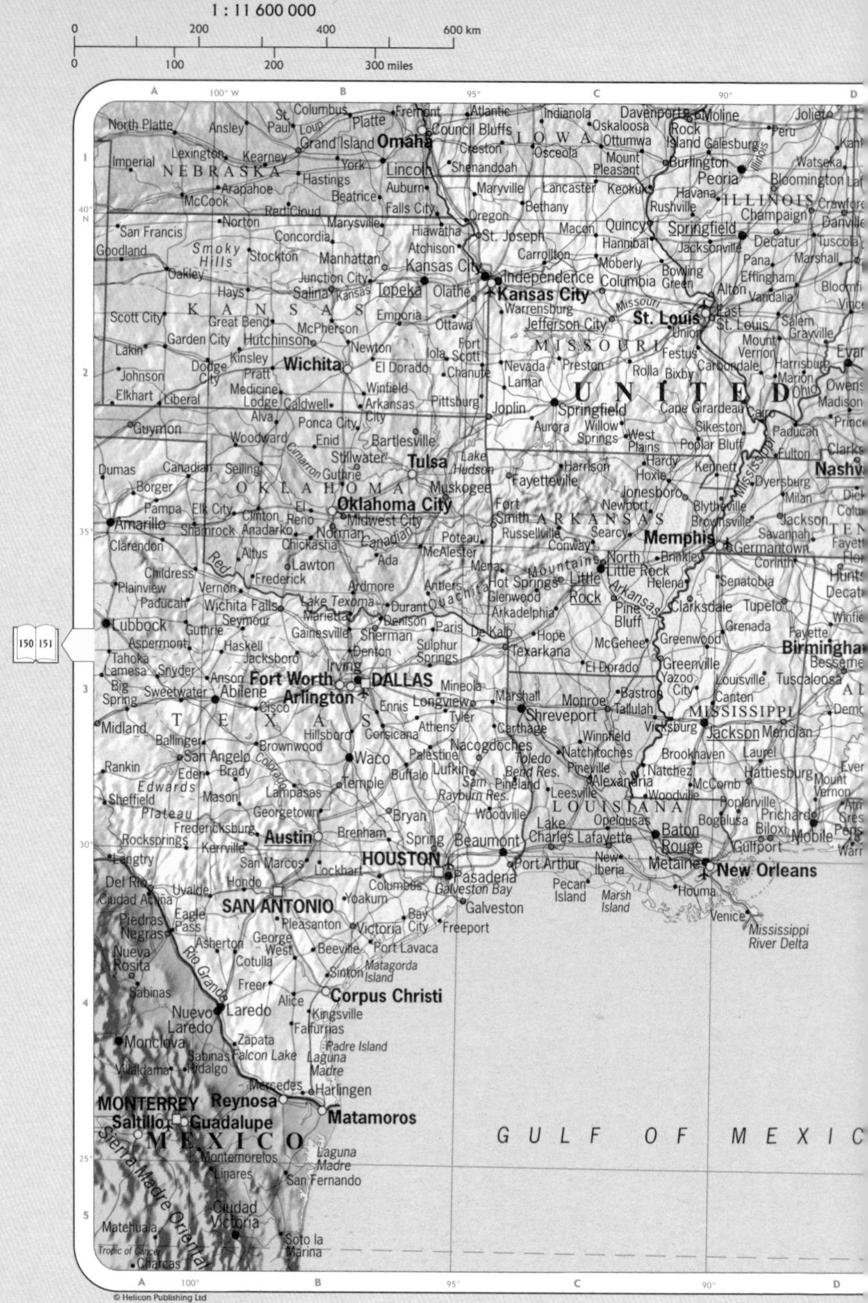
1 : 11 600 000
0
200
400
600 km
0
100
200
300 miles
A
100° W
B
95°
C
90°
D
1
2
3
4
5
40° N
35°
30°
25°
150 151
North Platte
Ansley
St. Paul
Loup
Columbus
Platte
Fremont
Atlantic
Council Bluffs
Grand Island
Omaha
Indianola
Oskaloosa
Ottumwa
Davenport
Moline
Rock Island
Galesburg
Joliet
Peru
Imperial
Lexington
Kearney
NEBRASKA
York
Lincoln
Creston
IOWA
Osceola
Mount Pleasant
Burlington
Illinois
Peoria
Watseka
Bloomington
Shenandoah
Hastings
Arapahoe
McCook
Red Cloud
Beatrice
Auburn
Falls City
Maryville
Lancaster
Keokuk
Havana
Rushville
ILLINOIS
Champaign
Crawford
Bethany
Oregon
Norton
San Francis
Marysville
Hiawatha
Atchison
St. Joseph
Macon
Quincy
Springfield
Danville
Decatur
Tuscola
Goodland
Smoky Hills
Concordia
Stockton
Manhattan
Kansas City
Hannibal
Jacksonville
Carrollton
Moberly
Pana
Marshall
Oakley
Junction City
Independence
Columbia
Bowling Green
Effingham
Hays
Salina
Kansas
Topeka
Olathe
Kansas City
Alton
Vandalia
Scott City
KANSAS
Great Bend
Emporia
Warrensburg
Missouri
St. Louis
East St. Louis
Salem
Grayville
McPherson
Ottawa
Jefferson City
Union
Garden City
Hutchinson
Newton
MISSOURI
Festus
Mount Vernon
Lakin
Kinsley
Wichita
Iola
Fort Scott
Nevada
Preston
Rolla
Carbondale
Harrisburg
Johnson
Dodge City
Pratt
El Dorado
Chanute
Lamar
Bixby
Marion
Elkhart
Liberal
Medicine Lodge
Winfield
UNITED
Ohio
Owens
Caldwell
Arkansas City
Pittsburg
Joplin
Springfield
Cape Girardeau
Cairo
Madison
Alva
Guymon
Ponca City
Aurora
Willow Springs
West Plains
Sikeston
Paducah
Woodward
Enid
Bartlesville
Poplar Bluff
Fulton
Cimarron
Stillwater
Tulsa
Lake Hudson
Harrison
Hardy
Hoxie
Kennett
Mississippi
Dyersburg
Nashville
Dumas
Canadian
Seiling
Guthrie
Borger
OKLAHOMA
Muskogee
Fayetteville
Jonesboro
Milan
Pampa
Elk City
Clinton
El Reno
Oklahoma City
Midwest City
Fort Smith
Newport
Blytheville
Amarillo
Shamrock
Anadarko
Norman
ARKANSAS
Brownsville
Jackson
Chickasha
Canadian
Poteau
Russellville
Searcy
Memphis
Savannah
Clarendon
Altus
McAlester
Conway
Germantown
Corinth
Red
Lawton
Ada
Mena
Mountains
North Little Rock
Brinkley
Childress
Frederick
Antlers
Hot Springs
Little Rock
Helena
Senatobia
Plainview
Vernon
Ardmore
Ouachita
Glenwood
Arkansas
Paducah
Wichita Falls
Lake Texoma
Durant
Arkadelphia
Pine Bluff
Clarksdale
Tupelo
Seymour
Marietta
Denison
Paris
Lubbock
Guthrie
Gainesville
Sherman
De Kalb
Hope
Grenada
Aspermont
Haskell
Denton
Sulphur Springs
Texarkana
McGehee
Greenwood
Birmingham
Tahoka
Jacksboro
Greenville
Bessemer
Lamesa
Snyder
Anson
Irving
El Dorado
Yazoo City
Louisville
Tuscaloosa
Big Spring
Sweetwater
Abilene
Fort Worth
DALLAS
Arlington
Mineola
Marshall
Monroe
Bastrop
Canton
Cisco
Ennis
Longview
Tallulah
MISSISSIPPI
Midland
TEXAS
Tyler
Shreveport
Vicksburg
Jackson
Meridian
Ballinger
Hillsboro
Corsicana
Athens
Carthage
Winnfield
Brownwood
Nacogdoches
San Angelo
Colorado
Waco
Palestine
Toledo Bend Res.
Natchitoches
Brookhaven
Laurel
Rankin
Eden
Brady
Buffalo
Lufkin
Pineville
Natchez
Hattiesburg
Edwards Plateau
Mason
Temple
Sam Rayburn Res.
Pineland
Alexandria
McComb
Sheffield
Lampasas
Leesville
Woodville
Poplarville
Georgetown
Bryan
Woodville
LOUISIANA
Prichard
Fredericksburg
Opelousas
Bogalusa
Biloxi
Mobile
Rocksprings
Kerrville
Austin
Brenham
Spring
Beaumont
Lake Charles
Lafayette
Baton Rouge
Gulfport
Langtry
San Marcos
HOUSTON
Port Arthur
New Iberia
Metairie
New Orleans
Del Rio
Lockhart
Pasadena
Ciudad Acuña
Uvalde
Hondo
Columbus
Galveston Bay
Pecan Island
Marsh Island
Houma
Eagle Pass
SAN ANTONIO
Yoakum
Galveston
Piedras Negras
Pleasanton
Victoria
Bay City
Freeport
Venice
Mississippi River Delta
Asherton
George West
Beeville
Port Lavaca
Nueva Rosita
Rio Grande
Cotulla
Sinton
Matagorda Island
Freer
Sabinas
Alice
Corpus Christi
Nuevo Laredo
Laredo
Kingsville
Falfurrias
Monclova
Zapata
Padre Island
Sabinas Hidalgo
Falcon Lake
Laguna Madre
Villaldama
Mercedes
Harlingen
MONTERREY
Reynosa
Matamoros
Saltillo
Guadalupe
MEXICO
GULF OF MEXICO
Sierra Madre Oriental
Montemorelos
Laguna Madre
Linares
San Fernando
Ciudad Victoria
Matehuala
Soto la Marina
Tropic of Cancer
Charcas
© Helicon Publishing Ltd

Southeast United States

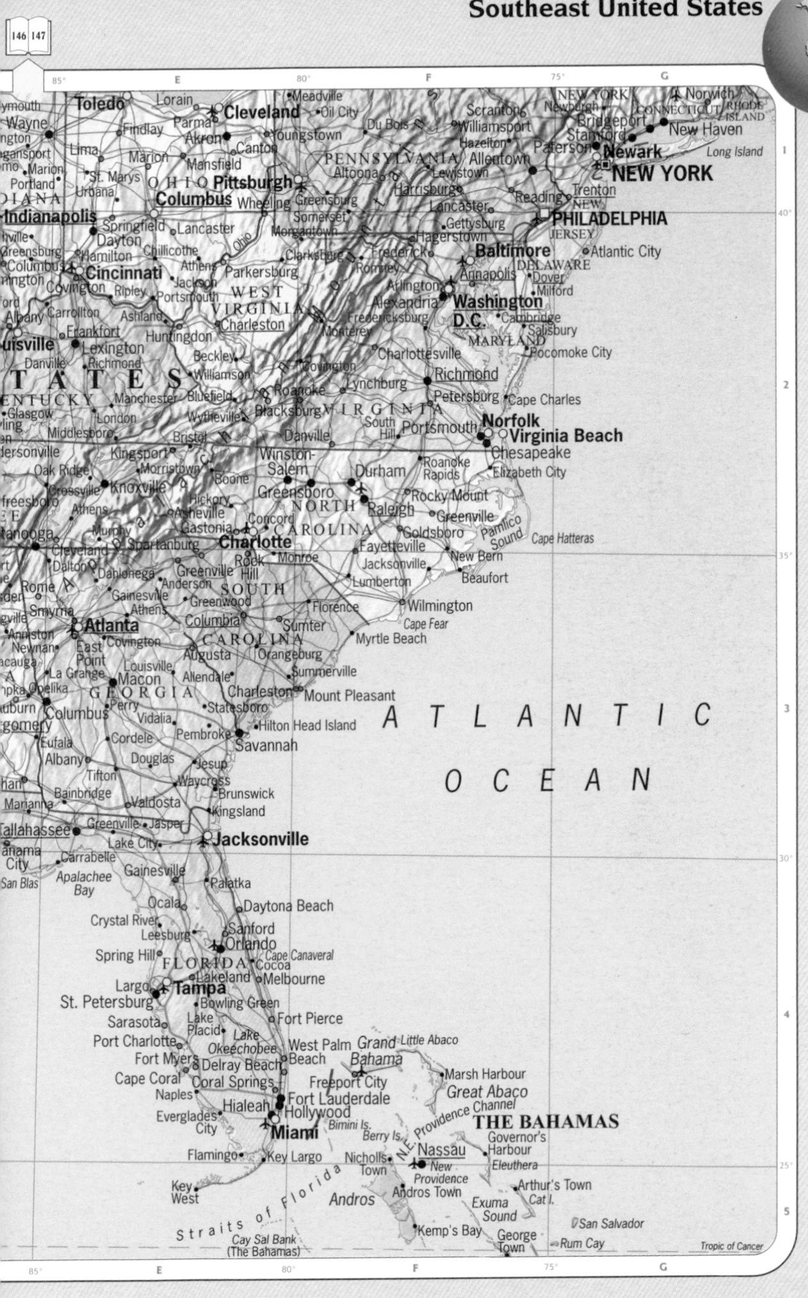

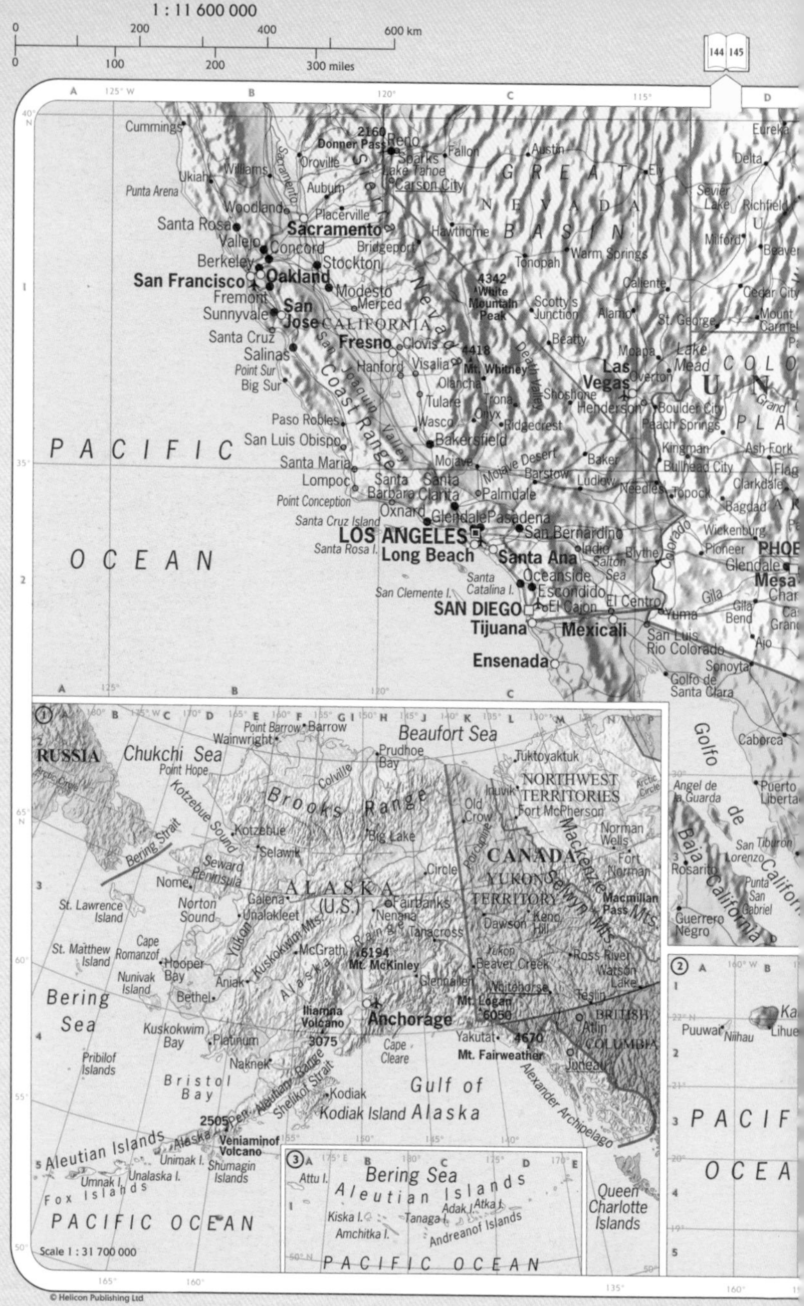
1 : 11 600 000
0 200 400 600 km
0 100 200 300 miles
144 145
PACIFIC OCEAN
San Francisco
Oakland
San Jose
Sacramento
Stockton
Modesto
Fresno
CALIFORNIA
Bakersfield
LOS ANGELES
Long Beach
Santa Ana
SAN DIEGO
Tijuana
Mexicali
Ensenada
Las Vegas
Reno
Carson City
GREAT BASIN
NEVADA
Sierra Nevada
Coast Range
San Joaquin Valley
Death Valley
Mojave Desert
4418 Mt. Whitney
4342 White Mountain Peak
2160 Donner Pass
Golfo de California
Baja California
Beaufort Sea
Chukchi Sea
RUSSIA
Bering Strait
Brooks Range
ALASKA (U.S.)
Fairbanks
Anchorage
6194 Mt. McKinley
Mt. Logan 6050
4670 Mt. Fairweather
Juneau
CANADA
YUKON TERRITORY
NORTHWEST TERRITORIES
BRITISH COLUMBIA
Bering Sea
Gulf of Alaska
Kodiak Island
Aleutian Islands
PACIFIC OCEAN
Scale 1 : 31 700 000
Bering Sea
Aleutian Islands
PACIFIC OCEAN
PACIF OCEA
© Helicon Publishing Ltd

148 149

152 153

1 : 25 900 000

0 400 800 1200 km

0 200 400 800 miles

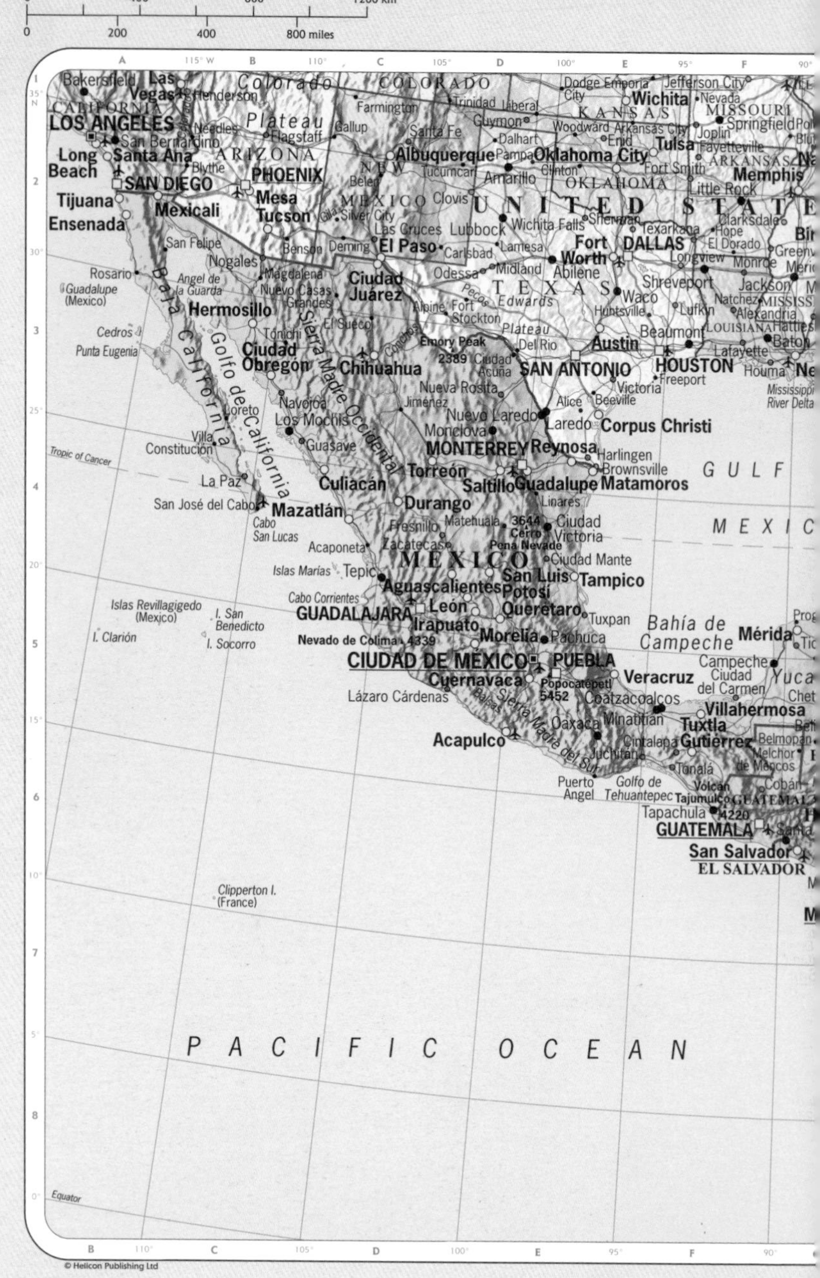

Central America and the Caribbean

1 : 45 000 000
0 400 800 1200 km
0 200 400 600 miles
Nassau
San Salvador
Tropic of Cancer
Florida Keys
Straits of Florida
Andros
Cat I.
Great Exuma
Long I.
Mayaguana
Acklins I.
Great Inagua
Turks and Caicos Is. (U.K.)
LA HABANA (HAVANA)
Santiago de Cuba
Windward Passage
Hispaniola
Puerto Rico Trench
8742
Mid-Atlantic Ridge
Yucatan Channel
Isla de la Juventud
Cayman Is. (U.K.)
I. de Cozumel
2005 Turquino
P. Duarte
3175
San Juan
Virgin Is. (U.S.)
Virgin Is. (U.K.)
Anguilla (U.K.)
Barbuda
Antigua
Kingston
PORT-AU-PRINCE
Cabo Beata
SANTO DOMINGO
Puerto Rico (U.S.)
Montserrat (U.K.)
Guadeloupe (France)
Martinique (France)
Greater Antilles
Swan (Honduras)
Caribbean Sea
Lesser Antilles
NORTH AMERICA
Tegucigalpa
Isla de Providencia (Colombia)
Isla de San Andrés (Colombia)
Punta Gallinas
Aruba (Neth.)
Netherlands Antilles
Isla La Tortuga
Isla de Margarita
Managua
BARRANQUILLA
P. Cristóbal Colón
5775
Golfo de Venezuela
Port of Spain
Golfo del Darién
Lago de Maracaibo
CARACAS
Boca Grande
San José
Panamá
VENEZUELA
Orinoco
Meta
Embalse de Guri
Georgetown
Paramaribo
Cayenne
MEDELLÍN
GUYANA
SURINAME
FRENCH GUIANA
ATLANTIC OCEAN
BOGOTÁ
Cordillera Occidental
Cordillera Oriental
I. de Coco (Costa Rica)
Isla de Malpelo (Colombia)
CALI
COLOMBIA
Guiana Highlands
3014 Pico da Neblina
Boa Vista
Negro
Macapá
Mouths of the Amazon
QUITO
ECUADOR
6310
Caquetá
Equator
MANAUS
Amazonas (Amazon)
BELÉM
GUAYAQUIL
Golfo de Guayaquil
Iquitos
Amazonas
São Luís
FORTALEZA
Teresina
Islas Galápagos (Galapagos Is.) (Ecuador)
Marañón
Madeira
BRAZIL
I. Fernando de Noronha
Natal
João Pessoa
Chiclayo
Trujillo
Chimbote
PERU
Pôrto Velho
Rio Branco
Araguaia
Barragem de Sobradinho
Chapada Diamantina
RECIFE
Maceió
Palmas
Callao
LIMA
Cusco
Cordillera Oriental
Lago Titicaca
La Paz
BOLIVIA
Cochabamba
Planalto do Mato Grosso
Cuiabá
Planalto
São Francisco
Aracaju
SALVADOR
Baía de Todos os Santos

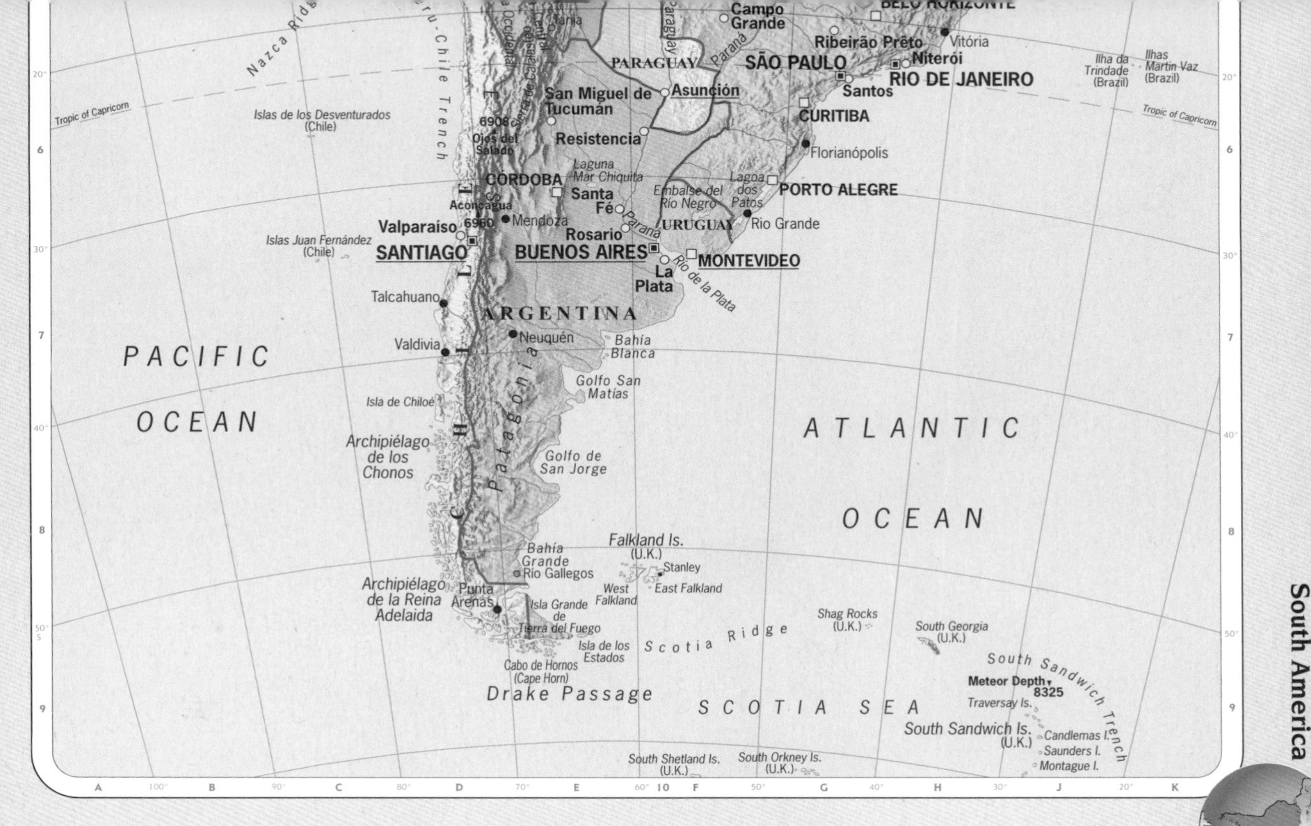
ATLANTIC
OCEAN
PACIFIC
OCEAN
SCOTIA SEA
Drake Passage
Scotia Ridge
South Sandwich Trench
Peru-Chile Trench
Nazca Ridge
Tropic of Capricorn
BELO HORIZONTE
Vitória
Niterói
RIO DE JANEIRO
Ribeirão Prêto
Santos
SÃO PAULO
CURITIBA
Florianópolis
Campo Grande
PORTO ALEGRE
Rio Grande
Lagoa dos Patos
MONTEVIDEO
Río de la Plata
La Plata
URUGUAY
PARAGUAY
Asunción
Paraguay
Paraná
Resistencia
San Miguel de Tucumán
Laguna Mar Chiquita
Santa Fé
Rosario
CÓRDOBA
Mendoza
BUENOS AIRES
Embalse del Río Negro
ARGENTINA
Bahía Blanca
Golfo San Matías
Neuquén
Golfo de San Jorge
Patagonia
Ojos del Salado
6908
Aconcagua
6960
Valparaíso
SANTIAGO
Talcahuano
Valdivia
Isla de Chiloé
Archipiélago de los Chonos
Archipiélago de la Reina Adelaida
Punta Arenas
Bahía Grande
Río Gallegos
Isla Grande de Tierra del Fuego
Isla de los Estados
Cabo de Hornos (Cape Horn)
Falkland Is. (U.K.)
West Falkland
East Falkland
Stanley
South Georgia (U.K.)
Shag Rocks (U.K.)
South Orkney Is. (U.K.)
South Shetland Is. (U.K.)
South Sandwich Is. (U.K.)
Traversay Is.
Candlemas I.
Saunders I.
Montague I.
Meteor Depth 8325
Ilha da Trindade (Brazil)
Ilhas Martin Vaz (Brazil)
Islas de los Desventurados (Chile)
Islas Juan Fernández (Chile)
Sierra de Calalaste
Cordillera Occidental
Cordillera Central

1 : 25 900 000
0
400
800 km
0
200
400 miles
CARIBBEAN SEA
Punta Gallinas
Peninsula de Guajira
Aruba (Neth.)
Netherlands Antilles
Willemstad
Lesser Antilles
Islas Los Roques
ST. VINCENT & THE GRENADINES
GRENADA
NICARAGUA
Isla de San Andrés (Colombia)
Ríohacha
Golfo de Venezuela
Coro
Isla La Tortuga
Isla de Margarita
Port of Spain
BARRANQUILLA
P. Cristóbal Colón 5775
MARACAIBO
CARACAS
Cartagena
Maracay
Cumaná
Golfo de los Mosquitos
Valledupar
Barquisimeto
Güiria
Maturín
COSTA RICA
San José
Canal de Panamá (Panama Canal)
Machiques
Valencia
Barcelona
Delta del Orinoco
Cerro Chirripó 3820
Golfo del Darién
Montería
Mérida
Acarigua
Calabozo
El Tigre
Volcán Barú 3475
Panamá
Barinas
Ciudad Bolívar
Ciudad Guayana
PANAMA
Turbo
Cúcuta
Apure
Orinoco
Cordillera de Mérida
Golfo de Panamá
Pamplona
San Cristóbal
San Fernando de Apure
Punta Mariato
Bucaramanga
La Paragua
El Dorado
MEDELLÍN
Puerto Berrío
Llanos
VENEZUELA
Tunja
Puerto Carreño
Quibdó
Meta
Caura
Paragua
Cabo Corrientes
Manizales
Guiana Highlands
2810 Mt. Roraima
Pereira
BOGOTÁ
San José de Ocuné
Ibagué
Cerro Marahuaca 2579
Isla de Malpelo (Colombia)
Villavicencio
Guaviare
Serra Pacaraima
Buenaventura
CALI
COLOMBIA
Cordillera Occidental
5750
La Esmeralda
Boa Vista
Neiva
Mesa de Yambí
Orinoco
Caracaraí
Tumaco
Popayán
Miraflores
San Carlos
RORAIMA
Pico da Neblina 3014
Pasto
Florencia
Mitú
Esmeraldas
Ipiales
Tres Esquinas
Branco
Taracuá
Santo Domingo de los Colorados
QUITO
Uaupés
Negro
Equator
Puerto Leguizamo
Caquetá
Manta
5896
Volcán Cotopaxi
Ambato
Barcelos
Bahía de Santa Elena
Portoviejo
La Pedrera
Japurá
GUAYAQUIL
ECUADOR
Napo
Putumayo
Fonte Boa
Salinas
Macas
Andoas
Santo Antônio do Içá
Golfo de Guayaquil
Cuenca
Amazonas
Pebas
Amazonas (Amazon)
Manacapuru
Machala
Iquitos
Caballococha
São Paulo de Olivença
Talara
Loja
Marañón
Leticia
Coari
Sullana
Carauari
AMAZONAS
Paita
Piura
Requena
Cordillera del Condor
Yavari
Jutaí
Purus
Bahía de Sechura
Jaén
Yurimaguas
Punta Negra
Chachapoyas
Canutama
Chiclayo
Tarapoto
Ucayali
Eirunepé
Humaitá
Cajamarca
Selvas
Trujillo
Pucallpa
Cruzeiro do Sul
Feijó
Chimbote
Tingo María
ACRE
Bôca do Acre
Madeira
Pôrto Velho
Islas Galápagos (Galapagos Islands) (Ecuador)
Isla Marchena
Isla San Salvador
Isla Fernandina
Isla Santa Cruz
Isla Isabela
Isla San Cristóbal
Isla Santa María
Cordillera Central
Cordillera Oriental
Sena Madureira
Rio Branco
Ariquemes
PERU
Xapuri
Guajará Mirim
Rondônia
Huacho
Cerro de Pasco
Iñapari
Riberalta
RONDÔNIA
Cobija
Callao
Madre de Dios
Cavinas
Guaporé
Manú
Mamoré
LIMA
Huancayo
Puerto Maldonado
Magdalena
Cordillera Occidental
ANDES
Chincha Alta
Ayacucho
Cusco
6394 Nevado Auzangate
Yacuma
Puerto Alegre
Paraguá
Ica
Chalhuanca
San Borja
Trinidad
San Miguel
Nazca
Nudo Coropuna 6425
Juliaca
Puerto Acosta
Lago Titicaca
BOLIVIA
Arequipa
Puno
La Paz
San Pedro
Camana
Mollendo
Cochabamba
Nevado Sajama 6542
Oruro
Santa Cruz
Samaipata
PACIFIC OCEAN
Peru-Chile Trench
Tacna
Lago de Poopó
Sucre
Bañados del Izozog
Nazca Ridge
Arica
Potosí
Iquique
Salar de Uyuni
Uyuni
CHILE
Tarija
Pilcomayo
Volcán San Pedro 6159
Tocopilla
La Quiaca
Calama
ARGENTINA
PARAGUAY
Filadelfia
152 153

Northern South America

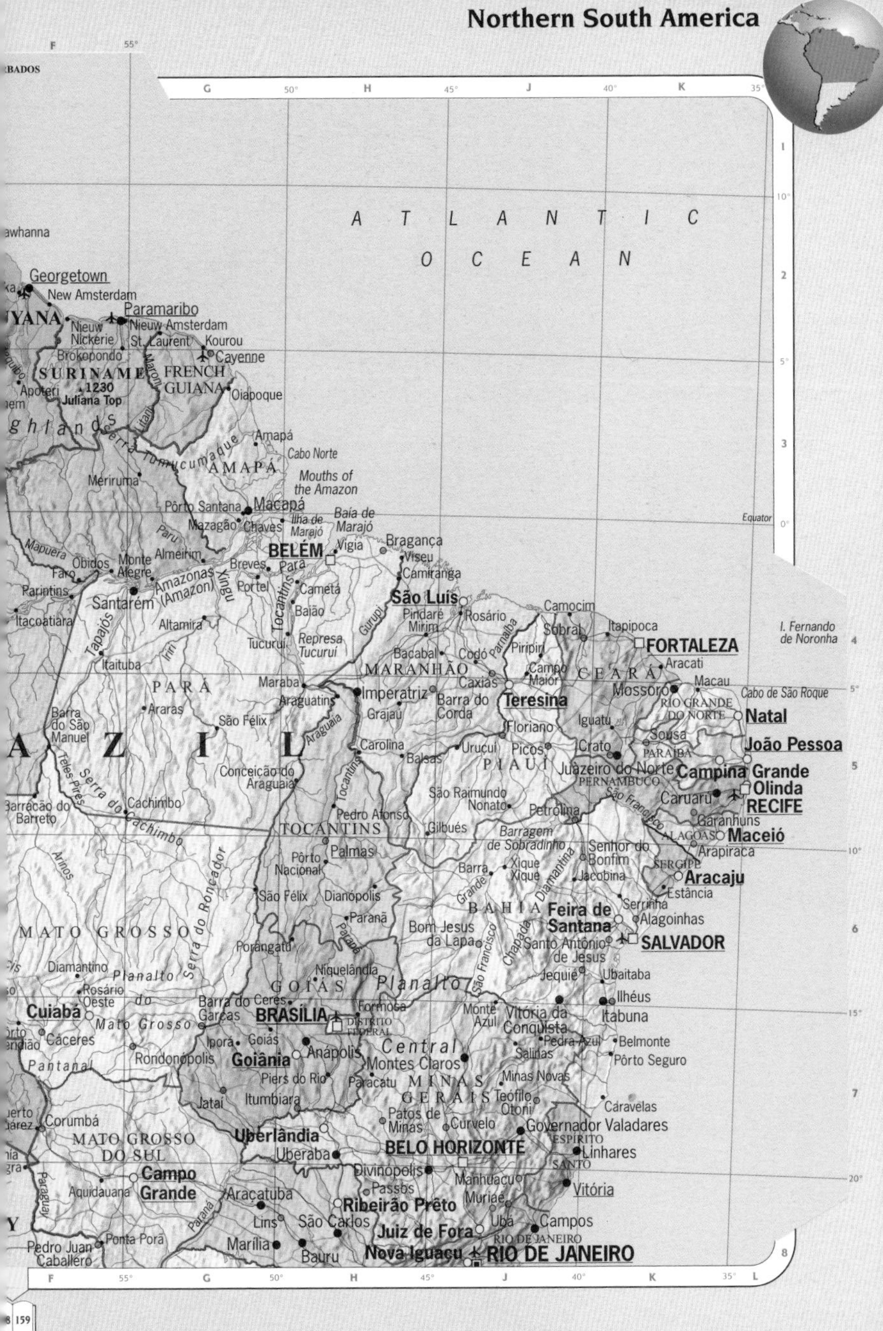

159

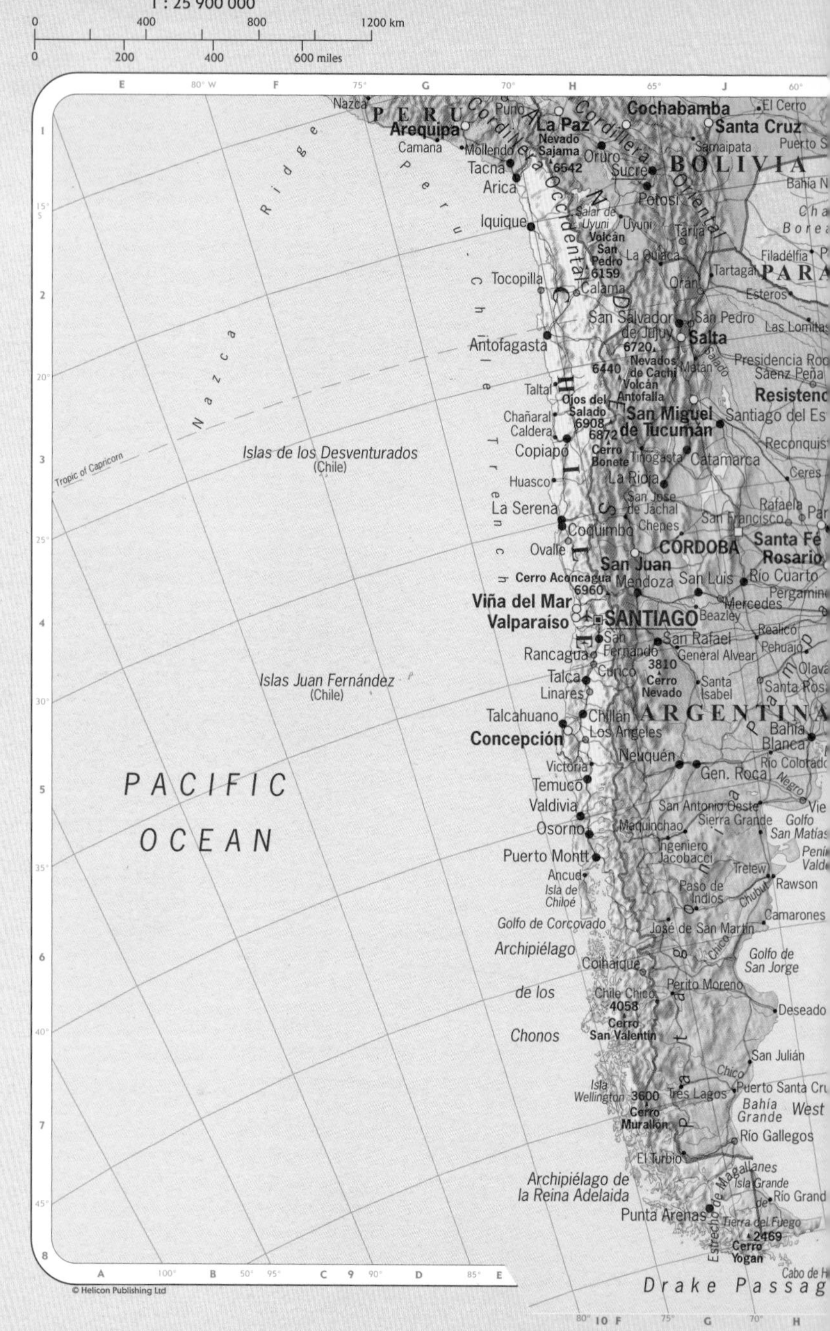

1 : 25 900 000
0
400
800
1200 km
0
200
400
600 miles
PACIFIC OCEAN
Nazca Ridge
Peru Chile Trench
Tropic of Capricorn
Islas de los Desventurados
(Chile)
Islas Juan Fernández
(Chile)
PERU
BOLIVIA
CHILE
ARGENTINA
Cordillera Occidental
Cordillera Oriental
ANDES
Pampas
Patagonia
Nazca
Arequipa
Camana
Mollendo
Puno
La Paz
Nevado Sajama
6542
Oruro
Cochabamba
Santa Cruz
Samaipata
El Cerro
Sucre
Potosí
Tacna
Arica
Iquique
Salar de Uyuni
Uyuni
Tarija
Volcán San Pedro
6159
La Quiaca
Tartagal
Filadélfia
Tocopilla
Calama
Orán
Esteros
San Salvador de Jujuy
San Pedro
Salta
Las Lomitas
6720
Antofagasta
Nevados de Cachi
6440
Metán
Salado
Presidencia Roque Sáenz Peña
Taltal
Volcán Antofalla
Ojos del Salado
6908
6872
Chañaral
Caldera
San Miguel de Tucumán
Santiago del Estero
Copiapó
Cerro Bonete
Tinogasta
Catamarca
Reconquista
Huasco
La Rioja
Ceres
La Serena
San José de Jáchal
Rafaela
Coquimbo
Chepes
San Francisco
Ovalle
CÓRDOBA
Santa Fé
Rosario
San Juan
Cerro Aconcagua
6960
Mendoza
San Luis
Río Cuarto
Viña del Mar
Valparaíso
SANTIAGO
Mercedes
Beazley
Rancagua
San Fernando
San Rafael
General Alvear
Realicó
Pehuajó
Curicó
3810
Cerro Nevado
Talca
Linares
Santa Isabel
Talcahuano
Chillán
Concepción
Los Angeles
Bahía Blanca
Neuquén
Gen. Roca
Río Colorado
Negro
Victoria
Temuco
Valdivia
San Antonio Oeste
Sierra Grande
Golfo San Matías
Osorno
Maquinchao
Puerto Montt
Ingeniero Jacobacci
Trelew
Rawson
Ancud
Isla de Chiloé
Paso de Indios
Chubut
Golfo de Corcovado
Camarones
José de San Martín
Archipiélago de los Chonos
Coihaique
Chico
Golfo de San Jorge
Perito Moreno
Chile Chico
4058
Cerro San Valentín
Deseado
San Julián
Isla Wellington
3600
Cerro Murallón
Tres Lagos
Puerto Santa Cruz
Bahía Grande
Río Gallegos
El Turbio
Archipiélago de la Reina Adelaida
Estrecho de Magallanes
Isla Grande de Tierra del Fuego
Río Grande
Punta Arenas
2469
Cerro Yogan
Drake Passage
© Helicon Publishing Ltd

156 157

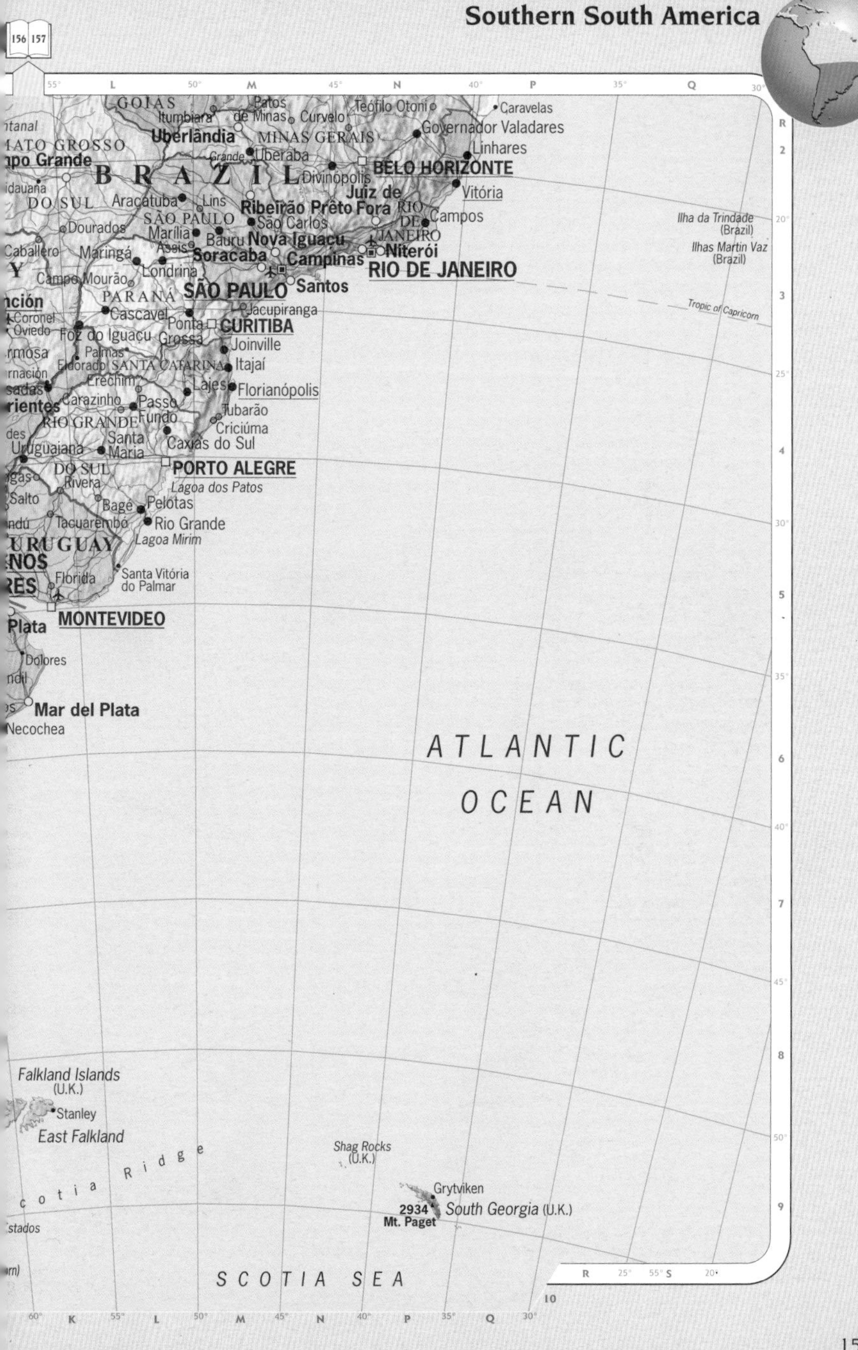
BRAZIL
GOIÁS
MATO GROSSO DO SUL
MINAS GERAIS
SÃO PAULO
PARANÁ
SANTA CATARINA
RIO GRANDE DO SUL
RIO DE JANEIRO
URUGUAY
Itumbiara
Patos de Minas
Curvelo
Teófilo Otoni
Caravelas
Governador Valadares
Linhares
Uberlândia
Uberaba
Grande
Campo Grande
Divinópolis
BELO HORIZONTE
Vitória
Juiz de Fora
Araçatuba
Lins
Ribeirão Prêto
São Carlos
Campos
Dourados
Marília
Bauru
Nova Iguaçu
Assis
Soracaba
Campinas
Niterói
Maringá
Londrina
RIO DE JANEIRO
Campo Mourão
SÃO PAULO
Santos
Cascavel
Jacupiranga
Ponta Grossa
CURITIBA
Foz do Iguaçu
Joinville
Palmas
Itajaí
Erechim
Lajes
Florianópolis
Carazinho
Passo Fundo
Tubarão
Criciúma
Santa Maria
Caxias do Sul
Uruguaiana
PORTO ALEGRE
Rivera
Lagoa dos Patos
Salto
Bagé
Pelotas
Tacuarembó
Rio Grande
Lagoa Mirim
Santa Vitória do Palmar
Florida
MONTEVIDEO
Dolores
Mar del Plata
Necochea
Ilha da Trindade (Brazil)
Ilhas Martin Vaz (Brazil)
Tropic of Capricorn
ATLANTIC OCEAN
Falkland Islands (U.K.)
Stanley
East Falkland
Scotia Ridge
Shag Rocks (U.K.)
Grytviken
2934 Mt. Paget
South Georgia (U.K.)
SCOTIA SEA
55° L 50° M 45° N 40° P 35° Q 30°
R 2 20° 3 25° 4 30° 5 35° 6 40° 7 45° 8 50° 9 10
R 25° 55° S 20°
60° K 55° L 50° M 45° N 40° P 35° Q 30°

Polar Regions

1 : 81 400 000

0 1000 2000 3000

0 500 1000 1500 miles

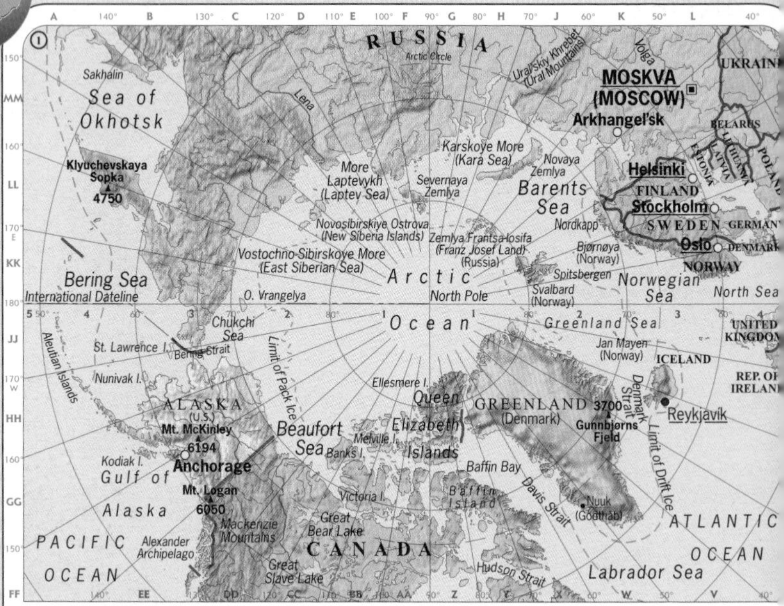

RUSSIA
Arctic Circle
Sakhalin
Sea of Okhotsk
Lena
Ural'skiy Khrebet (Ural Mountains)
Volga
MOSKVA (MOSCOW)
Arkhangel'sk
UKRAINE
BELARUS
LITHUANIA
LATVIA
ESTONIA
POLAND
Klyuchevskaya Sopka 4750
More Laptevykh (Laptev Sea)
Severnaya Zemlya
Karskoye More (Kara Sea)
Novaya Zemlya
Barents Sea
Helsinki
FINLAND
Stockholm
SWEDEN
GERMANY
Novosibirskiye Ostrova (New Siberia Islands)
Zemlya Frantsa-Iosifa (Franz Josef Land) (Russia)
Nordkapp
Bjørnøya (Norway)
Oslo
DENMARK
NORWAY
Vostochno-Sibirskoye More (East Siberian Sea)
Spitsbergen
Bering Sea
Arctic Ocean
Svalbard (Norway)
Norwegian Sea
North Sea
International Dateline
O. Vrangelya
North Pole
Chukchi Sea
Greenland Sea
UNITED KINGDOM
St. Lawrence I.
Bering Strait
Jan Mayen (Norway)
ICELAND
REP. OF IRELAND
Aleutian Islands
Nunivak I.
Limit of Pack Ice
Ellesmere I.
Denmark Strait
ALASKA (U.S.)
Queen Elizabeth Islands
GREENLAND (Denmark)
3700 Gunnbjørns Fjeld
Reykjavík
Mt. McKinley 6194
Beaufort Sea
Melville I.
Banks I.
Kodiak I.
Anchorage
Gulf of Alaska
Baffin Bay
Limit of Drift Ice
Mt. Logan 6050
Baffin Island
Davis Strait
Victoria I.
Nuuk (Godthåb)
Mackenzie Mountains
Great Bear Lake
ATLANTIC OCEAN
PACIFIC OCEAN
Alexander Archipelago
CANADA
Great Slave Lake
Hudson Strait
Labrador Sea

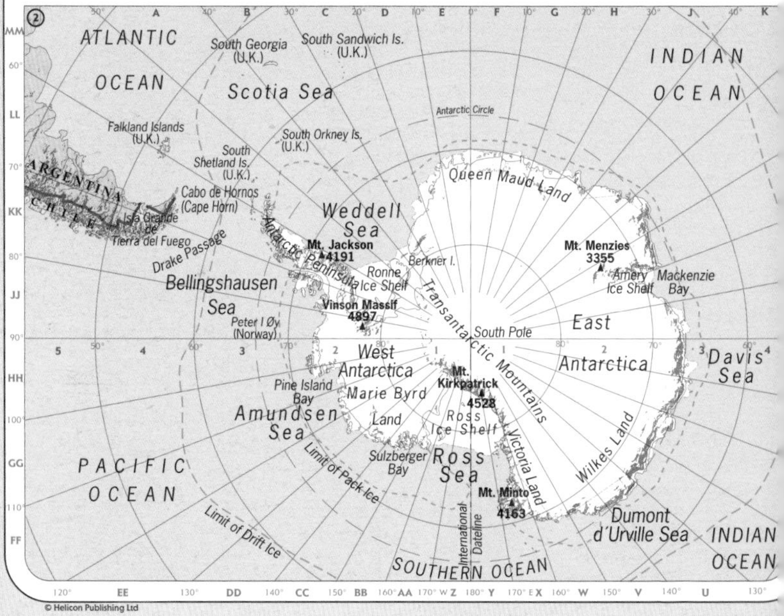

ATLANTIC OCEAN
South Georgia (U.K.)
South Sandwich Is. (U.K.)
INDIAN OCEAN
Scotia Sea
Antarctic Circle
Falkland Islands (U.K.)
South Orkney Is. (U.K.)
South Shetland Is. (U.K.)
ARGENTINA
CHILE
Queen Maud Land
Cabo de Hornos (Cape Horn)
Isla Grande de Tierra del Fuego
Weddell Sea
Drake Passage
Mt. Jackson 4191
Antarctic Peninsula
Mt. Menzies 3355
Berkner I.
Ronne Ice Shelf
Amery Ice Shelf
Mackenzie Bay
Bellingshausen Sea
Vinson Massif 4897
Transantarctic Mountains
Peter I Øy (Norway)
South Pole
East Antarctica
West Antarctica
Davis Sea
Mt. Kirkpatrick 4528
Pine Island Bay
Marie Byrd Land
Amundsen Sea
Ross Ice Shelf
Victoria Land
Wilkes Land
Sulzberger Bay
Ross Sea
PACIFIC OCEAN
Limit of Pack Ice
Mt. Minto 4163
Limit of Drift Ice
International Dateline
Dumont d'Urville Sea
INDIAN OCEAN
SOUTHERN OCEAN

INDEX

How to use the index

This is an alphabetically arranged index of the places and features that can be found on the maps in this atlas. Each name is generally indexed to the largest scale map on which it appears. If that map covers a double page, the name will always be indexed by the left-hand page number.

Names composed of two or more words are alphabetized as if they were one word.

All names appear in full in the index, except for 'St.' and 'Ste.', which, although abbreviated, are indexed as though spelled in full.

Where two or more places have the same name, they can be distinguished from each other by the country or province name that immediately follows the entry. These names are indexed in the alphabetical order of the country or province.

Alternative names, such as English translations, can also be found in the index and are cross-referenced to the map form by the '=' sign. In these cases the names also appear in brackets on the maps.

Settlements are indexed to the position of the symbol; all other features are indexed to the position of the name on the map.

Abbreviations and symbols used in this index are explained below.

Finding a name on the map

Each index entry contains the name, followed by a symbol indicating the feature type (for example, settlement, river), a page reference, and a grid reference:

Name — Reading, *U.K.* .... ● 82 M10
Reading, *U.S.* .... ● 146 E2
Realicó .... ● 158 J6
Symbol — Rechytsa .... ● 96 F4
Recife .... ● 156 L5
Recklinghausen .... ● 80 K3
Page reference — Recknitz **78** H3
Reconquista .... ● 158 K4
Red, *Canada/U.S.* 144 G1
Grid reference — Red, *U.S.* 148 B3

The grid reference locates a place or feature within a rectangle formed by the network of lines of longitude and latitude. A name can be found by referring to the letters and numbers placed around the maps. First find the letter, which appears along the top and bottom of the map, and then the number, down the sides. The name will be found within the rectangle uniquely defined by that letter and number. A number in brackets preceding the grid reference indicates that the name is to be found within an inset map.

Abbreviations

Al. .... Alabama	*Kans.* .... Kansas	*N.D.* .... North Dakota	*S.D.* .... South Dakota
Ariz. .... Arizona	*Ky.* .... Kentucky	*Nebr.* .... Nebraska	*Shetland Is.* .... Shetland Islands
Ark. .... Arkansas	*La.* .... Louisiana	*Nev.* .... Nevada	*Tenn.* .... Tennessee
Calif. .... California	*Mass.* .... Massachusetts	*Nfld.* .... Newfoundland	*Tex.* .... Texas
Colo. .... Colorado	*Md.* .... Maryland	*N.H.* .... New Hampshire	*U.K.* .... United Kingdom
Conn. .... Connecticut	*Me.* .... Maine	*N. Ire.* .... Northern Ireland	*U.S.* .... United States
Del. .... Delaware	*M.G.* .... Mato Grosso	*N. Mex.* .... New Mexico	*Ut.* .... Utah
Eng. .... England	*Mich.* .... Michigan	*N.Y.* .... New York	*Va.* .... Virginia
Fla. .... Florida	*Minn.* .... Minnesota	*Oh.* .... Ohio	*Vt.* .... Vermont
Ga. .... Georgia	*Miss.* .... Mississippi	*Okla.* .... Oklahoma	*Wash.* .... Washington
Ia. .... Iowa	*Mo.* .... Missouri	*Oreg.* .... Oregon	*Wis.* .... Wisconsin
Id. .... Idaho	*Mont.* .... Montana	*Orkney Is.* .... Orkney Islands	*W. Va.* .... West Virginia
Ill. .... Illinois	*N.B.* .... New Brunswick	*Pa.* .... Pennsylvania	*Wyo.* .... Wyoming
Ind. .... Indiana	*N.C.* .... North Carolina	*S.C.* .... South Carolina	

Symbols

- Continent name
- Country name
- State or province name
- Country capital
- State or province capital
- Settlement
- Mountain, volcano, peak
- Mountain range
- Physical region or feature
- River, canal
- Lake, salt lake
- Gulf, strait, bay
- Sea, ocean
- Cape, point
- Island or island group, rocky or coral reef
- Place of interest
- Historical or cultural region

A

B

C

D

F

H

I

J

L

M

N

P

S

U

V

W

Z